MANAGING THE HUMAN SERVICES
IN HARD TIMES

DAVID A. BRESNICK
DIRECTOR—CENTER FOR MANAGEMENT
DEVELOPMENT & ORGANIZATION RESEARCH
BARUCH COLLEGE, CUNY

HUMAN SERVICES PRESS
200 EAST 24th STREET
NEW YORK, NY 10010

To Naomi, Ellen, Blanche, Denise and Dick
and the other staff of the
Center for Management, who made
this book possible

361.3
B75m
130924
Feb 1985

Human Services Press
200 East 24th Street
New York, New York 10010

Library of Congress Catalog Card Number: 83-80211   ISBN 0-9610834-0-9
Printing Number 1 2 3 4 5

Preface

This book is intended to provide practitioners in large and small human services agencies with common language, concepts and techniques. Jobs at federal, state and city levels are very different from those in not-for-profit and proprietary organizations which carry out a major portion of service delivery functions. Yet there is a growing recognition that they all need to apply a common management approach. *Managing the Human Services in Hard Times* is designed to aid those heroic individuals who must produce more with less to serve the growing human needs of the 80s.

Managing the Human Services in Hard Times derives from my experience in directing a large scale management training project for what is probably the largest integrated human service agency in the world—the New York City Human Resources Administration. HRA combines social services, family and adult services, special services for children, income maintenance, child support, day care and medicaid. In designing a training program involving over 1,000 participants from these diverse backgrounds we found a great desire to understand and apply management techniques. We also found that a program which made the connection by specific examples—case studies, role plays and exercises—between the abstract concepts of management and the every day tasks of human service managers was enthusiastically embraced. This book adopts such an approach.

These have been exciting years in the management of human services. Attention to management has increased and the training of top-level managers has diversified. While the bulk of top-level managers still come up the social work ladder, others come from public administration, private management and data processing. This cross-fertilization has had a beneficial impact on the quality of human service management, though the institutionalization of systematic management approaches is still in a formative stage.

This book is an attempt to contribute to that systematization. It is intended to provide practitioners in large and small agencies a common language and set of concepts, recognizing that many practitioners have not had systematic management education and that others have not been able to keep current with developing practice in this dynamic field. As an introduction to the field of human service management the book cannot do everything for everybody. Yet I feel strongly that an overview is important to help establish a common framework and lexicon, and that this book will be useful to the vast majority of human service managers.

While *Managing The Human Services In Hard Times* is a primer, the need for volumes on a variety of specialized topics is evident. We are planning such a series. The topics of program evaluation, management information systems, accounting, project planning, policy analysis and contract administration leap to mind. If you have suggestions for authors or topics please let me know.

Also, if you have comments and suggestions for future revisions of this volume, I would appreciate receiving them.

DAVID BRESNICK   NEW YORK CITY   1983

Acknowledgements

This particular book carries more than its share of indebtedness. The late Dean of the Baruch School of Business and Public Administration, Samuel Thomas, made the original suggestion that I embark upon the large scale management training project that formed its basis. Three directors of the Office of Human Resources Development of the New York State Department of Social Services supported the project: Mel Kelsey, Al Snyder and Bob Donahue, as did three directors of the Office of Staff Development of the New York City Human Resources Administration: Jackie McKinney, Mary Pratt and Walter Dix. Jim Chard, Jack Krauskopf and Carlotta Brantley provided additional support.

I owe a special debt to the project staff many of whom contributed directly to materials development. Many of the charts in this volume either directly or in revised form derive from the project. This is particularly true of the materials in Chapter 4 on Project Planning and Control. Regular staff members included: Penny Haile, Frank Farren, Hillel Schiller, Norma Turner, Eleanor Evans, Bernard Iatouro, Blanche Berk, Russell Nutter, A. J. Scipio, Delores Pazos, Harvey Bass, Ed Thompson, Barbara Fisher, Anne Miles, Debbie Bassinger, Naomi Cooperman, Magdi Badawy, Yohan Jeffereis, Doug Muzzio, Jay Bostwick, Dick FitzPatrick, Ellen Goldner. Part-time consultants included: Richard Kopelman, Gary Yukel, Jim Guyot, Jack Ukeles, Michael Zisser, Sara Silbiger, Al Booke, Andrew Lavender, James McKeever, John Trinkaus, Ted Abramson, Sam Ryan, Shel Zalkind, Art Levine, Jacqueline McMickens, Marilyn Ullman, Leo Barnett, Amar Dev Amar, Noreen Brierton, Trudi Hill, Lise Liepmann, Paul Register, Lewis Friedman, Michael Krasner, Frederick Shiels, Leon Mysch, Vincent Marasia, Eugene Cistaro, Nancy Murray, Wilbur Rich, John Dempsey, William Fortunato, Mahmoud Wahba, Philip Borello, Bonnie Osinski, Mark Berenson, Richard Curcio, David Levine, and Jeff Brown.

Managing the Human Services in Hard Times

Overview

Chapter 1. Introduction to Human Services Management

1. What is Human Services   1
2. Service Delivery Organizations   6
3. The Management of Human Services   11
4. Toward Improved Performance   13

Chapter 2. Goal-Setting and Planning

1. Defining Mission and Direction in a Service Delivery Organization   17
2. Goals for Human Service Organizations   20
3. Communicating and Effectuating Organizational Goals   25
4. Planning and Policy Analysis   33

Chapter 3. Problem-Solving and Decisionmaking

1. The Manager as Problem Solver   36
2. Understanding the Context   41
3. Deferring, Delegating, Routinizing   43
4. Alternatives and Criteria   44
5. Implementing Solutions   49

Chapter 4. Project Planning

1. Work Process Documentation   53
2. Scheduling Work   56
3. Network Analysis and PERT   58
4. Project Management   62

Chapter 5. Staff Performance

1. Authority Relationships   67
2. Motivating Individuals   71
3. Behavior Modification   75
4. Self-Administered Feedback   78

Chapter 6. Communications

1. The Centrality of Communications   81
2. The Elemental Skills   83
3. Coaching and Other Interviewing Techniques   89
4. Conducting Meetings   92
5. Team Building   95

Chapter 7. Organization Building

1. Staff Selection and Termination   98
2. Staff Development and Training   104
3. Planning for Staff Development   108
4. Organization and Development   112

Chapter 8. Representation and Resources

1. The Representational Role   115
2. Bargaining Techniques   119
3. Influencing Governmental Decisionmaking   121
4. Public and Community Relations   126
5. Obtaining Resources   128

Chapter 9. Resource Acquisition

1. Planning for Resource Acquisition   131
2. The Budget Submission   134
3. Special Grants   139
4. Marketing the Human Services   144

Chapter 10. Resource Control

1. Managerial Control of Resources   147
2. Operational Budgeting   151
3. The Accounting System   153
4. Relating Benefits to Costs   159

Chapter 11. Information Systems

1. Management and Information 163
2. What Is an Information System? 165
3. Client-Based Systems 166
4. Designing and Implementing Automated Systems 168
5. Management Information Systems 171

Chapter 12. Program Monitoring and Evaluation

1. What Is Program Evaluation? 177
2. Measuring Goal Attainment 178
3. Data Collection Techniques 180
4. Quasi-Experimental Design 187

Chapter 13. Survival in Hard Times

1. Toward a Developmental Approach 191
2. Environmental Uncertainty and How to Cope 192
3. Effective Implementation Through Self-Analysis 194
4. Strategies for Creating A Responsive Organization 197

Appendix A. The Human Services

1. Social Security and Public Welfare 199
2. Child Welfare 205
3. Education 208
4. Employment and Training 212
5. Health 213
6. Mental Health 216
7. Corrections 218
8. Care of Special Groups 219
9. Operating in the Human Services 220

Chapter 1.

Introduction to Human Services Management

1. What Is Human Services

America has a schizophrenic attitude toward the human services. It is a humane country that has always sought to care for its own, but it has also stressed self-help. The definition of which services should be provided collectively through government or non-profit organizations and which services individuals should be responsible for has been raised anew by President Ronald Reagan. To many it appears that the human services are in for hard times. Others assert that a new sense of social responsibility at the state and local levels, assisted by corporate responsibility and private philanthropy, will result in more effective delivery.

Human services is a term that has become more and more familiar to the general public and public managers. Many local and state governments have established Departments of Human Services. In 1980 when the U.S. Department of Health, Education and Welfare was disbanded and a separate Department of Education created, the new name chosen was the Department of Health and Human Services.

Behind the increasing popularity of the term, "human services," is a recognition that the range of services provided by government to directly assist its citizens has greatly increased. We have come a long way since the Federal government, in the midst of the Depression, enacted the Social Security Act of 1935 to establish a national system of unemployment insurance and pensions and agreed at the same time to help states provide welfare services.

Many local and state governments were at or near bankruptcy and the tradition of Federal avoidance of social welfare programs was breached only with the greatest hesitancy. In 1982, despite scepticism toward government operations and popular support for cutbacks in government expenditures, the demands for human service programs continue. When cutbacks are announced in day care programs, public outcries are heard. When the possibility of decreases in aid to education are mentioned, politicians receive volumes of mail. And a major contender for the Democratic presidential nomination in 1980, Senator Edward Kennedy, accused the incumbent President of failing to initiate a national health program adequate to the needs of the country. Even the new Conservative Republican President Ronald Reagan has been forced to retract proposed cutbacks in social security programs and proclaim his acceptance of their basic purpose.

Human services in the United States are a bewildering range of programs, funded, regulated and delivered by a mix of governmental and non-governmental organizations. In talking about the human services system, caution must be exercised. The human services system is an amorphous concept. Its definition depends in part upon who is articulating it. Yet in spite of the ambiguity of the term, a group of services do exist which are meant to better the life and life opportunities of American citizens, are coordinated more or less well and are administered by organizations which share common managerial perspectives and tasks.

During the time of the Great Society in the mid-late sixties enabling legislation authorized massive social programs. In the aftermath, it was clear that those enunciating basic policies often did not understand the intricacies of policy implementation at the service delivery level.

Delivery of human services is often the responsibility of non-governmental organizations. Many hospitals, nursing homes, senior citizen centers, youth homes and employment and training programs are administered by not-for-profit or proprietary organizations. On the other hand, many human service delivery organizations are run by government bureaus directly. Social Security centers, for example, are run by the Social Security Administration within the U.S. Department of Health and Human Services. The Employment Service is run by the states depending heavily upon federal funding. Income maintenance centers are administered by cities and counties, or directly by states.

The current human services system reflects the idiosyncratic development of human services in this country. Three major aspects of this growth are: 1) a basic commitment to private philanthropy and voluntarism in delivering services to the needy; 2) intervention by the government as a last resort; 3) increasing Federal funding for programs, often through a back-door approach, and in pursuit of what are initially perceived as national security needs.

Federal involvement in the human services has resulted in a large number of categorical programs, which often overlap. While many of these programs are administered by the Department of Health and

Human Services, the Departments of Education and Labor, and the Veterans Administration also have major responsibilities for human service programs. In fact, every major Federal department is responsible for significant human services programs.

The growth in funding levels over the period 1950-1976 for major human service programs, in the areas of income maintenance, health, education and welfare in both the public and private sectors is indicated below.

NO. 519. PUBLIC AND PRIVATE EXPENDITURES FOR SOCIAL WELFARE: 1950 TO 1978

[In billions of dollars, except percent. See headnote, table 518. "Public" refers to Federal, State, and local governments; "private" to nongovernmental agencies]

TYPE OF EXPENDITURE	1950	1960	1965	1970	1972	1973	1974	1975	1976	1977	1978, prel.
Total, net [1]	35.4	78.7	117.8	209.3	268.2	298.5	332.1	392.3	447.6	497.7	548.9
Public	23.5	52.3	77.2	145.9	191.4	213.9	239.4	290.1	332.0	361.6	394.5
Private	12.2	27.8	42.7	67.4	82.1	90.6	99.6	109.4	125.2	146.8	166.0
Income maintenance	10.7	29.8	42.6	72.5	98.7	112.3	126.4	152.5	177.6	194.4	209.2
Public [2]	9.8	26.3	36.6	60.8	83.8	95.7	107.6	131.7	153.0	166.6	177.8
Private	1.0	3.5	6.0	11.7	14.8	16.6	18.7	20.9	24.6	27.8	31.4
Health	12.0	25.9	38.9	69.2	86.7	95.4	106.0	122.2	139.7	164.5	187.0
Public	3.1	6.4	9.5	25.4	33.5	36.7	41.5	50.9	59.0	67.3	76.2
Private	9.0	19.5	29.4	43.8	53.2	58.7	64.5	71.4	80.8	97.2	110.8
Education	11.0	21.8	34.1	61.7	73.1	80.0	87.1	96.5	109.5	116.2	124.1
Public	9.4	18.0	28.1	51.9	61.3	67.4	73.7	82.3	93.1	98.3	104.6
Private	1.6	3.7	6.0	9.9	11.8	12.7	13.4	14.2	16.4	17.9	19.5
Welfare and other services	2.0	2.7	4.3	9.8	15.0	16.8	19.3	24.6	30.4	33.2	40.2
Public [3]	1.3	1.6	2.9	7.8	12.7	14.2	16.4	21.6	27.0	29.3	35.9
Private	.7	1.1	1.4	2.0	2.3	2.6	2.9	3.0	3.4	3.9	4.3
PERCENT PUBLIC											
Total [4]	65.8	65.3	64.4	68.4	70.0	70.2	70.6	72.4	72.6	71.1	70.4
Income maintenance	91.0	88.1	86.0	83.9	85.0	85.2	85.2	86.3	86.1	85.7	85.2
Health	25.5	24.7	24.5	36.7	38.6	38.4	39.1	41.6	42.2	40.9	40.8
Education	85.3	82.8	82.5	84.0	83.9	84.2	84.6	85.3	85.0	84.6	84.3
Welfare and other services	65.8	59.1	68.0	79.6	84.7	84.5	85.0	87.8	88.8	88.4	89.3
PERCENT OF GNP [5]											
Total, net [1]	13.4	15.8	17.9	21.8	24.1	24.1	24.4	26.7	27.5	27.1	26.9
Income maintenance	4.0	6.0	6.5	7.5	8.9	9.1	9.3	10.5	10.9	10.6	10.2
Health	4.5	5.2	5.9	7.2	7.8	7.7	7.8	8.4	8.6	9.0	9.2
Education	4.1	4.4	5.2	6.4	6.6	6.5	6.4	6.6	6.7	6.3	6.1
Welfare and other services	.8	.5	.7	1.0	1.4	1.5	1.4	1.7	1.9	1.8	2.0

[1] Total expenditures adjusted to eliminate duplication resulting from use of cash payments received under social welfare programs to purchase medical care and educational services.   [2] Includes cash benefits and administrative costs under social insurance, public assistance, supplemental security income, and veterans' and emergency employment programs. Excludes cost of medical services provided in conjunction with those programs and for other welfare programs. See Table 524.   [3] Includes food stamps, surplus food for the needy and for institutions, child nutrition, institutional care, child welfare, economic opportunity and manpower programs, veterans' welfare services, vocational rehabilitation, and housing.   [4] Before adjustment for elimination of duplication.   [5] Gross national product; see text, p. 417.

Source: U.S. Social Security Administration, *Social Security Bulletin*, May 1980, and earlier issues.

At the state level, separate departments are the rule for administering welfare, education and health programs. Additional departments may exist for mental health, corrections, higher education and youth services. A number of states have Departments of Human Services which combine administrative responsibility for several of the human services.

At the local level great variation exists, in part reflecting the diversity of local government forms. Both cities and counties perform varying human services depending in large part upon the particular state. Independent boards of education usually preside over the elementary and secondary education system. A state board usually has jurisdiction over public and private institutions of higher education.

Why have the human services become so prominent, not only in American society, but in Western Europe, the industrialized societies as a whole, and indeed in the less developed countries as well? The existence of high technology and industrialization have placed before humankind the possibility of mass prosperity. The quest for better conditions has kept pace with the possibilities for attaining them. People around the world now expect government to ensure that' they are fed, clothed, and educated. The development of mass communications has surely facilitated the worldwide transfer of knowledge and expectations. Political leaders have generally accepted the obligation to provide these material benefits. We live in a world with high expectations about life conditions and a general belief that society should provide the conditions for individual success. A large number and variety of organizations have developed to ensure these conditions. Insofar as they focus directly on assisting individuals attain these conditions, they are in fact human service organizations—organizations providing services to individuals to achieve better living conditions through better health, greater knowledge and skills, and higher earning power.

These changed expectations also reflect the increasing recognition that the failure of individuals to lead lives which provide the basic necessities may not be of their own doing. Individuals operate within society and their failure to attain certain minimal standards may be a reflection on the general society. It becomes a common obligation to help people attain these benefits. This expectation has been reinforced by modern social science research which indicates the possibility of improving the conditions of individuals through collective action.

Within the United States, the Great Society programs adopted under President Lyndon Johnson reflected this worldwide trend and the American government's belief that it could improve social welfare through programmatic efforts. The *Economic Opportunity Act (EOA) of 1964* was the early symbol of the War Against Poverty, incorporating a variety of programs including the Job Corps, College Work Study, Project Headstart, Community Action, Volunteers in Service to America, and the Work Experience Program for AFDC Families. Other prominent legislation usually considered to be part of the Great Society were the *Civil Rights Act of 1964*, the *Voting Rights Act of 1965*, the *Social Security Amendments of 1965*, *Public Law 89-97 (Medicare and Medicaid)*, the *Public Works and Economic Development Act of 1965*, and the *Elementary and Secondary Education Act of 1965*

The Great Society, begun in the aftermath of President Kennedy's assassination and impelled forward by it, bears the unmistakable stamp of President Lyndon Johnson. His personal desire to contribute a "second" New Deal and his consummate legislative skills provided the force behind the legislative program and sustained its momentum in the next several years. Yet the roots of this legislation lay in the staff work undertaken in the Kennedy years. In fact, the trend toward Federal assumption of greater responsibility for human services programs was clearly discernible during the 1950s and early 1960s. During the 1950s major initiatives resulted in Federal acceptance of responsibility for support of the disabled, Federal sharing of medical care costs under state programs of public assistance, and Federal help to education in the *National Defense Education Act of 1958*. In the early 1960s these trends continued as eligibility for Aid to Dependent Children was extended to families with unemployed fathers; an executive order created the Food Stamp Program and the *Appalachian Redevelopment Act of 1961*; the *Manpower Development and Training Act of 1962* addressed economic development and job training.

As these programs and others continued to mushroom in a climate favoring greater payments to those without sufficient funds, Federal transfer payments skyrocketed. Grants to state and local governments went from $2 billion in 1950 to $78 billion in 1978, including a rise in social investment and service expenditures from $800 million in 1950 to $53 billion in 1978. Increases in cash assistance were not limited to welfare for the poverty stricken, but included social security, workman's compensation, veterans benefits, and unemployment insurance. In the mid-sixties a whole range of social legislation was adopted which strengthened the commitment of the government to social programs. One effect was the proliferation of programs, and the greater attention paid to them. As the extent and overlap of these programs became evident, the need for greater coordination arose. Efforts at integrating these services developed and gave rise to the use of human services terminology as a way of conceptualizing the need for service integration. Thus, a series of reports and efforts developed to integrate human services, including an initiative to create special legislation.

Human services is a term that has different meanings for different people. To workers in mental health it signifies an expansion of the traditional hospital for the mentally ill to a community-based institution concerned with a broader range of human needs. To social workers it signifies an expansion of the social services directed at welfare recipients to include child care and care of the aged. To state officials, it suggests bringing together diverse federal grant programs in a state agency. To local officials, it signifies the establishment of multi-service or referral centers to help the poor. To the federal government, it represents the reorganization resulting in the establishment of the Department of Health and Human Services.

These diverse definitions of the scope of human services can be generalized to include a range of organizations both private and public which provide services aimed at improving the life and life opportunities of people. These organizations provide social services, cash benefits, rehabilitation, counseling, health care, vocational training and general education. They have common managerial problems associated with their highly professional staff, their orientation to client problems and their need to appeal to both the government and to the free market for funding. These service delivery organizations and the overseer, regulatory and support agencies that are closely associated with them interact in significant ways. An understanding of their operation requires an overview of what may be termed the human services system as well as an understanding of the basic unit of service delivery. The service delivery organization (referred to henceforth as the SDO) forms the core of the human services system and its effective management is central to the success of the human services system.

2. Service Delivery Organizations

SDOs range in size from one person entities to large hospitals and correctional institutions which house thousands of individuals and employ more than a thousand staff members. Many of the basic management processes like budgeting and personnel selection are similar regardless of size. While we focus on organizations that have at least one level of management above the first line supervisor, much of what is discussed will be applicable to smaller organizations, too. The difference is the extent to which the manager will interact with individuals who themselves have supervisory and management responsibilities.

Some examples of SDOs are the income maintenance center which determines eligibility and approves payments, the residential facility for foster care or abused children and the training facility for unemployed minorities attempting to learn job skills. The SDO is surrounded by a complicated network of funding sources and regulatory bodies.

An income maintenance center approves payments to families with dependent children that derive from a combination of Federal, state and local funds. In return for providing funds, the Federal and state governments impose regulations regarding the determination of eligibility and grant level. The foster care center may be run by a local governmental unit or a community agency with funds provided by the Federal government and state governments subject to regulations developed mostly by the state. The training facility could be run by a private company, a community agency or a local governmental unit, including a board of education, but it would be accountable to the prime sponsor, a unit of state or local government approved by the Department of Labor. Regulations developed by the Department of Labor provide detailed ground rules for running such programs.

Human service organizations are just like other organizations in that their ability to attain their objectives and the quality of the services they provide depends in large part upon their management. But their objectives may be more ambiguous than those of other organizations and their basis of support is rarely limited to marketplace purchases. Most human service organizations receive all or part of their funding from government sources. Convincing community and political leaders of their usefulness is often the key to their marketing success. Increasingly though, managers of human service organizations recognize the importance of generating support among clientele groups and general public opinion.

Since SDOs provide services to people, they are ordinarily organized in an institutional setting, which may be either residential or non-residential. Nursing homes, colleges, and mental health facilities are ordinarily residential facilities, although many senior citizen centers, junior colleges and out-patient clinics provide similar services to a non-residential population.

The institutional setting ordinarily includes a physical facility with a full-time staff. While sometimes human services are delivered without a physical facility or a full-time staff, such situations are not the norm and will not be the focus of our discussions.

Even within institutionally-based SDOs a tremendous variety exists. The distinction between residential and non-residential services is an important one. Organization size is also important. Human service organizations may vary from senior citizen centers serving relatively small populations with a staff director as the sole staff member to hospital complexes serving thousands of individuals, or school systems serving hundreds of thousands. Obviously where the staff is relatively small, the differentiation of management responsibilities is less well defined. But even in very small organizations, those who are responsible for their direction will benefit from an understanding of the management function and how it can best be carried out.

The staff of SDOs often includes a high proportion of professionals. School teachers in schools, social workers in service centers, and doctors and nurses in hospitals are professional groups with considerable influence. Their shared educational background results in a common base of knowledge, techniques and shared values. Their sense of professionalism has a variety of organizational effects, including a desire for autonomy and a resistance to hierarchical organization. Given the values and norms of their professional training, they can provide an invaluable asset in pursuit of organizational goals. But they also have an external set of values and attitudes which affect their functioning in organizations. Managers of human service organizations must be aware of the professionals with whom they work and develop an ability to focus their energies toward common organizational goals.

Another characteristic of SDOs is their dependence upon government funding. This has tremendous consequences for the operation of these organizations. Their future depends upon a continuation of the funding supplied by these agencies. They become dependent upon the government budgeting process and its cycle to sustain and increase their operations. This cyclical dependence is different from the discipline of the marketplace where changes tend to be on a more continuous basis. Marketing strategies directed at the general public are replaced by operations in the arena of politics. Even human service organizations that operate in the marketplace must be sensitive to government budgeting cycles.

Human service managers must understand government budgeting and the ways to be successful in the budget process. In the first instance this requires an understanding of who holds the budget strings and how to deal with these persons. Many grant programs are responsible to individual administrators who must approve annually of their funding. In other programs the manager's attention may be directed toward other officials with broader responsibility such as legislators or elected executives.

Since people are the products and these people are citizens in a democratic governmental system, the clients have a role in determining the manager's success in the political arena. A principal running an elementary school or the supervisor of an income maintenance center knows that the institution's constituents are actors within the political system and can complain through a variety of mechanisms if they are dissatisfied. Even managers of private and not-for-profit institutions are subject to close scrutiny, as nursing home administrators learned during the 1970s. An unruly constituency can disrupt the opportunities for political success and budget renewal.

The potency of the political constituency can be an asset as well as a liability. If properly managed, constituent support can be a powerful tool in the development and continuation of human service organizations. Contacts with political officials and direct action such as forcefully keeping facilities open, can sometimes rescue human service organizations from funding cuts.

Human service organizations provide services to individual citizens. They are "helping" organizations. They achieve their results by affecting people. Some human service organizations such as income maintenance centers, drug rehabilitation centers and unemployment centers are directed at individuals with acute needs and limited resources. Others such as social security offices, hospitals and schools, serve all citizens regardless of financial need. Managers of these institutions have an especial obligation to understand these human needs and to meet them. They must be interested in people and their betterment. Whether involved in education, institutional care or individual counseling, human service organizations are attempting to improve the lot of individuals. Managers need to focus on these basic goals and be sensitive to them. They need to be familiar with and interested in the people affected by their organizations.

One of the difficulties of dealing with the management of human services organizations is their variety. Our approach will focus on middle-sized institutions such as colleges and lower schools, training facilities, health care facilities, senior citizen and day care centers, facilities for youths in need of special guidance, income maintenance and social service centers and government bureaus of a regulatory or general nature. A variety of professional programs are currently training individuals for careers in the management of human service organizations. These programs are at the masters level and sometimes at the undergraduate level in the fields of health, community psychology, social work, public administration, business administration, human services, and urban planning.

One of the primary concerns of SDOs is their effectiveness in carrying out their stated goals. To what extent is it realistic to expect a prison to rehabilitate an adult who has successfully led a life of crime and is now middle-aged? To what extent is a student educable who, by the time of his entrance into high school, has not learned to read and do basic mathematics? What are the proper goals of a nursing home dealing with individuals over 80 who have contracted terminal cancer? The managers of human service organizations are time and again confronted by situations where they have precious little ability to effectuate their goals with respect to individuals who bring with them a lifetime of experience and are only minimally in contact with their organizations. Yet a realistic understanding of the difficulties of effectuating changes in individuals and their behavior should not serve as an excuse for benign neglect. In the face of the obstacles to successful change, managers of human service organizations must nonetheless persevere and exhibit a realistic optimism. They must believe in human potential and exploit its possibilities.

Effectuating change in humans, in the best of circumstances, is difficult. It is complicated by the difficulty of specifying objectives and measuring success. To what extent is a particular school program successful in improving reading levels, given the effects of television and parental guidance in developing reading skills? To what extent should a day care center focus on group skills as opposed to individual children's cognitive or creative abilities? How can we measure the effectiveness of a training program in bolstering the earnings of an individual, given the extent to which general skills, knowledge and attitudes developed elsewhere, not to speak of personal contacts, will affect job success. The process of specifying and evaluating the output of human service organizations is a formidable task.

Yet it can be done. The problem in theory is much the same as that encountered by industrial organizations. In managing a factory the focus is always on the product, its quality and its cost. Since the output of most factories is sold on the marketplace there is a built-in corrective against products which are shoddy, too costly, or not useful. It should be remembered, however, that the market mechanism often breaks down. A company that is not subject to market discipline may be able to produce and sell products that are shoddy and costly. A company may lose its position in the market through neglect. All of us are familiar with the failure of the American automobile industry to anticipate market demands for small, low-consumption, high-quality automobiles and their subsequent loss of market share.

It should also be noted that in human services a market does appear to be emerging, although slightly different from the marketplace in which consumer products are sold. In addition to the availability of varied suppliers and increasing consumer choice, for example, in shopping for health care or schooling, grantors and regulators are becoming more demanding in their requirements for demonstrative evidence that the services provided are needed, are of high quality, and are not too costly.

In the operation of a factory, the questions of quality and cost are the most pressing. Need is usually in the province of the market researchers and advertising professionals. While in industry the need issue is often reduced to one of whether people can be convinced through an advertising campaign to buy a product, in the human services the justification of need must be presented directly to policymakers. While we don't object if people spend their personal resources in frivolous ways, we want to be certain that government funds are spent for justifiable purposes. But this determination of need or usefulness of a particular service or product should be separate in our analysis from questions of quality and cost which are generally much more straightforward in concept and calculation.

The quality of service provided is analagous to the quality of a product provided. Does the service work well? What is its unit cost? Are the consumers satisfied with the service? Are those providing the service skilled? Is it reliable? Does it meet the basic requirements of the individuals being served? Such questions about the quality of service can be measured and presented without major conceptual problems or difficulties.

Finally, measures of the impact of the service and its need and usefulness are necessary. However, we sometimes confuse measures of service quality with those of impact of service. Part of the success of industrial production is separating these issues. Similarly in service evaluation, it is the regulators and grantors that should have primary responsibility for determining whether the services rendered are having the impacts desired. The service provider can best concentrate efforts on providing high-quality and low-cost services.

This should not be interpreted to mean that the provider should not look at the impact of programs where that is appropriate. But these questions are often of a different magnitude and require the kind of systematic data collection, research and development activities which such a provider cannot be expected to undertake.

3. The Management of Human Services

The juxtaposition of the terms "management" and "human services" appears contrived to some. Particularly to those focusing on the direct delivery of services and client contact, management raises the spectre of business, rather than helpfulness. To some extent this objection is based upon misunderstanding, though the need to differentiate the management of industrial organizations from human service organizations should be manifest. That some striking similarities exist should also be apparent. Another source of misunderstanding in the use of the term "management" with respect to the human services occurs because of the frequent use of the term by budget cutters. Those working within human service organizations are all too familiar with budget cutters on boards of directors, in legislatures and on the editorial pages of major newspapers who call for better management to absorb the damage caused by cuts in appropriations for human services. Meanwhile, many of those working in human service organizations know the stringent conditions in which they operate and feel that much greater, not less, resources are needed. Better management becomes an excuse for the inability to provide adequate resources. The antipathy which many human service managers have for the term "management" is readily understood in this context.

Another source of discomfort over the management orientation is that it becomes associated with a down-grading of the objectives of the organization and concern with organizational processes. Many of those working within human service organizations and especially those emerging from professional education in social work are oriented toward service delivery. They view their task as providing direct services to clients. Concern with management may come to be viewed as tangential to or even competitive with the concern for the delivery of services.

In reality of course, managers do spend a good deal of their time with other workers, rather than in direct service delivery. Their job is to ensure that services are delivered efficiently and effectively rather than to deliver those services themselves. While it is important for human service managers to understand and believe in the service delivery goals of their unit, they spend most of their time ensuring that these services are delivered by others. Of course, there is a danger of managers becoming too far removed from the service delivery function of their organizations. There is the additional danger that in a given organization the emphasis given to management and administration will be out of proportion to the need. But by far, the greater danger today in human service organizations is that those with management responsibility will not understand their jobs and persist in delivering direct services themselves rather than focusing on the management systems and techniques necessary to achieve effective service delivery.

Human service organizations, then, like industrial organizations, have an authority structure and an identifiable group of individuals charged with their direction. These individuals must formulate realistic goals and be given the capacity to obtain those goals. In understanding the job of the manager of a human service organization there is much that can be learned from the job of managers generally. But there are also specific knowledges, skills, and attitudes that help facilitate success in human service organizations.

Current understandings of the behavior of managers is based upon studies using such techniques as direct unstructured observations, structured interviews and self-report diaries. Earlier views of management which emphasized a number of functions of management, for example, those represented by the acronym, POSDCORB, are generally viewed as inadequate today. While planning, organizing, staffing, directing, coordinating, reporting, and budgeting are activities that managers engage in, they do not constitute a comprehensive catalog of management behavior. A strong pedagogical emphasis on the six or eight management functions excludes the full range of managerial behavior.

A more comprehensive conceptualization of management behavior is provided by Leonard Sayles, Professor at the Columbia University School of Business. He argues that managers are responsible for regulating the work-flow of their organizations. They lead the individuals in the work unit toward some set of goals, while monitoring their behavior to improve performance. And they represent the work unit in interactions with other work units within and without the organization. For each of these broad categories, Sayles has provided detailed lists of specific activities in which managers engage.

But how can this broad characterization of the work of managers be made appplicable to those leading human service organizations and their subunits? How can they be expected to direct large numbers of professionals who resist hierarchical organizational patterns? How can they set realistic goals given the resistance of human beings to change? How can performance standards be set and met given the ambiguous and conflicting goals of human service organizations? What techniques can be used for dealing with the volume and complexity of data that needs to be considered? How can complex projects be successfully planned, executed and monitored?

This book is aimed at answering these questions and improving the performance of managers in human service orgnizations. As mentioned above, SDOs of moderate size—income maintenance centers, senior citizen centers, social security offices, drug rehabilitation facilities, schools, housing facilities, and day care centers, will be taken as our focus. We will ordinarily suppose that a manager must deal with staff specialists in such areas as personnel, budgeting, and data processing and one or two levels of supervisors in an hierarchical setting. Many organizations are smaller and flatter. The manager of a human service organization may be directly responsible for personnel and budgeting. All staff may report directly to the manager without any intervening levels of management. In those cases the challenge of management may be greater because of the diverse talents required of a single individual. Similarly, executives in multi-tiered institutions will find additional challenge in dealing with a larger number of staff and a more formidable hierarchy.

Also a large number of human service managers work for government or the not-for-profit sector as regulators or grantors. The huge Federal commitment to human services has necessitated a substantial corps of individuals who administer grant programs. Similarly, states and in some cases, local governments have had to create agencies to oversee grant programs. Private foundations and not-for-profit agencies, especially organizations like the United Way, also engage in fund granting and seeking activities. Often grant seeking agencies assign specialized staff to secure additional funds. The largest number of regulators are at the state level. Regulators may operate where little or no government funds are directly committed. Thus states have established agencies to regulate schools, day care facilities, and nursing homes to mention a few areas of interest.

These regulators and grantors and the management personnel associated with them form an important part of the human services management network. Their work will be described from the perspective of the human services manager who must deal with them. These individuals tend to have less contact with clientele groups and often are at status and pay levels comparable to managers of human service organizations without comparable direct supervisory and management responsibilities. Nonetheless, their need to understand human service organizations engaged in service delivery is critical. They constitute the support network within which these service delivery organizations function.

4. Toward Improved Performance

Improved organizational performance is the goal of most managers. To improve performance in human service organizations a manager must develop specific skills and knowledge and possess an overall management strategy.

While skills, knowledge and management strategy are important to any manager, the human services manager has particular needs. A thorough understanding of the particular program and its relationship to similar human services programs is critical. Translating organizational mission into organizational goals and individual objectives is especially demanding since human service organizations often have conflicting and ambiguous goals and large numbers of autonomous professionals. Providing direction in an organization which is pulled in opposing directions is a formidable task. Attempts to improve staff performance are often frustrated by a highly autonomous structure reinforced by professional autonomy and conflicting personal philosophies. Paper flow problems may be enormous and an understanding of how to use information systems may be critical, as well as how to use the services of appropriate consultants.

The human service manager must be able to communicate effectively and develop effective communications within the organization. Appropriate project planning techniques should be used when needed. The ability to implement programs in spite of conflicting and competing forces is critical. Human service managers cannot survive for long without a lively sense of how to bargain with competitors for resources. A manager should understand the principles of program evaluation and apply them to organizational decisions. Cost control techniques and information technologies need to be understood. Finally, the manager should have a firm understanding of current developments and future directions. The ability to understand human services management and master the knowledges and skills required will be an important determinant of success.

The elusive goal of improved performance is within the grasp of most human service managers. Much of the knowledge and many of the skills necessary for managerial effectiveness will be described in the coming chapters. The knowledge will be more easily gleaned from this book than the skills. But the manager who knows his or her own developmental needs will find the means to overcome them. Unfortunately, human service organizations have not traditionally devoted the resources needed to develop managerial talent. It may be necessary to seek outside assistance.

The excuse that management techniques are unnecessary or unknown for human service organizations is no longer an acceptable response. The human service manager of tomorrow will be a skilled and knowledgeable operative, perhaps more laboriously trained and more finely tuned than the industrial manager. The management of human service organizations, with all their complications and complexities, is the greatest managerial challenge facing contemporary society.

Selected Bibliography

Aiken, Michael et al. *Coordinating Human Services.* San Francisco: Jossey Bass, 1975.

Anderson, Wayne T., Frieden, Bernard J., and Murphy, Michael, eds. *Managing Human Services.* Washington, D.C.: International City Management Association, 1977.

Council of State Governments. *Human Services Integration: State Functions in Implementation.* Lexington, Kentucky: Council of State Governments, 1974.

Gans, Sheldon and Horton, Gerald. *Integration of Human Services: The State and Municipal Levels.* New York: Praeger, 1975.

Harshbarger, D. and Demone, H. W., eds. *A Handbook of Human Service Organizations.* New York: Behavioral Publications, 1974.

Hasenfeld, Yeheskel and English, Richard. *Human Service Organizations.* Ann Arbor: University of Michigan Press, 1974.

Mikulecky, Thomas, ed. *Human Services Integration.* Washington, D.C.: American Society for Public Administration.

Miringoff, Marc. *Management in Human Service Organizations.* New York: Macmillan, 1980.

Murphy, Michael J. and Glynn, Thomas. *Human Services Management: Priorities for Research.* Washington, D.C.: International City Management Association, 1978.

Project SHARE. *Managing the Human Service "System." What We Have Learned from Services Integration.* Human Services Monograph No. 4 Rockville, Maryland: Aspen Systems, Inc.

Steiner, Richard. *Managing the Human Service Organization: From Survival to Achievement.* Beverly Hills: Sage Publishers.

Chapter 2.

Goal Setting and Planning

Goal setting, the most central of managerial tasks, becomes progressively more important as one moves up the ladder of management responsibility. The ability of an individual to perceive the direction in which an organization can make important contributions and articulate that direction, differentiates the outstanding leader from the run-of-the-mill manager. Phillip Selznick has emphasized the importance of institutional leadership and characterizes it as the ability to set direction at the critical time and reach beyond the routine matters of the organization.

Sometimes this ability is described as vision: to be able to discern the proper course for an organization. The ability to bring that vision into practice is what management is all about. Managers of human service organizations need to master such basic skills as work scheduling, project management and employee motivation in order to make their visions work for them.

Successful managers must know when to take the initiative and how to assert themselves. They must know how to take command of a staff meeting at an appropriate moment and explain why a new direction is needed. The individuals who led the Young Men's Christian Association (YMCA) away from a purely religious orientation toward a recreational and service function ensured its survival and prosperity. They displayed both vision and the ability to command. The manager who acknowledges the dire financial circumstances of an organization, institutes appropriate cutbacks in staff, and devises a new funding strategy allows the organization to survive. Sometimes leaders make mistakes and their organizations suffer. But by providing appropriate direction at the right moment they can turn their organization in the right direction and achieve prosperity and continued service.

The effective manager must be able to discern direction, articulate goals and convince others of the appropriateness of those goals. The human service manager must convince peers and subordinates who often have strong views of their own. Eventually in a private corporation the decision may reach the Board of Directors. Similarly in many not-for-profit organizations a board of directors or board of trustees will make ultimate decisions. In public sector organizations the elected executive and at times legislative leaders will become involved.

The selling job of a human service manager extends beyond individuals within the organizational hierarchy, to a multitude of public and community leaders. These include government and not-for-profit officials who have a responsibility to approve continued funding.

Most managers recognize goal definition and attainment as their most important task. The last chapter described some impediments to goal attainment in a multi-leveled, multi-purpose human services system. But let us cast aside for the moment the complexities of the human services system as a whole and focus our attention on individual service delivery organizations (SDOs): the income maintenance center, the school, the hospital, the rehabilitation center for youthful offenders. How does the manager of such an organization set the goals and ensure that they are met?

A range of goal setting activities are within the purview of management. These include long range and middle range organizational planning having a time frame of years, and annual goal setting incorporating the individual objectives of subordinates. In discussing goal setting for the manager of the SDO, attention will be given first to mission statements and annual goals. Less detailed treatment of middle and long range planning will follow.

1. Defining Mission and Direction in a Service Delivery Organization

Perhaps the first task of any manager is to develop a sense of the overall mission of the organization. This is equally true for managers of service delivery organizations (SDOs). Often this overall purpose will be captured in a written mission statement, approved by superiors whether they be higher level executives, legislators or a board of directors. But whether or not it is written down, a basic understanding of organization mission is the beginning of effective management.

Mission statements are often general and subject to implementation in a variety of ways. Often the mission of an organization will be unchanged for many years. When a manager assumes his position, one of the first tasks should be to review any existing mission statement and make sure it reflects current reality.

An income maintenance center is a typical SDO, providing services to individuals who qualify for welfare payments under the programs of Aid to Families with Dependent Children and Home Relief. Such a center determines the eligibility of individuals and their benefit levels and ensures that they are paid.

Thus the general mission of a particular income maintenance center might be stated as follows:

The X income maintenance center is responsible for authorizing payments and determining eligibility and payment levels for individuals living within Y area who may be entitled to receive benefits under the programs of Aid to Families with Dependent Children and Home Relief.

The mission statement should capture the main purpose of the SDO, although it does not usually indicate the priorities of a particular center. It is a broad statement of function. Individual income maintenance centers differ in their service areas and their program responsiblilities. Many states define the role of income maintenance centers broadly offering other services within the same setting. Until the separation of income maintenance from social services during the 1960s, the two were performed out of the same centers by the same people. Now federal regulations encourage the separation of the function, but they are still housed in common facilities in many locations.

Related SDOs should have similar mission statements. Thus a social security office would have the responsibility for determining eligibility benefits for recipients under the provisions of the Social Security Act. A mission statement might look like this:

The X branch office of the Social Security Administration is reponsible for authorizing payments and determining eligibility and payment levels for individuals residing in the Y area who may be entitled to receive benefits under the programs for Old Age, Survivors and Disability Benefits.

Consider a nursing home which takes care of elderly individuals who cannot live on their own. A possible mission statement might be: to house, clothe, feed and minister to individuals over the age of 60 who cannot live on their own and who qualify for admission to the home. Many other human service organizations, such as hospitals, correctional institutions and half-way houses have as their mission caring for individuals. They would have similar mission statements.

In addition to maintaining individuals at some given level, many human service organizations seek to improve their health or capabilities. Most hospitals for example are meant to improve the health of individuals through surgery or other treatment. Half-way houses for drug users, institutions for juvenile offenders and vocational training for those with disabilities are all meant to improve the individual's potential for a successful productive life. A half-way house for drug users might have the following mission statement: To enable residents to stop taking drugs and leave the facility to function productively in society.

Employment and training programs seek to enable individuals to gain new abilities to function productively. A mission statement for a vocational training program might read: To provide individuals with the requisite skills so that they can function in productive jobs.

Of course, sometimes the mission of a particular organization may involve several of the goals outlined above. In such a case the mission statement would need to be expanded. Many human service organizations have similar missions and therefore similar mission statements. The most common missions of human service organizations are listed below.

Missions of Service Delivery Organizations (SDOs)

Type of SDO	Examples	Mission
cash benefit	income maintenance social security	to determine eligibility and level of benefits; monitor benefit flow
in-kind benefit	medicaid foodstamps	to determine eligibility and benefit level; monitor benefit flow
child welfare	foster care facility	to provide residential care; or placement for needy children
training	vocational education co-op education	to develop skills of participants to qualify for job placements
rehabilitation	half-way house for addicts or alcoholics	to permit individuals, following treatment, to resume a normal life
health	community clinic hospital	to cure the effects of organic malfunctions

The mission of many human service organizations is apparent. In such cases a written document merely states what is generally acknowledged. But there are some situations in which the definition of mission becomes a major concern of the manager. This is particularly true for multi-purpose organizations. A classic study of the Young Men's Christian Association (YMCA) tried to account for the success of the organization over a period of more than 100 years. One of the critical ingredients was the ability of this multi-purpose human service organization to redefine its purpose from a religious organization to a recreational organization serving both men and women.

Human service organizations with multiple purposes are better able to survive over time as the needs of those seeking assistance change. Closely connected with such shifts are society's decisions about which services to support as reflected in public policies. The ability of a manager to perceive the changing needs that an organization may fulfill and the ability to implement changes in organizational mission can be an invaluable asset at certain critical periods in the life cycle of human service organizations. More often, however, the exercise of leadership to redefine organizational direction will take place within the confines of the existing mission.

Within the human services system changes in mission are often imposed from above. As we have noted the human services system is a multi-layered system deriving in large part from legislative and executive action at the federal and state levels. Numerous examples can be cited of the ways in which state and local agencies and SDOs at the local level have been created and modified by legislative and executive acts. The Social Security Act of 1935 gave tremendous stimulus to recasting statewide public welfare departments. HEW initiatives during the early 1970s stimulated the development of integrated state departments of human services. The Manpower Development and Training Act of 1962 and its successor, the Comprehensive Employment and Training Act of 1973 created a system of state and local prime sponsors and local contractors to provide employment and training services.

While any individual SDO may have some latitude in redefining its mission, this is more generally true of a non-governmental unit. A government agency derives for the most part from legislation which establishes its mission. Of course, a government agency may attempt to change its mission. The executive often plays an active role in preparing both initial and revised legislation to govern the agency's purposes. In addition government agencies will often influence the missions of subordinate agencies. The separation of income maintenance and social services functions at the state levels was largely the result of federal agency initiatives. The limitation of community action agencies established under the Economic Opportunity Act of 1964 was largely the result of efforts by local officials to curtail their power.

Given the constraints on altering basic organizational mission, most of the effort of managers to provide direction in SDOs is not in recasting the mission, but in redefining the mission through the choice of specific, time-bound goals which the organization pursues. But as will be seen below the ability to set annual goals or goals with other time frames is a very far-ranging power.

2. Goals for Human Service Organizations

In moving from broad mission statements to time-bound goals, the complexity of managing human service organizations becomes clearer. Whereas mission statements set forth general purposes, annual goal statements set forth specific goals. These become the basis of accountability and managers themselves are judged by their ability to contribute to specific organization goals. In formulating annual goals the starting point is the mission statement, but that is only the beginning. The purposes of an organization must be captured at a particular moment and projected into the future in a realistic fashion. Human service organizations have service goals just like industrial organizations have production goals.

Instead of producing 100 cars like an auto plant, a human service organization provides service to 100 individuals. Selecting service goals and monitoring their completion is, in the first instance, the manager's task. In some cases goals are readily identifiable, in others their identification is difficult.

If goal-setting is the first task of the manager, it also points up the distinctiveness of the human service manager. While in an industrial setting the goals of a particular factory are to produce a quantity of products within certain quality constraints, the human service organization must provide a quantity of services at a given quality level.

In SDOs the targets are not products, but services. For example, a hospital or long-term care facility might register 30,000 patient days at the end of a time period. Just as the quality of a product can be measured, the quality of service can be measured. How clean were the premises during that time? Was there overcrowding? Were medical and dental examinations made when necessary? A school or training facility might set a goal of 1,000 person training days. Then questions of quality can be posed? How many subjects were offered? At what level did the instruction occur? Were the clients satisfied with the level of services? An income maintenance center or referral center might have a goal of determining eligibility or referring 500 people over the course of the month to other service agencies. Then questions of quality can be asked about the accuracy and appropriateness of eligibility determinations and referrals.

The problem of equating product quality with service quality is that the former can usually be technically defined through a small number of tests. Determinations of levels of service quality which involve interactions among people and a number of indeterminate factors are more difficult. Yet these differences should not be overstated. Within bounds service outputs can be measured and quality can be determined. The problem often arises that the target populations of SDOs are different from each other so that the services delivered to them are difficult to equate. But so long as the target populations are more or less comparable, comparisons among SDOs offering similar services can be made.

Once quality of service has been judged, the question of cost arises. While industrial organizations disciplined by a competitive market have engaged in extensive cost accounting techniques, human service organizations have not typically developed such approaches. Their monopoly position and reliance upon public funds have protected them to some extent. In recent years, however, increasing attention is being given to cost calculations. Not only has competition increased among these organizations, but government itself has demanded more systematic cost data as a precondition for continued funding. The questions of cost and financial accountability are considered in Chapter 11.

Another complicating factor in the management of human service organizations is the need to measure service impact. Since industrial products are sold on the open market we tend to view this question as superfluous. If someone is willing to pay for a product the need and impact are considered obvious. That people may be manipulated by clever advertising campaigns to develop extraordinary needs is usually not considered. The elimination of these issues greatly simplifies the task of industrial management. The need for and impact of particular products and services is much more difficult to determine than their quality. The figure below summarizes the major conceptual distinctions in developing standards for service and product quality. In setting standards for product quality a clearly defined set of technical specifications is ordinarily available. In judging service quality the standards usually require professional judgment and may be more difficult to quantify. Consumer satisfaction with a product is registered through the marketplace purchase. Consumer satisfaction with government services that do not have a market place are registered through the political process. The usefulness of a product to further certain goals is analogous to the impact of a service on its recipients. Often the efficacy of a material product is more easily determined than that of a service, particularly those which have the goal of effectuating changes in individuals.

Standards of Quality

Service	Product
1. Professionally defined elements	1. Technical Specifications
2. Recipient Support	2. Consumer Purchases
3. Service Impact	3. Product Usefulness

The manager of an SDO is often required to demonstrate both need and impact. To the extent that it is possible to reserve such questions for the grantor and regulator agencies and their managers, burdens on the SDOs are greatly reduced. In practice this often occurs. Yet when public monies are being spent on the human services and the organizations providing them are not in a competitive situation, our concern with the need for and impact of these services is much greater. The result is that the manager of the SDO may find a portion of time spent on demonstrating need and impact. This is one burden that those involved in industrial production ordinarily pass on to someone else.

This demand for demonstrating the impact of human services finds its expression in the development of program evaluation techniques. Unfortunately, the design and implementation of such techniques may be quite complicated and the answers they provide inconclusive. Yet in many areas the use of program evaluation techniques has yielded helpful results, particularly when those evaluations have been conducted over extended periods of time. Program evaluation techniques will be fully treated in Chapter 12.

An added difficulty in implementing and evaluating human services is the expectation that they will be developmental: that they will result in better jobs for trainees; move welfare clients off welfare, and cure those who submit to treatment. SDO managers need to be concerned with the impacts of their services. However, just as factory managers are best able to obtain information about the quality of the services they actually deliver. The demands on the human service manager or outcome and impact data, however, may be tremendous, making the job just that much more difficult.

The specification of outcome goals for human service organizations requires ingenuity and persistence. Several rules will help in developing outcome statements: (1)Keep in mind the clear distinction between service goals and outcome goals, and include both; (2) Select outcome goals that lend themselves to comparison with other organizations and comparisons over time within the same organization; (3) Avoid limiting goals which may distort resources by establishing a narrow orientation, and forcing the abandonment of other important goals.

This last rule is especially important, because it presents a particular danger to human service organizations, where less important service and outcome goals may be easier to measure. Suppose that in a preschool class emphasis was placed on reading readiness because of the ease in establishing a quantitative measure. If a more important goal related to the development of social skills for young children who have had little contact with other children, that goal might be difficult to state in quantitative terms and monitor. If such a goal remained unstated the tendency of the organization might be to focus attention on reading readiness which might in fact have been a less important goal.

Clearly, minimizing inaccurate eligibility determinations is an admirable goal for an income maintenance center. But it does not reflect the misery of those who might have been denied assistance. Why not add some measure to determine those who were eligible but were denied benefits? And what about the goals related to getting people off the welfare rolls?

A residential rehabilitation center certainly wants its target population to become self-sufficient. But it also wants to make sure that those who are released will do well on the outside. One danger of an outcome measure focusing on the number of releases is that individuals will be released prematurely. Another is that to improve the success rate individuals with only minor problems may be accepted into the program.

Consider the goal that everyone in a school should achieve a one year improvement on a specified standardized test within the next year. Here the school is being compared with all other schools across the country. But such a comparison is probably not appropriate since we already know that the single greatest determinant of a school's reading level is the socio-economic status of its student body. A more accurate measure would match this school with all other schools in the same socioeconomic grouping.

A variety of processes are available to the human services manager for generating goal statements. At times a process may be mandated by a board of directors, legislature or higher executive. In fact such processes do exist in many governmental jurisdictions. In some organizations no formal process for goal-setting may be in place, while in larger organizations an elaborate procedure may be in effect. The manager must take these existing procedures into consideration in developing a process for a specific organization. The manager must decide what degree of formality the process should have and what the role of specific individuals should be. Discussions with superiors and subordinates can aid in making such a determination.

No organization can afford not to have a process for goal setting. And that process should at minimum include the promulgation of written organizational goal statements, consultation in the development of the goal statement and a formal presentation to staff of those goals. The organizational goals should represent a consensus as to the direction of the organization. They should be stated in a way that individuals can relate their own jobs to the stated goals. They should allow for a determination at the end of some time period, preferably a year, the extent to which they have been met. These goals should focus on the central service delivery targets for the organization and include outcome goals. They should reflect some improvement over the previous year and provide for the growth and development of the individuals in the organization. They should provide realistic targets for improvement and growth. Where the organizational goal-setting process is part of a larger planning process it should be designed to reinforce that larger process and capitalize on that larger process for greater impact.

Consultation in the setting of goals can range from individual discussions with a small number of people and research into statements made by individuals to an active process of interaction and feedback. Forums should be available where those expected to contribute to the organizational goals have an opportunity to discuss them. These should include both open-ended forums, where a variety of individuals can participate, for example at a large staff meeting or public meeting, and smaller meetings, for example the weekly meetings of top staff. Consultation of course means that goals will be presented and/or discussed prior to their final designation. This consultation in the setting of goals, begins the process of goal communication, which can be pursued in a variety of ways.

The development of an organizational goal statement is only the first step in a process of establishing direction in an organization. In order for these goals to be realized, they must be acted upon by management and indeed many individuals within the organization. The recognition that goal statements by themselves are only a beginning and that the incorporation of such statements into the every day activities of the organization may be difficult, proceeds from an understanding of the complexities of organizations and the obstacles to individual pursuit of organizational goals.

3. Communicating and Effectuating Organizational Goals

In a complex organization goals will be perceived differently in different parts of the organization. An explicit and carefully worked out process for disseminating organizational goals minimizes these differences in perception. During the 1950s the need for more explicit organizational communication and interaction in annual goal-setting was recognized within business organizations and led to the popularity of Management-by-Objectives (MBO). The idea behind MBO is that the goals of an organization need to be disseminated and translated into individual objectives for those working in the organization. (For purposes of clarity we shall adopt the convention of referring only to goals for organizations and objectives for individuals.) In this sense MBO may be considered shorthand for any explicit, periodic repetitive process during which goals are formulated and translated into individual objectives for the managers in the organization.

During the first phase of MBO, organizational goals are formulated in a process which ordinarily includes a range of staff. This could involve a written questionnaire, an open forum or small group meetings. On the basis of input from members of the organization, the top management comes to some agreement about the major goals for the organization during the subsequent time period, usually one year.

After the organizational goals have been formulated each individual division formulates goals and the managers responsible for these divisions formulate personal objectives based upon these goals. The process reaches down to the appropriate level in the organization, depending upon the sophistication of the workers, the applicability of an objective setting process, and the needs of the organization. It is particularly useful to include professional staff within the process, since it provides an effective method for internalizing organizational goals.

The heart of the MBO process lies in translating organizational goals into individual objectives and then ensuring that those objectives are realized. The critical formal stages in this process may be characterized as an Objective Setting-Meeting and periodic Review Meetings. Ordinarily the Objective-Setting Meeting will be held immediately following the adoption of the Annual Goals for the organization and its subdivisions. The frequency of Review Meetings will vary from organization to organization. A quarterly review process is often used which would require four Review Meetings in addition to the Objective-Setting Meeting. Of course the formal meetings are only one aspect of the monitoring process. If properly developed the individual objectives form the basis for guiding employee effort and providing a basis for interaction during that period. They provide the manager with the basis for focusing on the most critical aspects of the subordinate's performance. They become an important part of a strategy of performance improvement.

The Objective-Setting Meeting

The purpose of this meeting is to arrive at a "contract" between the manager and the subordinate detailing the performance expected of the subordinate over the coming year. This "contract" and its revisions will then form the basis of the evaluation of the subordinate's performance. This meeting presents both tremendous opportunities and some potential pitfalls. If conducted well it can greatly facilitate the task of supervision. It can also turn out to be a useless exercise or even the source of distrust and suspicion.

While the success of an Objective-Setting Meeting depends upon the cooperation of the subordinate, the major responsibility for the meeting rests with the manager. The way in which the meeting is approached is critical in influencing the attitude of the subordinate. Particularly when such meetings are first instituted great care must be taken to ensure that the subordinate understands the purposes of the meeting and is prepared for it. It is usually advisable to announce well in advance that such meetings will be held and explain to individuals the purpose for the meeting. A written explanation of the process should either be handed out at the same time or supplied beforehand.

In preparing subordinates for the Objective-Setting Meeting, the mutuality of the process must be stressed. This will have been reinforced if these same individuals were previsously involved in the process of organizational goal-setting. The Objective-Setting Meeting is a process of reaching agreement about performance expectations on the part of the subordinate and manager. It is a process of clarification and bargaining in which a subordinate presents a series of objectives for the specified time period and the manager may either accept, revise or prepare new objectives.

In this sense the Objective-Setting Meeting should be the culmination of an ongoing process between the manager and subordinate. It began with a job clarification meeting when the subordinate first started working and has continued through informal and formal meetings. The Objective-Setting Meeting should be part of an organic communication process which serves to highlight certain annual objectives and arrives at an explicit written contract which will be referred to throughout the year.

Perhaps the greatest danger in the Objective-Setting Meeting is that it will be perceived as essentially a bargaining process, rather than a mutual clarification session. Particularly in organizations where ongoing commuication is weak or the setting of objectives is linked to a formal evaluation or appraisal system, the meeting may be an occasion for tension. The danger exists that the subordinate will react defensively and seek to limit the expectations of the manager, by suggesting only those objectives that pose little risk of not being met, minimizing the value of the Objective-Setting Meeting.

The success of Objective-Setting Meetings, then, depends upon their acceptance by subordinates, which in turn depends upon the organizational climate and the manager's overall relationship with the subordinate. The manager is much better served by creating an atmosphere of cooperation than by threatening punishments for performance failures. The manager needs to stretch the subordinate and insist upon mutually agreeable standards for judging whether objectives are met. It might be added that this task is particularly difficult in human services organizations where objectives are difficult to specify and evaluate and individuals often operate autonomously.

The purpose of the Objective-Setting Meeting, then, is to arrive at an agreed list of objectives committed to writing which will be the basis of the mutual performance expectations of the manager and the subordinate. These objectives represent the priority areas for involvement of the individual and the specified performances expected.

Initially objectives should be prepared by the subordinate, flowing naturally from the process of ongoing communication. They should incorporate both the priorities of the individual position and the organizational priorities. A difficult area in some cases is differentiating ongoing responsibilities from new departures. In any objective-setting process the departures tend to take precedence since they are the matters which require a new focus of attention. Care should be taken, however, to recognize ongoing and continuing responsibilities and performance levels as the major element in most annual review processes.

The art of writing and specifying objectives requires a good deal of experience with the process and an understanding of the individuals involved. It is treated below in Chapter 7, as more generally a part of written communication skills.

The proficient use of the Objective Setting Meeting is a skill learned over time. For those who wish to improve through self- analysis a checklist is included below. If an individual seeks to improve skills in this area, special courses are available. When a new MBO system is implemented in an organization, especial care should be given to providing training and supplementary assistance to those requiring it.

A Checklist for An Objective Setting Meeting

1. Were adequate efforts made to inform the subordinate ahead of time of what would be expected?
2. Was a non-threatening atmosphere created by the initial interactions?
3. Was prior communication such that a dialogue had already been set in motion about objectives?
4. Was the subordinate involved in setting organizational goals?
5. Were the objectives stated an accurate reflection of organizational priorities? The manager's priorities? The subordinates' priorities?
6. Were the objectives stated in behavioral terms?
7. Were the objectives realistic, but challenging?
8. Were the objectives linked to performance indicators that could be measured?
9. Were plans for implementing the objectives discussed?
10. Were both parties convinced that the objectives were fair, and related to their own personal jobs, the organizational goals and their own conceptions of how to implement these goals successfully?
11. Were both parties enthusiastic about implementing the objectives that were stated?

The Objective-Setting Meeting is only the formal beginning of the annual process of setting individual objectives to match organizational goals. Its success depends upon successful follow-up on the part of the subordinate. The manager can be helpful here too. Monitoring the performance of individuals is a central function of managers. The process must continue throughout the year. Yet MBO requires in addition to ongoing effort a system of formal review of the "contract" entered into at the Objective-Setting Meeting. Such formal reviews should occur at least twice during the year, and often are held on a quarterly basis. The factors determining the frequency of the meetings include the nature of the organization, the people involved and the environmental uncertainty. Structuring the process of review is the manager's responsibility, though in large organizations the number of formal reviews is often specified on an organization-wide basis.

The purpose of the formal Review Meeting is to assess attainment on an interim basis and provide additional counseling and direction. The importance of maintaining a cooperative, rather than an adversarial atmosphere is as evident here as in the Objective-Setting Meeting. To the extent that the earlier meeting has succeeded in developing that spirit it is easier to maintain. The focus should be on counseling and support.

It is preferable that Review Meetings be scheduled at the time of the Objective-Setting Meeting so that they are acknowledged as occasions for assessing progress. The scheduling of these meetings puts interim time frames on the attainment of objectives or portions of objectives and automatically draws attention to progress at periodic intervals. Both parties, however, should feel free to continue ongoing communication and if necessary schedule additional formal review sessions. Obviously the review sessions take on special importance where managers do not interact with subordinates on a regular basis.

Conduct of Review Meeting

The manager should begin the Review Meeting by stressing a spirit of cooperation and setting the subordinate at ease. An order should be established for reviewing each objective, recognizing that progress will differ from area to area. Since the purpose of the meeting is to support and counsel, the greatest time should be spent on those objectives which can benefit from the advice of the manager. It is not necessary to spend extended effort on objectives which are being attained or which are not being attained if the manager is unable to help in any way. Managers should be careful to praise as well as criticize and recognize that support is just as important as censure. When objectives are not being met in a timely fashion, the reasons for delay and measures to overcome delay should be discussed. Undue attention should not be given to criticizing failures, particularly when these are out of the control of the subordinate.

A critical purpose of the Review Meeting is to recognize how to update the written objectives originally adopted. It may well be that different priorities now confront the individual and organization or that attempts to implement objectives have been frustrated. Changes in objectives should be incorporated in a revised written "contract." Another important function of the Review Meeting is to revise implementation plans. As an aid to self-evaluation, a checklist for Review Meetings is provided below.

Checklist for Review Meeting

1. Was the Review Meeting scheduled far in advance, preferably during the Goal Setting Meeting?
2. Was a supportive, counseling atmosphere created?
3. Did interim measures such as monitoring and counseling on an informal basis set the stage for the Review Meeting?
4. Was attention focused on those objectives and implementation plans which might be improved through discussion
5. Was praise as well as criticism offered by the manager?
6. Were objectives and implementation plans revised in light of changing circumstances and projections?
7. Was agreement reached as to future direction, while maintaining a cooperative spirit?

Like the Objective-Setting Meeting, the Review Meeting is a complicated procedure and one in which experience is often the best teacher. Experience can be misleading, however, especially in cases where organizations have not developed established procedures. In organizations where a good process is in place, managers will learn from one another.

Opportunities off the job should also be available to develop skills needed for the successful conduct of a Review Meeting. In organizations just beginning such a process, a series of orientations including skill building sessions are a necessity. Also training courses focusing on Review Meetings are available. Sometimes within the MBO process, the final review session will be a performance appraisal session in which an explicit evaluation of the subordinate's attainments are discussed and become part of the personnel file. This approach must be treated with circumspection. The introduction of performance appraisal dimensions into the MBO process can run directly counter to the rationale for MBO as articulated by leading proponents. In their view a critical element of MBO is the open and non-threatening character of the goal setting process. This results in individuals taking seriously the need to shape their own objectives in terms of organizational goals. If formal evaluation is added there is the possibility that individuals will be more concerned about protecting themselves against a harsh evaluation than in establishing realistic individual objectives. If progress toward reaching objectives is going to be used as a basis for evaluating performance, a strong incentive develops to state objectives which can be easily met. So rather than stretching the individual and promoting organizational goals, it can become an impediment to individual initiative and organizational progress. The result might be a meaningless exercise where ritualistic objectives would be met, because they would probably have been met in any case.

The problem posed by incorporating formal evaluations into a process of management by objectives is complicated in a public organization where the process may be difficult to limit to those directly involved. A written statement of objectives may become available to the general public and again inhibit a stretching process in favor of a safe, limiting process. The integration of these two disparate processes: setting individual objectives related to organizational purposes and evaluating individual performance must be handled circumspectly.

Another question to be considered is the linkage of annual review processes. The final Review Meeting might well turn into the Objective-Setting Meeting of the next cycle. Certainly the following year's objectives should follow from the status of the previous year's objectives. On the other hand mixing the functions of the Review Meeting with the Objective-Setting Meeting can cause additional problems.

In structuring a multi-year process both of these questions are critical. Below we propose two alternative schemes, though many variations are possible. In the first, four meetings take place each year, one a combined final Review Meeting and Objective-Setting Meeting. In the second model five meetings take place each year with the final Review Meeting treated as a Performance Appraisal Meeting. A suggested addition to either approach might be a discussion during the third Review Session of future individual objectives and proposed new organizational goals for the following year.

Two Schedules for Review Meetings

A. Integrated Quarterly Review		B. Separated Quarterly Review	
Y1 M1	Review/Objective-Setting	Y1 M1	Objective-Setting
Y1 M3	Review	Y1 M3	Review
Y1 M6	Review	Y1 M6	Review
Y1 M9	Review	Y1 M9	Review
		Y1 M12	Review/Appraisal
Y2 M1	Review/Objective-Setting	Y2 M1	Objective-Setting
Y2 M3	Review	Y2 M3	Review
Y2 M6	Review	Y2 M6	Review
Y2 M9	Review	Y2 M9	Review
		Y2 M12	Review/Appraisal
	Y=Year	M=Month	

The use of an explicit goal and objective-setting process requires organizational resources. It must compete with other demands for the time and energy of managers. The decision whether to use such a process and the amount of resources that should be devoted to it may be mandated or is at the discretion of the manager. If used properly it can be invaluable. Used in a perfunctory way, it consumes time and gives little return.

Of major importance in determining the specific character of any program utilizing MBO or its variants is the orientation of the organizational leadership. Since the program affects the basic operations of the institution, resistance among managers is not unusual. Much of the discussion of MBO in the literature addresses itself to the problems of implementation. The consensus is that if a new departure like MBO is to succeed, it must be strongly backed by top leadership. Furthermore, it must become an organic part of organizational operations, not just a cosmetic procedure.

MBO raises another basic question in a service organization staffed by professionals adhering to externally imposed standards and cherishing individual professional judgment. Will MBO provide the most effective means of motivating employees of SDOs? In such a situation the necessity of submitting written objectives, holding conferences and then being evaluated on these objectives may become associated with a narrowing, rather than a broadening of initiative. MBO may be perceived by many professionals as an attempt to impose administrative strictures. Since the professionals spend so much time unsupervised and since performance standards are unclear, the effect of MBO may be to restrict the breadth of job performance rather than to enlarge it. Finally, the accessibility of human service managers to public scrutiny makes the implementation of an evaluation system more difficult. The potential for confidential objectives and results to find their way into public view may compromise the integrity of the process.

While the basic difference between human service organizations and industrial organization is striking it should not be exaggerated. Many other organizations, involved in the production and distribution of goods and services can be found that have similar difficulties in defining their goals. But it is probably true that goal definition is more difficult for human service organizations than for most other organizations. How difficult depends upon the nature of the task and the target group being serviced.

This difficulty in specifying goals, then agreeing on goals and finally achieving control over their attainment, has often discouraged human service managers from engaging in goal setting activities. But just as production organizations have been driven to systematic goal setting by the demands of the marketplace, human service organizations are being asked by funding sources to specify goals and then demonstrate they have reached those goals. Evidence of this tendency is the increasing demand that human service organizations establish accountability systems and institute performance appraisals to ensure that managers attain the goals they set. The usefulness of specifying goals for human service organizations is beyond question. Incorporation into a successful management process is still an ideal for most human service organizations.

4. Planning and Policy Analysis

For the purposes of simplification we began this chapter focusing on the determination of goals by the SDO. In describing in detail an approach to systematic organizational goal setting and individual formulation of objectives on an annual basis, the most useful planning process for most human service organizations has been described in detail. Another type of planning related to goal setting and objective-setting is project planning which will be described in Chapter 4. For most SDOs long-range planning is the exception rather than the rule. The demands of service delivery and the constraints imposed from above militate against a long-range perspective.

Long-range planning requires realistic projections of the future: both with respect to the problems which will need to be met and the resources which will be available. Many human service managers complain that given the constraints of an annual budget process at the several levels of government and within other funding agencies, planning beyond annual goal setting is difficult if not impossible. Furthermore, the process of documenting and justifying current activities to satisfy current funding agencies may be extremely time consuming, leaving little time for planning activities. But a counter- argument can be made that because of the great uncertainty in demands and resources in the human services, planning for the future is even more critical.

Human service organizations are more like publicly-held corporations with boards of directors or divisions of conglomerates than they are like individual entrepreneurial businesses, where the owner can be relatively free-wheeling. The result is that that manager's annual goal-setting efforts and long-range projections must anticipate policies determined above. Also since human service organizations are invariably dependent at least in part on grant funds, they must be responsive to donor organizations. Almost invariably grants come with guidelines and regulations that must be followed. These constraints limit the process of planning. Yet they also present a considerable challenge to the ingenuity of the human service manager. Unfortunately, given its difficulties, disregard of planning may be a tempting option.

Given the ever-changing landscape of the human service system, the failure to look ahead, anticipate new sources of revenue and changing needs may be a blueprint for organizational disaster. An increasing number of not-for-profit organizations recognize the advantages of diversification. By organizing several services under a common organizational umbrella, the organization can withstand sudden changes of emphasis by government and private philanthropy which might otherwise threaten organizational existence. In addition coodination among these activities may result in better service delivery to the client.

But given the small size of many SDOs, the resources available for planning are minimal. An ad hoc approach may be the most successful. A small group of individuals can be designated as a task force on long range goals, or stategic planning or simply information gathering. An individual with research skills might be selected as task force leader. A major function of a task force may be to develop sources of reliable forecasts. Regular publications, conferences and periodic reports from government agencies can often provide forecasting information. Current sources to be checked include: Regional Bureaus of Labor Statistics, State Departments of Social Services, and Project Share and its bibliographical resources.

Planning beyond annual goal setting might involve multi-year plans, specific development of new projects or assessments of past and future activities. Most SDOs will not have special units to carry out these tasks although a larger one such as a hospital might.

The manager and a small group of assistants should engage in planning on an individual and group basis. If regular staff meetings are held, one purpose can be to consider strategic planning questions. And of course, ad hoc arrangements can be made to look at specific questions. This latter course has particular appeal since it results in an involvement throughout the agency. The manager may convene a task force or special committee to look at special problems or one as general as the next five years at the organization.

The choice of mechanisms for planning is the choice of the manager and the success of planning is largely the result of the manager's personal efforts. In any organization, but particularly human service organizations, the emphasis is on day-to-day service. The demands of many human service organizations are enormous, and the staff is rightly oriented toward service delivery. But no matter how great the burdens of the day, the organization that does not reserve time for consideration of the future is making a serious mistake.

SDOs are not free to determine their own organizational goals. In the private and not-for-profit sectors SDOs usually are responsible to boards of directors. In the public sector managers of SDOs report to higher agency officials and indirectly to the executive, and the legislature. Organizational goals are thus subject to numerous constraints.

Planning of human services in fact takes place during the various policymaking processes that go into the development and passage of legislation, executive orders and administrative regulations, and foundation directives. Legislative committees and their staffs in conjunction with executive staffs at the federal, state and local levels are the primary locus for planning for the future and policymaking. In the past in a number of instances legislators have been surprised at the consequences of major social policies they enacted partly because the processes of prediction are not well developed. When problems arise committee hearings may be held and ad hoc legislative task forces or interdepartmental task forces may be created. In some instances citizens' groups are appointed to survey a problem and make policy recommendations. At the federal and state levels agency planning has important impacts on the ways that legislatively determined policies are implemented. Especially at the federal level, special units focusing on policy analysis and planning are common.

The human service system is characterized by considerable fragmentation, a reflection of the competition among different levels and agencies of government as well as the patchwork of special categorical legislation. Major initiatives at the national level tend to originate in the Executive Offices or the responsible Congressional Committees, while initiatives to regularize programs often develop within the Departments. Recently the new Congressional Budget Office has been assuming an important planning function in undertaking multi-year analysis and coordinating projected spending levels.

The human service manager must recognize the primacy of higher level organizations in planning and policy analysis. But the manager who opts out of such activity abdicates an important part of the leadership role.

Selected Bibliography

Anthony, Robert. *Planning and Control Systems: A Framework for Analysis.* 1965.

Drucker, Peter. *The Practice of Management.* New York: Harper and Row, 1954.

Horton, Gerald T. *Alternative Approaches to Human Services Planning.* Arlington, Virginia: Human Services Institute for Children and Families, 1974.

Kahn, Alfred. *Social Policy and Social Services.* New York: Random House, 1973.

Odiorne, George. *Management by Objectives.* New York: Pitman Publishing Corp., 1951.

Selznick, Philip. *Leadership in Administration.* New York: Harper and Row, 1957.

United Way of America. *UWASIS II. A Taxonomy of Social Goals and Human Service Programs.* Alexandria, Virginia.: United Way, 1976.

Zald, Mayer N. and Denton, Patricia. "From Evangelism to General Service: The Transformation of the YMCA," *Administrative Science Quarterly,* 1963, 8:214-34.

Chapter 3.

Problem Solving and Decision Making

1. The Manager as Problem Solver

Although attention to the goals and direction of the organization is an important responsibility of managers, the resources devoted to organizational planning are usually small. The manager spends most of the time responding to day-to-day problems. This is especially true for the SDO manager.

A manager influences the direction of the organization through these frequent actions and minor decisions that involve readjustments of the organizational operations on almost a daily basis. The manager both as the buffer between the organizational unit and the outside world and as the coordinator of the work unit is called upon to deal with unusual situations which are not met by the preprogrammed responses of the organization. In performing this role, referred to by Mintzberg as disturbance-handler or problem-solver, the manager attempts to reestablish the work flow so that intervention is no longer necessary.

The way in which the manager handles this role is critical to successful leadership and organizational effectiveness. Possible responses range from deferral of any action to careful convening of elaborate decisionmaking bodies to apply sophisticated decision techniques. The skill of the successful manager depends upon the ability to choose the proper response to a particular problem and either apply the prescribed technique or delegate that task to others. A pervasive difficulty is reconciling the need to react quickly, with the need to use the most sophisticated techniques where they will improve the quality of the decision. A combination of pragmatic leadership and rational decisionmaking is the ideal that managers seek to attain.

The nature of the managerial job exposes the manager to a never-ending series of new problems that require solutions. Yet it is important to remember that the environment in which the manager operates, and this is especially true for the human service manager, is constantly changing. The picture that emerges from recent social science research is that of the active manager who must respond constantly to a range of stimuli. Often situations are messy and complicated.

During the last thirty years, many studies of managerial behavior, including those by Sayles and Mintzberg, have been undertaken. They have focused on the types, location, patterns, and duration of managers' activities and their interactions with others. Questionnaires, interviews, activity sampling, structured and unstructured observation, as well as various self-report instruments, have all been employed singly or in conjunction with one another. What emerges is a view of the active manager where problem solving and decision making merge with a myriad of ad hoc responses.

In the first major diary study of managerial activities, Carlson described the activities of nine European executives. He attributed differences in frequencies of activities to differences in organizational structure and in the manager's physical proximity to subordinates. Stewart used work diaries to conduct a study of the activities of 160 middle managers. Differences in the amount of time managers spent on activities were generally attributed to the degree that a manager's position was specialized, the extent to which the manager was concerned with problems outside the work unit, the extent to which the manager was involved in daily activities of the larger organization, and the organization's size. Those managers whose positions were specialized or whose major concerns were with problems within their own department were more apt to spend more time on paper work than the "general" manager, and less time in discussions with others. The amount of time spent in discussion also increased with organizational size and with the rate of organizational change. The type of job held by the manager was also linked to the amount of time spent alone or with others.

Dubin and Spray used a diary to obtain data about the jobs of eight executives employed by three different organizations. They attributed many of these differences among managers to either their rank in the organization or to the degree to which their positions were specialized. Those managers with functional specializations tended to spend more time alone than the other managers in the study. The use of oral communications increased and written communication decreased as the executives rose in rank. The number of contacts the executives made with individuals outside of the organization also increased with the executive's rank. However, the type of organization also affected the frequency of the manager's external contacts. Managers in client-centered organizations spent a good deal more time with persons outside of the organizations.

While studies of managerial behavior have not specifically focused on human service organizations, public and service-oriented organizations have been included to some extent. While type of organization will clearly affect managerial behavior, other variables are also important, including: 1) the individuals involved; 2) the specific function they perform within the organization; and 3) the level within the organization at which they perform.

Management involves frequent interpersonal contact and frequent interruptions and deviations from the expected. It is not a job for the faint-hearted or phlegmatic. These findings are consistent with subjective feelings of many managers that they are constantly in a "time-bind." Managers invariably wish for more hours in the working day and frequently spend long hours completing their many tasks. The seemingly never ending demands on the manager are merely a part of the job. Managers have open-ended jobs that, in a sense, never reach completion. Managers are constantly interacting with their subordinates, peers and superiors. They must attack problems which arise on a continuing basis. If their communications with these various individuals are functioning well, they will be receiving a constant flow of information suggesting where their intervention may be helpful. Perhaps the most important part of a manager's job is deciding when and where to intervene. When is intervention required to regularize the work-flow? When does a situation become the manager's problem? When are decisions needed? Associated with these questions about managerial intervention are others about how the manager spends time. In attempting to secure monies or implement new programs, what strategies are most effective? Should written guidelines be developed? Should a series of meetings be held with subordinates? Should the public relations dimension be emphasized? Much more than other organizational actors, the manager's time is unstructured, subject to change and must be adapted to the current organizational priorities. In a basic sense, decisions about how to spend time are very closely connected with the task of the organizational unit in which the manager is functioning. This is particularly true for individuals who head SDOs.

The art of self-control, structuring one's own work schedule to reflect the current needs of the organization may be the managers's most important task and the one most closely related to on-the-job success. Yet, unfortunately, no simple rules are available to tell a manager how to program the day. The best use of time is dependent upon the organization goals, the manager's function, the manager's individual strengths and weaknesses, the abilities of the rest of the management team and the members of the work unit. In the final chapter, ways of analyzing one's own managerial activities will be described and some guidelines will be suggested for making better use of the manager's scarcest resource, time.

Since an important part of management is to regularize the work flow in the organization, the manager's task becomes dealing with interruptions in the work flow. These interruptions may be viewed as challenges to the smooth flow of organization processes. The manager becomes a disturbance-handler or a problem-solver. A large part of the manager's job is to deal with problems as they arise.

Problems come in all shapes and sizes. A member of the work group is absent or not functioning well. The quality of work output, as indicated by a periodic report, is below standard. The work unit must accept new responsibilities. Supervisors in the organization have demanded a report be prepared for tomorrow or the day after.

Higher level managers often deal with problems by delegation. Then they may establish a priority listing for those remaining. The ability to reduce problems, anticipate problems and routinize the response to problems is a valuable asset in every level of the organization. Still, a certain number of problems demanding attention will arise within the area of responsibility of any manager functioning as manager.

Often such problems are complex and need to be analyzed more carefully. The outlines of rational problem-solving and decisionmaking are generally agreed upon, though individuals may differ slightly in the way they define stages and the importance they attach to each. One approach to systematic problem-solving and decisionmaking is described below.

Systematic Problem-Solving

Stage 1. *Scanning the Environment:*Survey the significant factors within the work group environment related to the problem.

Stage 2. *Defining the Problem:*Clearly identify the problem, limiting its scope as much as possible to simplify its solution.

Stage 3. *Deferring, Delegating, Routinizing:* Many problems are simply deferred while others are assigned to subordinates or dealt with in a pre-established routine manner.

Stage 4. *Generating Alternatives:* A number of options should be thought up and considered.

Stage 5. *Establishing Criteria:* The basis for choosing among alternatives should be clarified.

Stage 6. *Evaluating Alternatives Against Criteria:* The necessary analysis and calculations to choose among alternatives must be made.

Stage 7. *Developing and Selling Recommendations:* A strategy for gaining acceptance of the alternative selected must be adopted.

In order to explain the sequence of steps in a rational approach to problem solving, it will be useful to refer to a realistic situation confronting human service managers. The case study which follows involves a rather specialized function within a large city agency, bound by civil service law and procedures. In this sense it represents an attempt to revise lax disciplinary procedures in special circumstances. But in a broader sense, it involves the creative resolution of a difficult and sensitive problem of employee discipline, in a particularly opportune circumstance. It presents the possibility for creative problem solving in an area in which it is ordinarily very difficult to operate.

The Dilemma of Louise John

On July 1, 1985, Louise John, an upcoming middle level manager was promoted to head of the Disciplinary Unit in the Office of Personnel of a large human service agency in Central City. Carl Zanof, who had taken office on February 1, 1985, as Commissioner of Human Services, called Louise John into his office after the swearing in ceremony. "Louise," he said, "I consider you a bright young woman. You are taking over a sensitive area. One in which I think improvements are possible. But you must also realize the potential dilemmas that you will face and the importance of maintaining good relationships with the unions representing the employees. I know you will do what is right."

In the first month after taking office, Louise noticed that Carl Zanof altered several decisions of the hearing examiners by imposing more stringent penalties. About one month after taking office the supervisor of the four hearing officers appeared in Louise's office.

"Ms. John," he began, "we hearing officers have served seven Commissioners faithfully. We have called the cases before us as we have seen them. We believe we have much to offer the Department of Human Services, but find the position of the Commissioner in reversing and changing our decisions unacceptable. Either we are the hearing examiners or he should conduct the hearings himself. I can retire at any time. Two of the hearing examiners are in a similar situation and the other two have five more years until retirement. Unless the Commissioner meets with us and finds a way of resolving this impasse, I and the other two hearing examiners eligible for retirement intend to take our story to the press and resign, explaining that this Commissioner does not respect the civil service system and its provisions for 'fair hearings and due process.'"

What would you do if you were in Louise John's position?

2. Scanning the Environment and Defining the Problem

Problems which arise in the operation of organizations must be viewed within their larger context. Why has the problem arisen and what is the manager's relationship to its solution? Clearly Louise John must recognize that the problem is very closely connected with herself and her own career. She has recently received a promotion and her abilities are being tested. A classic conflict between her superiors and her subordinates has developed and she is clearly the woman in the middle of a very difficult situation. Her performance in this situation will probably have an impact on her career out of proportion to its own significance. She is in a highly visible position, having just taken over a new job and dealing with an issue which not only commands the interest of the Commissioner, but may explode onto the front pages of the newspapers.

The significance of this issue, of course, is not limited to those individuals already mentioned. The issue of treatment of employees is one in which the unions representing those employees will certainly be involved. In fact the continuing municipal budget cuts in Central City have increased the militancy of all the employee unions. Unable to secure large wage increases for their membership, the unions have been very difficult to deal with on other issues. A resignation by hearing examiners on the issue of civil service standards would almost certainly be taken up by local union leaders.

An underlying element in the possible conflict is the Mayor himself. The Commissioner's strong stance on employee discipline in part reflects the Mayor's position. The Mayor has taken a hard line against the unions and argued for greater efforts by civil service workers. On several occasions he has condemned shirkers. On the other hand the Mayor will be up for reelection in one year. Since the last round of collective bargaining negotiations, the Mayor has been more tame in his criticism of the unions. He is hoping to get their support for reelection, or at least convince them to remain neutral. The Mayor also has a history of abandoning Commissioners in their time of need. If a confrontation is brought on between the unions and the Mayor, it is difficult to predict what the Mayor would do and whom he would surprise.

Finally, the media have recently been emphasizing potential controversies, in preparation for the Mayoral election. Their actions, and public reactions might be inflammatory.

More generally, in viewing any problem, a variety of contextual elements must be investigated. These elements are in large part determined by the human services system. But even among human service organizations considerable differences occur. In each case, scanning the environment is a critical element in successful action.

An important distinction can be made between human service organizations which are part of the governmental structure, such as income maintenance centers, public schools, public hospitals and public rehabilitation facilities and their private or not-for- profit counterparts. The central differences is that the public agency is directly responsible to appointed and elected public officials, while the private or not-for-profit agency is directly responsible to its board of directors and its funding sources.

Part of the skill of managing a human service organization is the ability to understand twhich part of the human services system is involved when a particular problem develops and which parts are likely to react to a particular course of action. The skilled human services manager must develop an almost intuitive skill which allows for subtle reactions to environmental stimuli. The skill and knowledge necessary for appropriate response in these situations is developed over a period of time. Part of the distinguishing aspect of working within human service organizations is the similarity of the context in which problems arise. When the response to a problem involves interaction with actors outside the immediate organization, the manager exercises the representational role which is described at greater length in Chapter 9 below.

Sometimes analyzing the context of the problem will point to an easy solution. A statement by a mayor or a member of the board of directors may be seen as part of some larger issue, which is best left without response. The perceived problem is now viewed as merely a statement by an influential individual, not justifying direct oreganization response. But more often the contextual analysis will serve only to clarify what are the interests or the stakes of the individuals involved or potentially involved. Further clarification and definition of the problem is ordinarily necessary before taking any action.

The problem presented to Louise John may be viewed on three levels. In the first instance she must deal with the demand of her subordinate for an audience with the Commissioner. But in the longer view, she must deal with the conflict between two approaches to employee discipline. Her superior seems to be pressing her for a more stringent procedure, while her existing employees seem satisfied with the approach they have developed over many years. While she must address the first problem first, the second is clearly at the heart of the problem. And a third problem lurks in the background. What should be her attitude toward the threatened resignation? Such an action could open new alternatives to bring in new personnel and reorganize hearing procedures.

3. Deferring, Delegating, Routinizing

Having defined the problem, a response becomes possible. The vast majority of problems are resolved in a straightforward way. Perhaps the most common approach is to defer a problem. Since the volume of problems presenting themselves to a manager is very high some measures must be taken to reduce the numbers that are being dealt with at any given time. Some can be solved almost automatically since they represent typical problems which may be anticipated and for which a standard response has been developed on the basis of experience. Others can be deferred, at least temporarily. In fact knowing when to defer a problem is one of a manager's most useful skills. In addition to strategies for delay, the manager also will attempt to limit the possible impact of a problem.

A skillful manager attempts to deal with problems by pushing back the time frame in which they must be solved and in limiting their impact to a smaller number of individuals. But even a manager skillful at limiting strategies must be able to deal with problems that do not respond to readily available solutions and may not be deferred. In the case above Louise John might not do anything. Perhaps her employee was overwrought because of a personal problem. Or perhaps he will forget he raised the issue. Indeed, the most common solution to problems is ignoring them. Many will go away.

While good managers ignore problems which don't need solutions, they also identify problems which present opportunities. If Louise John runs the risk of damaging her reputation, she also has the opportunity to demonstrate her ability. Her choice of whether to act or defer action will in part depend upon her estimate as to the likelihood of the problem disappearing. Indeed, this particular problem would appear to be an unlikely candidate for disappearance.

Remembering once again the high activity levels that are characteristic of managers, it should be apparent that deferring problems may be an inviting strategy. Deferring the wrong problems can of course result in dire consequences.

If deferring a problem is not possible it may be possible to delegate it to someone else, since a manager works through others. Delegation can be healthy and positive, if the problem is within the power of a subordinate to solve. Actually in the first instance the problems that are soluble at lower levels should not ordinarily come to the attention of the manager. But problems which can properly be considered by others within the organization do often come to the attention of the manager. In this case delegation can be appropriate and effective.

Delegation can also be a strategy for avoiding responsibility or deferring a problem while also being able to report that something is being done. "It's in her hands." The danger of delegation as bluff is that it either will not succeed, or the demoralization to your subordinate will be too great. This is a course to be pursued carefully and sparingly.

In the case of Louise John delegation would be difficult, since the problem is being generated by a subordinate specifically for her attention. Also it involves an issue that is directly in her competence and one which involves both her superior and her subordinate directly.

What about routinization? A large number of problems can be resolved in preestablished ways. Client appeal procedures are an attempt to routinize potential problem areas. Problems which can be anticipated such as those involving the operation of payroll and payment systems can be eliminated by correcting the systems themselves and anticipating the problems. A shrewd manager will always attempt to anticipate problems and establish regular procedures for dealing with them. To the extent that problems can be routinized they can be dealt with quickly and without danger to the work process. In this particular situation one routine solution might be to ask for a written statement of the problem. This is a standard bureaucratic procedure, which places the burden on the complainant and at least in some cases results in the elimination of the problem without actually confronting it directly.

4. Alternatives and Criteria

Problems that are not amenable to being deferred, delegated, or relegated to routine solutions, demand more vigorous problem solving activity. In solving such a problem the generation of alternatives is a critical step, for it determines the ultimate range of possibilities which will be considered. As the manager moves to more formal and complex approaches, expertise becomes of increasing importance. The manager may be forced to draw upon others within or without the organization who can provide this expertise. In large organizations problems which require formal analysis may be sent to a special unit that specializes in problem-solving.

Remember that the manager is constantly searching for ways to reduce time demands. The manager therefore seeks the most expedient way of dealing with a particular problem. Often the number of alternatives to be considered is severely limited by the need to act quickly.

The longer and the more elaborate the procedure for generating alternatives, the more time is consumed in this activity. Moreover, additional time is required to evaluate and compare a large number of alternatives. With this understanding let us consider the ways in which an effective manager can generate a range of alternatives for consideration. Perhaps the easiest place to begin is the case we have considered involving the hearing examiners.

Suppose that Louise decides to respond first by ignoring the demands made upon her for a meeting. Then the demand is renewed and she asks for a written request. Then she is confronted with the issue once again and calls the supervisor in to reason together. But the supervisor presses his demands to meet with the Commissioner. So far Louise has been pursuing a cautious limiting strategy. Now she goes to the Commissioner, explains the situation, and asks the Commissioner's advice.

The Commissioner suggests that indeed the meeting take place and that it be seen as an opportunity. If the supervisor and two hearing examiners want to leave, let them. Perhaps a solution can be found to change the nature of the decisions of the hearing examiners by taking some other approach. Perhaps hiring new lawyers for this job will reach the results needed. On the basis of the Commissioner's advice, the meeting is held and the Commissioner very shrewdly acknowledges his differences, suggests they have served the agency well and offers to ease their retirement. They acquiesce and the Commissioner tells Louise she now has a harder problem to solve: how to make the hearing examiner system work more in keeping with agency needs. Of course she must solve the problem within the existing budget constraints. The current personnel budget for the hearing examiners is $120,000. In addition, a freeze on hiring outside personnel to full-time agency lines is in effect.

Louise makes some contacts within the agency and comes up with three potential pools of staff with which to fill the vacancies: 1) Managerial (Salary: $23,000-$38,000); 2) Staff Analyst (Salary: $15,000-$23,000) 3) Attorneys (Salary: $19,000-$33,000). Then, in a chance conversation with a friend working in another Central City agency, a practice comes to light that seems to present a possible alternative course of action. It seems that one city agency hires hearing examiners under a contract and pays them on a per diem basis.

In this particular situation a creative alternative developed out of a chance contact with a friend. But how can creative alternatives be generated in a systematic way? It is difficult to determine what makes for creativity, but an effective manager must be exposed to a broad range of approaches to problems and be open and receptive to new ideas. While individual inspiration can result in creative impulses and solutions, cultivating creative and knowledgeable peers can also be helpful.

Like Louise who had friends in other city agencies, the astute manager will cultivate friends within his or her own agency and similar agencies. They can provide an important source of ideas. Another source of new approaches is professional journals which report on new approaches. In the human service area specifically, some journals include: *Social Service Review* and *American Public Welfare Journal*. *Public Administration Review* is a general public sector journal that may be helpful and *Administrative Sciences Quarterly* is a technical journal that may provide some good ideas. Another strategy for generating new approaches is to attend conferences. Sometimes group brainstorming techniques can yield surprising results. Individuals are encouraged to come up with new ideas by creating an affirmative environment, using some simple principles of group facilitation.

Once the alternatives have been generated to solve a particular problem, one of them must be selected for implementation. We have discussed above how a series of alternatives were used to attempt to resolve the problem of the hearing examiners before actually calling a meeting of the interested parties. Once this meeting was called and completed, the resolution moved to another level. The problem of establishing a new group of hearing examiners took center stage.

As this problem developed a number of constraints were placed upon its solution. Meeting these constraints was a prerequisite to a satisfactory solution. The Commissioner stated a strong preference that managerial class employees not be used for this particular job. The legal office of the Human Services Department made it be known that it could not afford to give up any attorneys. The money available for the positions was $75,000 plus 37% fringe, the personnel costs of the three retiring examiners. And the ban on hiring new staff was already mentioned.

Another criteria ordinarily imposed on solutions in human service organizations is that they not be strongly opposed by any important political force. Agency heads, mayors and boards of directors are hesitant to adopt particular courses of action which have strong political opposition.

In addition to all of the specific constraints in this situation and the more general one of political feasability, it is an implied rule that in almost every decision the benefits accruing should be greater than the costs of the undertaking and that no less costly alternative will yield as great a benefit.

Yeheskel Dror has formulated this rule as the optimization of Net Output = Benefits-Costs. It can at times be a difficult quantity to calculate, but often may be simplified if the benefits or costs of different alternatives are roughly equivalent. It may be possible in such a case merely to compare that aspect which is not equivalent.

In general, then, the criteria for evaluating the desireability of a particular alternative or course of action concern the following three issues: 1) How effective is it? How likely is it to bring about the desired result? 2) What is its cost? Are there other programs resulting in the same or similar results at lower costs? and 3) Are there any untoward consequences of the alternative?

In the case above, a series of options were rejected outright. The use of managerial employees was forbidden by the Commissioner. The Office of Legal Affairs refused to allow its lawyers to be considered for transfer for use as hearing examiners. The only viable alternative using internal staff that remained was the use of staff analysts. Let us refer to this as Alternative A. This alternative could then be compared to the alternative of using independent hearing examiners on a contract basis, Alternative B. The costs associated with Alternative A would be between $45-$69,000, plus 37%. The costs associated with Alternative B would be $78,000 for 780 person days.

Although in this instance the respective benefits cannot be precisely quantified it would appear that the benefits of hiring the independent contractors are overwhelming. The only real advantage of hiring the staff analysts would be their experience in the agency. But this, in fact, might be a detriment if they had already been familiar with the old way of doing things. Furthermore, it is probably impossible to secure individuals with hearing experience or with substantive knowledge of the procedures and rules. A training program would have to be established. On the other hand the independent contractors are lawyers who are familiar with the procedures and whose background and abilities can already be judged by reference to their work for other agencies. It also appears that hiring these individuals will result in a savings of money. Clearly the control exercised over these individuals is much greater since they will have no permanent status within the agency.

As this example illustrates, benefits of particular courses of action may be difficult to measure. Other, more complicated examples can be cited. How does one compare the relative benefit of institutionalization of debilitated persons as opposed to placement in private homes? In that case, again the costs are probably more easily calculated.

Another complicating factor in the calculation of benefits and costs is the necessity of calculating the present value of future benefits. Suppose it could be determined that by entering a particular training program an individual would earn an average of $100 a year more over a 10 year period. What expenditure of current monies would justify such an earning increase in future years? Calculating present value is one of the techniques that is central to benefit/cost analysis and is discussed below in Chapter 12.

The use of mathematical techniques for computing the effects of programs is at the heart of what is termed modeling or operations research. A mathematical model allows for the abstract representation and estimation of major factors so that the effects can be calculated. In its simplest form a mathematical model can be a single equation. As a simple example, consder the question of how large an office space is needed to accommodate a given population of welfare recipients using a social service office. Suppose the number of recipients that can be accommodated in an office is given by the equation X=Y where X is the number of recipients being served by a social services center and Y is the number of square feet in the center. Suppose the equation incorporates the historical experience of a certain city over the past ten years. Can you think of any circumstances which might make this prediction inaccurate? Can you think of any ways of ensuring that the office would remain cost-effective if the number of recipients changes? How would you estimate the number of recipients anticipated in five years? Suppose you obtained estimates of changes in the numbers over the last five years, would this estimate be a good prediction of the future?

Needless to say, mathematical models are often much more complicated than a single equation. Often several equations are involved. A technique known as linear programming allows for finding solutions to a series of equations which constitute a model. One interpretation of such a group of equations is a decison problem in which each equation represents a constraint limiting the decision alternatives.

So far we have considered situations in which the impacts of a number of alternatives can be calculated and compared. When decisions are made under these circumstances they are classified as decisions under conditions of certainty. Many decisions, particularly calculations about the future may not involve certainty. For example, a particular decision about holding an event out of doors may be contingent upon whether or not it will rain. A decision about whether to investigate a particular father accused of non-support may rest upon whether the individual is likely to be earning income at some time in the future. A decision to release someone on probation may involve the probability of rearrest. Where firm information allows for a calculation of the probability of a particular event occurring, we refer to decisionmaking-under-risk. Where the probability is not known or is subject to an educated guess, the decisionmaking is said to take place under conditions of uncertainty. Under such circumstances, certain assumptions are possible to allow for the selection of the better alternative.

While an optimal solution, providing the best course of action is the goal, it cannot always be realized. Even where theoretically such a solution is possible such as under conditions of certainty, some information may not be available. Although Herbert Simon urges us to seek efficiency and Yehezkel Dror favors the concept of net output, such calculations are often not possible.

Herbert Simon introduced the term "satisficing" to describe solutions which are not optimal but are very good ones. According to Simon a calculation of the impacts of all alternatives is usually not practical. Time constraints require quick response and a comprehensive solution is often not possible. Incremental decisionmaking often results from informational and time constraints as well as political pressures to maintain the status quo.

5. Implementing Solutions

Solutions to problems are rarely self-implementing. In a small percentage of cases the manager who arrives at a solution to a problem need only give a "nod of the head." Sometimes the solution may require an elaborate sequence of activities. In such cases the project planning techniques described in the next chapter will be invaluable.

Whether or not the implementation effort requires a project plan, however, the solution ordinarily involves the efforts of other individuals who must either actively participate or at least give their acquiescence. A manager with a "bright idea" for resolving a problem must sell the idea to a varied audience. Even in cases where the manager has the formal authority to act independently, and often this is not the case, a skillful selling job may be needed to convince those affected or with some interest that the proposed solution is correct.

In arriving at a proposed solution, it is often useful to make sure that the requisite authority for implementing the solution is ensured from the outset. A manager may check with superiors. Where oversight boards are involved, formal proposals may be made prior to arriving at a proposed solution. And individuals who must provide approval may be brought into the problem solving process. Even individuals who are not in a position of formal authority may be usefully involved in the process, helping ensure that their support will be forthcoming at a later stage. Even where preparations have been made to involve others, additional efforts are often required once a solution has been identified.

Where extensive analysis has been undertaken, the selling of the solution may be clothed in complicated and sophisticated concepts. It is the job of the manager and staff to translate their decision into language and logic which is clear. A solution which is eminently sensible can easily be undermined by a reluctant audience.

In the human services selling solutions is particularly important. Everyone, including the clients, feels that they have their own ideas about how things should be done. Professional groups such as social workers, doctors and teachers have their own perspectives and approaches. And the system tends to be diffuse. For a manager to get ideas acted upon requires perseverance and persuasiveness.

Persuasiveness may require formal written presentations or oral presentation before boards or public meetings. The manager with strong written and verbal communication skills is in the best possible position to convince others of the worthiness of the cause. The ways in which these skills can be developed are covered below in Chapter 6.

The techniques of persuasion must adapt to the appropriate audience. Superiors and subordinates respond to internal approaches based upon regular contacts over a relatively long period of time. Outsiders require attention getting devices. But human service managers must be ready and willing to address a variety of audiences in a variety of ways.

Human service organizations are, to an extraordinary extent, dependent upon public and community support for their operation. Without public support, welfare programs will not flourish. Drug rehabilitation centers are not able to exist without community support and willingness to encounter some local inconvenience. Hospitals and income maintenance centers require public support and cooperation for their effective operation.

In the case above the selling was easy and obvious. It is not always so. Nor are human service managers always in a position to argue as strongly as they might. No other groups of managers are as held accountable by so many monitors for what they are doing. The public wants to know, the government wants to know, the grantors want to know.

Selling the solution is not the end either. For the solution must then be implemented, sometimes, by a complicated project plan. The development of such plans is the subject of the next chapter.

Selected Bibliography

Carlson, Sune. *Executive Behavior; A study of the Workload and the Working Methods of Managing Directors.* Stockholm: C.A. Stroberg Aktiebolag Pub., 1951.

Dror, Yeheskel. *Public Policymaking Reexamined.* San Francisco: Chandler Publishing, 1968.

Dubin and Spray. "Executive Behavior and Interaction". *Industrial Relations*, 3 (1964), 99-108.

Hoos, Ida. *Systems Analysis in Public Policy: A Critique.* Berkeley: University of California Press, 1960.

Mintzberg, Henry. *The Nature of Managerial Work.* New York: Harper and Row, 1973.

Rivlin, Alice. *Systematic Thinking for Social Action.* Washington, D.C.: The Brookings Institution, 1971.

Sayles, Leonard R. *Leadership: What Effective Managers Really Do. . . . and How They Do It.* New York: McGraw-Hill, 1979.

Simon, Herbert. *Administrative Behavior.* New York: Free Press, 1945.

Stewart, Rosemary. *Contrasts in Management.* London: McGraw Hill, 1976.

Stewart, Rosemary. *Managers and Their Jobs.* London: MacMillan, 1967.

Williams, Walter and Elmore, Richard, eds. *Social Program Implementation.* New York: Academic Press, 1976.

Chapter 4.

Project Planning and Control

Decisions, whether involving organizational goals, resource allocation or day-to-day operations have to be acted upon to take effect. Sometimes action is minimal. For example, the decision to award a contract may only require a letter to become operative. Conversely, if an organization is considering whether or not to submit a bid, the decision may be the culmination of a long process which results in the simple act of mailing a letter. A decision to hire a certain individual may result in a letter of appointment and then a series of routine actions carried out by the personnel division.

But decisions also may initiate complex sets of events. Suppose it was the decisionmaker's responsibility to prepare a schedule for monitoring completion of the contract awarded. Or the decisionmaker had first to begin to generate a proposal involving input from a large number of individuals. Or suppose the decisionmaker was responsible for creating a system for putting someone on payroll for the first time in a new organization without any personnel system.

Management decisions radiate consequences, some more complicated than others. Many of these consequences may have been programmed in the past and the appropriate actors may do their part quickly and efficiently in a coordinated manner. Often the processes used by bureaucracies to implement decisions are time-consuming and inefficient.

Any group of activities directed toward implementing a decision or carrying out some specific objectives may be viewed as a project which can be planned and executed in a systematic way using a group of planning techniques that assist in the analysis, scheduling and control of the project. Viewed as a whole, this process may be labelled project planning.

It may seem unusual to associate project planning techniques with human services management. They have ordinarily been associated with private sector production activities and processes. They have been frequently used in documenting and improving industrial processes and in overseeing construction projects, where the work of a number of subcontractors must be orchestrated to achieve timely completion. More and more these approaches are being used in human service management. And rightfully so. Many of the tasks undertaken in human service organizations involve complex series of interrelated tasks that require explicit and detailed treatment.

While not every manager of a SDO needs to be expert in the details and techniques of project planning, an understanding of these techniques can prove invaluable. Every manager is involved in task analysis and work scheduling, although often informal approaches are used. Often these may suffice. Increasingly, though, in today's complex world of human services the techniques of project planning may prove useful. Even those managers who do not need to prepare Milestone Charts, GANTT Charts and PERT diagrams will benefit from an understanding of the systematic principles behind these project planning aids.

Suppose a new income maintenance center or facility for children is being established. The clients must be transferred. The staff must be hired and relationships with contractors must be established. Suppose a new Federal regulation mandates a change in the processes for determining welfare eligibility which requires the reorganization of all the county's income maintenance centers. Suppose a deadline is established for eliminating the backlog in processing a certain form under threat of loss of reimbursement. All of these situations involve complex sets of activities that must be coordinated over a specified period of time. Can the manager afford to rely on memory and staff meetings to ensure that the activities are all executed in an orderly and timely fashion by the deadline?

Project planning techniques permit the systematic delineation, scheduling and execution of a complex series of tasks which may be viewed as a project. This process of analysis can also be used for analyzing ongoing activities of some particular unit. Often the explicit process of project planning or some of the activities associated with it, results in a streamlining of ongoing processes. Systematically describing and documenting a process can result in substantial increases in efficiency. Ordinarily the objectives will be at least tentatively defined prior to the designation of the project manager and team members.

Experience has shown that a series of discrete steps can be outlined leading to a systematic approach to the planning and execution of such projects. These steps involve: 1) Project Definition; 2) Task Specification; 3) Task Analysis; 4) Work Scheduling; 5) Supplementary Analysis; and 6) Execution. In carrying out these steps, particularly 2, 3, 4, and 5, a series of specific techniques are available.

The individual who is responsible for the implementation of the project is referred to as the project manager. Where projects are sufficiently large, a project manager may be temporarily relieved of other assignments to undertake the specified project. The first undertaking of the project team becomes the explicit identification and agreement on project objectives. Once the project objectives have been identified, task specification can occur. The specification of tasks is the first step in developing a detailed project plan. Where the number of steps is small, the specification of tasks, which is technically referred to as a Work Breakdown Structure (WBS) may be all that is needed. Most projects worth directing special attention to, however, involve greater complexity so that techniques such as Milestone Charts, Responsibility Charting, Workflow Diagrams, GANTT Charts, Network Analysis, Critical Path Method, and Program Evaluation and Review Technique (PERT) may be applicable.

1. Work Process Documentation

Once objectives have been set, the process of task specification begins whereby the tasks and subtasks required to attain the agreed objectives are written down and numbered. The actual description of each step usually involves some research on the part of the project team. This process of research can be useful in clarifying the tasks that are actually performed. When a complete task and subtask list is generated the number and variety of tasks can be surprising. The completed listing of tasks and subtasks is referred to as a Work Breakdown Structure (WBS). The example below shows a WBS for the release of a patient from a hospital to a halfway house.

Work Breakdown Structure (WBS)
Releasing a Patient to a Halfway House

1.0 The hospital decides the person is ready to move to a less protected environment.
    1.1 The nursing staff reports to the director of the team, the psychiatrist, that the patient is ready for discharge.
    1.2 The psychiatrist reviews the client's records.
    1.3 The psychiatrist evaluates the patient.
    1.4 The psychiatrist meets with the unit team.
    1.5 The unit team decides the patient is ready for a halfway house.
    1.6 The patient is notified.
    1.7 The application forms are completed.
    1.8 The forms are send to CDPC.
2.0 The hospital gets approval for transfer to a halfway house from the district office (CDPC).
    2.1 The forms are received by CDPC.
    2.2 The forms are reviewed.
    2.3 A decision is made as to whether or not the client should be placed in a halfway house.

    2.4 CDPC writes a memo to the hospital stating the decision.

    2.5 The memo is sent to the hospital.

3.0 If the client is to be placed, the director of the halfway house program identifies a placement.

    3.1 CDPC sends a memo to the director of the halfway house program requesting a placement.

    3.2 The director of the program calls CDPC to discuss the case.

    3.3 The director of the program reviews the data on the houses to ascertain where space is available.

    3.4 The director of the program calls the houses to double check for available space.

    3.5 The director decided which house will accommodate the client.

    3.6 The director sends a memo to CDPC notifying them of the available placement.

4.0 Final approval of the placement is made.

    4.1 CDPC receives the memo.

    4.2 CDPC decides whether or not the placement is acceptable.

    4.3 CDPC notifies the director of the halfway house program of the approval.

5.0 The client is placed in the house.

    5.1 The director of the halfway house program notifies the house.

    5.2 The director of the program notifies the psychiatrist at the hospital.

    5.3 The psychiatrist notifies the client.

    5.4 The house arranges logistics with the psychiatrist.

    5.5 The client is placed in the halfway house.

One of the nice features of this particular WBS is its sequential order. Each one of the tasks specified occurs after the task immediately preceding it. In many work processes events occur simultaneously, leading to a more complex situation and a scheduling problem of greater difficulty. Incidentally, of course, the value of analysis can be much greater in such situations.

The development of a WBS is a way of systematically stating each and every step that must occur in order to carry out a particular project. The use of a WBS ensures that, at least initially, every aspect of the project will be considered. The WBS also indicates the range of individuals responsible for completing tasks and subtasks, but it does not deal with the ambiguities of individual responsibility for specific tasks.

Very often more than one individual will have some responsibility with respect to a specific task. In order to clarify individual responsibility a technique known as responsibility charting can be used. A responsibility chart consists of three elements: a list of tasks (or responsibilities); a list of actors (either individuals or units); and a code indicating the degree of responsibility. The responsibility chart below is based upon some general activities engaged in by the staff of the Halfway House and their supervisors.

RESPONSIBILITY CHART

Actors Respon- sibilities	Commis- sioner	Regional Director	Assis- tant Director	House Director	Coun- selor	Nurse
Setting Policy	R	A				
Hiring		AP	R	R		
In-taking Clients				AP	R	A
Managing Day-to-Day Operations			AP	R	A	
Providing Direct Service				A	R	R

CODE: R = Responsible A = Assist AP = Approve I = Inform C = Consult

The specification of the tasks comprising a project and charting responsibility for them are the first steps in developing a schedule. Another preliminary technique that may be used is flowcharting. Flowcharting indicates the sequential pattern of activities. It also may be used to indicate delays, halts in the work flow, movement from one actor to another, decisions and inspections. The flowchart, or work flow diagram, is also an important tool in itself. Flowcharting of work processes can lead to work simplification, including the elimination of unnecessary steps, changes in sequence to expedite completion of the project, and suggestions as to the best sequence to follow.

A specific application for work flow diagrams are the procedures for submission of forms for approval which are so prevalent in human service organizations. By pointing up duplication and sources of delay, this technique can help reduce unnecessary and redundant procedures. In general, work flow diagrams can point up: 1) long sequences without task accomplishment; 2) dual performance of the same or similar tasks; 3) too many waits or delays; 4) unnecessary back and forth movements; 5) superfluous inspections; 6) movement in a backward direction. The instructions and the symbols used in making a work flow diagram are set forth below.

SYMBOLS FOR A WORK FLOW DIAGRAM

Symbol	What It Indicates
⟶	the direction of the work flow
◯	work activity or operation (typing, filling out a form, telephone, etc.)
D	a delay that is unforeseen
▽	a storage, wait, or halt in the work flow that is necessary or inherent to the task
⟹	movement from one actor or department to another (sometimes a sequence of activities is performed by the same actor and no movement occurs; other times, when a sequence of sub-tasks are performed by different actors or department, there is movement)
◇	a decision (including "yes" or "no," a formal approval, etc.)
▭	an inspection (of records, physical plant, etc.)

An example of a work flow diagram, based upon the same project described earlier in the WBS, follows.

2. Scheduling Work

Sometimes the process of task analysis ends with a WBS, a Responsibility Chart or a Work Flow Diagram. More often, once these beginning analytic tools are used, work scheduling is undertaken. It is the work schedule that places the complex series of tasks constituting the project within an acceptable time frame and establishes a basic system for monitoring interim task completion. The actual scheduling technique that is used is up to the project manager. It depends in part upon the complexity of the project and the detail with which progress is to be monitored. In many cases, a simple Milestone Chart will be sufficient; while in others the greater capabilities of Program Evaluation and Review Technique (PERT) will be needed. The use of Milestone Charts has become quite common in human services management. The Milestone Chart is a simple approach to accountability which is easily conceived and is often used in contract and grant relationships to make a timetable explicit. A Mile-

WORK FLOW DIAGRAM: "TAKING A CLIENT INTO THE HALFWAY HOUSE"

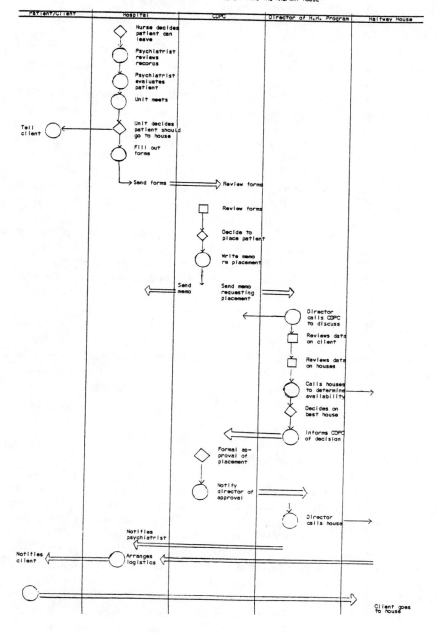

stone Chart merely associates time frames with the completion of critical activities. The basic format of a Milestone Chart is to list activities on the left side of the page and indicate dates across the page. Then for each activity a starting and completion date are indicated. Sometimes symbols for anticipated and actual slippage will be used.

The Milestone Chart can be a powerful tool for project planning and control. It allows a manager to have an overview of the entire project and create an overall project design. A Milestone Chart will indicate when each task begins and when it should end. It allows for checking on proper sequencing. Overlap may be reduced, unnecessary tasks eliminated, and unrealistic deadlines avoided. A Milestone Chart indicates to the manager when time and effort should be spent on specific aspects of the project. The result is to minimize delay and unrealistic expectations.

Typical steps in the construction of a Milestone Chart, include: (1) Identify the project for which the schedule is to be charted; (2) Identify the activities necessary for the completion of the project that requires monitoring. (When identifying the activities involved in a sequential task, perform a task analysis.); (3) Determine the appropriate units of time for the schedule (days, weeks, months, etc.); (4) Estimate the amount of time it should take to complete each activity, including the starting date and the completion date; (5) Illustrate the estimated time span on the milestone chart.

An example of Milestone Chart follows.

A GANTT CHART is a modified Milestone Chart, with one additional piece of information: the ability to record on a continuing basis the degree of completion of each task. This is accomplished by placing on the Milestone Chart, in the place of straight lines indicating tasks, boxes which can be cross-hatched to indicate what proportion of a common task has been completed. An example is set forth below.

3. Network Analysis and PERT

In large scale projects the techniques described above prove to have certain shortcomings. They don't represent the interrelationships among tasks and they don't provide a mechanism for accounting for the uncertainties of time. Program Evaluation and Review Technique (PERT) was a technique developed as an outgrowth of the U.S. Navy's Polaris submarine missile program which allows for the more effective management of large scale projects. Its widespread use by the Department of Defense has increased its popularity. In the Polaris Project it allowed the Department of Defense to coordinate and monitor 11,000 individual contractors, a job far outreaching the capabilities of traditional scheduling techniques.

KEY MILESTONE CHART

Project Title: Taking Clients into the Schenectady Halfway House
Project Manager: _____
Location: _____
Phone No.: _____   Date Prepared: July 23, 1980

Key
Start Date
Completion Date

Milestones	Jan	Feb	Mar	Apr	May	Jun	Jul	Aug	Sep	Oct	Nov	Dec	Jan	Feb	Mar	Apr	May	Jun
° Hospital staff determines that client is ready for transfer																		
° Hospital gains approval for transfer from CDPC																		
° Placement is identified																		
° Final approval of placement is made																		
° Client arrives at the halfway house																		

EXAMPLE OF A GANTT CHART

Project Title: Placing a Client in a Job

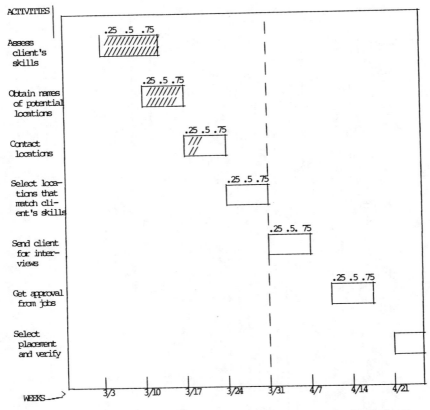

PERT is particularly well adapted for one-time projects where the time required for the completion of activities cannot be accurately forecast. It allows for estimating times and then adjusting the schedule based upon periodic updates. This is made possible by its ability to interrelate discrete events which occur in sequence. The use of networks, sequences of events, and its emphasis on the selection of sequences which take the least time, make it an important aid in reducing the time necessary for the completion of a complex series of events.

A scheduling technique is only as good as the time estimates it incorporates. PERT allows for the estimation of time, the incorporation of probability estimates and the readjustment of projections of later events based upon the completion of earlier events. The selection of "critical paths" allows for a concentration of control effort on those events which have the greatest impact as an important reference point in completing the project.

The basic elements making up a **PERT** network are events, sequences and activities. An event is the start or completion of a task. In a network diagram it is represented by a circle. Activities are the actual performance of work involved in a project. They are represented by lines with directional arrows connecting the circles representing events. A **PERT** network consists of sequences of events connected by activities which are associated with certain estimated times for completion. In the figure below, a network is illustrated consisting of 5 events, 6 activities and their associated estimated times.

FIVE   EVENT   NETWORK

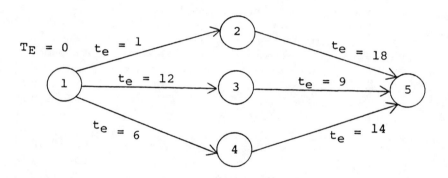

Now try your own hand at constructing a PERT network. After reading the case study below, construct an events list and a PERT diagram including both events and activities.

The Food Stamp Project

At present, a cumbersome and time-consuming approach is used for issuing and replacing food stamp authorizations through a manual process. Forms authorizing food stamp benefits are hand delivered by messenger to a central receiving point, after which they are forwarded by truck delivery to the Food Stamp Central Office. Then they are forwarded to the Office of Data Processing for mailing. You are appointed project manager in charge of creating an automated system. Although you are not a data processing specialist, you know that a computer program must be designed and tested. You also know that the forms used for inputting data must be revised and that written instructions for completing these forms must be developed. The forms must then be printed. Then a pilot program must be instituted and finally expanded to the other centers.

Try to construct an events list, based upon the narrative above. Then check it against the following suggested events list: 1. Project begun; 2. Program specifications written; 3. Program specifications tested; 4. Current documents revised; 5. Preparation of written instructions completed; 6. Arrangements with print shop completed; 7. Training of staff of pilot center completed; 8. Testing of computer hardware use in pilot completed; 9. Pilot system installed; 10. Training of staff of other centers completed; 11. System installation in other centers completed.

Now construct a PERT Network indicating the sequencing of these tasks. Compare your solution with the figure below.

As mentioned earlier, a critical aspect of PERT networks is the use of a time estimate, since the time for completion is often uncertain. The time estimate as indicated by the formula below is calculated by combining three elements: optimistic time, the minimum time in which an activity can be completed; pessimistic time, the maximum possible period of time it would take to accomplish the activity; and most likely time, the best estimate of the period of time in which the activity can be completed. By combining these estimates an expected time $t(e)$ is derived. The following symbols are used: a=optimistic time; m=most likely time; b=pessimistic time, $t(e)$=estimated time. Then $t(e) = (a + 4m + b) \div 6$.

Now refer to the Food Stamp Case and see if you can calculate the estimated time. For each event calculate $t(e)$, then calculate the overall $t(e)$.

In addition to the expected time several other concepts are critical to the use and analysis of PERT networks. Earliest expected time, $T(E)$, is the earliest possible time that an event can be completed; $T(S)$ is the completion or contractual obligation date; $T(L)$ is the latest time by which an event must be completed to keep the project on schedule. Slack is a measure of the excess time available in reaching an event. Slack = $T(L)$—$T(E)$. A critical path is the path that has a minimum of slack.

Once a PERT network has been set out, it can be used as a decision aid. The analysis will lead to a projection of the earliest date for completion. This will allow for a determination of the probability of completion within the scheduled completion dates. The analysis will also point up the critical activities and events. A manager can then monitor more effectively.

A further extension of PERT network analysis is known as PERT/COST and allows for the determination of estimated costs and the analysis of tradeoffs between the competing values of time and money. Computer programs are available for undertaking such analyses.

4. Project Management

The techniques that have been described are useful tools in planning projects and sequencing component tasks. But they are only tools. They

PERT NETWORK

Project: Data Input of Non-Recurring Food Stamp Authorization

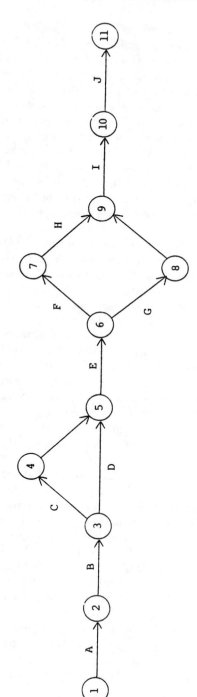

NOTE THE ERROR(S) IN THE NETWORK. CAN YOU ELIMINATE THEM?

help the project manager to develop a logical organization of work processes. They provide a graphic technique for monitoring progress and maintaining control over the actual completion of specific tasks. They also help identify potential bottlenecks and delays. But the development of a logical, streamlined task structure is only the beginning.

Successful project planning and control requires the successful management of people. Individuals must accept responsibility for tasks and the project manager must receive continuing feedback so adjustments in the plan can be made as necessary. Insofar as project planning is a more rigorous and defined approach to planning and control, it provides the manager with more regular feedback and greater control. But the task of getting team members to do what they are supposed to do is dependent upon the same supervisory skills that other less structured task sequences require. Subordinates will react differently to project planning techniques. Some will welcome their specificity, others will be annoyed.

The terminology of project manager and project team that has been used in describing project planning indicates a debt to the somewhat specialized field of project management. Although the terms project planning and project management are sometimes used interchangeably, project management has a special meaning. It refers to a particular sort of project planning and control in which a project is defined which cuts across existing organizational units. Rather than assign the project to an ongoing unit, an ad hoc group called the "Project Team" is selected with members drawn from among various work units. Individuals may be assigned on a part-time or full-time basis. A project manager is designated, the project objectives are agreed upon and a time frame is set for the selection of the project team and the completion of its tasks. After that date, the project team will be dissolved and the members will return to their original units.

One advantage of such an approach is that a special group is designated which can draw individuals of diverse talents to complete a particular task while the ongoing organizational activities are only minimally affected. Since the project team is not part of the permanent organization, other units are less inclined to look upon it competitively. The perspective of its members is likely to be more innovative and open to change because of its ad hoc nature and the ability to select individuals with specialized technical skills and more free-wheeling styles. Often the project management approach is used for the design and implementation of new information and appraisal systems.

If the selection of team members is sufficiently broadbased, its task of implementing new systems will be facilitated by representation from diverse units. Once the system is operating, the team members return to their respective units and become interpreters and advocates of the new system.

In project management situations, the ad hoc nature of the organization makes the task analysis and work scheduling procedures described above particularly valuable. The project team does not have a history of routine process to draw upon for its own operation. Very often a complicated set of existing routines needs to be documented. And, since individuals are not familiar with one another, a process that explicitly lists required tasks and assigns responsibility is particularly important.

In addition, the time constraints on the completion of the project are often such that the tasks and subtasks must be carefully coordinated and closely monitored in order to ensure that deadlines will be met. For all these reasons project management undertakings are particularly likely to adopt the techniques of task analysis and work scheduling.

The effective project manager, heading an ad hoc organization with a time bound project, must meet special demands. The project manager is not dealing with a group of subordinates who have developed loyalty over a period of time. The members of the project team are temporarily assigned and in fact may be at high professional levels, comparable to that of the manager. In addition, the project manager inevitably spends a good deal of time dealing with individuals outside the project team. And finally the project manager may have only a small portion of the technical expertise necessary for a complete understanding of the project.

The project manager, in other words, operates in a much more uncertain, unpredictable and uncontrolled environment than the traditional manager. The project manager must be especially skilled in getting things done through persuasion and bargaining rather than command. And of course, the skills of task analysis and work scheduling are especially useful to the project manager. The time frame is critical and the project manager is constantly concerned with keeping the project on target so that the complex set of tasks is completed on schedule. Project management is a particularly important application of project planning.

The human services manager, like any other manager, has a major responsibility for scheduling work and controlling the completion of sequential tasks. First line supervisors can often undertake these tasks in an informal and unstructured manner. But as a manager moves up the hierarchy the chances that complex tasks, including those amenable to project planning techniques, will arise is greatly increased. While most managers will not themselves become proficient in the more sophisticated graphic and numerical techniques, all managers need to understand the basic project planning methodology.

Selected Bibliography

Battersby, A. *Network Analysis for Planning and Scheduling.* New York: John Wiley & Sons, 1970.

Chapman, Richard. *Project Management in NASA*. Washington, D.C.: National Aeronautics and Space Administration, 1973.

Cleland, D. I. and King, W. R. *Systems Analysis and Project Management*. New York: McGraw-Hill, 1975.

Wiest, J. and Levy, F. *Management Guide to PERT-CPM*. Englewood Cliffs, N.J.: Prentice-Hall, 1972.

Chapter 5.

Staff Performance

1. Authority Relationships

The challenge faced by the project manager was, having developed a project plan, to implement that plan, working through others. A manager can choose the most ideal goals and develop the most clever implementation plan. But without the coordinated efforts of others, the plans will not be met.

Most of the manager's time is spent on day-to-day occurrences which involve informal interaction with other organizational members. The manager has a particular responsibility to shape these interactions to result in productive organizational activity. Ordinarily a primary work group of individuals who are in more or less constant contact and who report to the manager can be identified. Often these individuals take part in regular staff meetings which reinforce their relationships to the manager and to each other.

While the effective manager must learn to work with all members of the organization and, indeed, many individuals outside of the organization, the patterns of interaction with this primary work group are particularly important. They constitute the extension of the manager. Since no manager can function autonomously, the ability to count on the performance of this primary work group is critical to managerial success.

One of the most common mistakes that managers make is to assume that providing direction is equivalent to issuing commands. Providing direction means much more than issuing commands. A classic recognition of the difficulty of getting subordinates to follow directions is the statement attributed to President Truman upon turning over the reins of the national government to President Eisenhower. Truman suggested that Eisenhower, entering civilian life after a distinguished military career, would issue commands and see that they were not obeyed. The task of the President is to persuade others to do his bidding, rather than ordering them. Indeed Truman probably exaggerated the ease of command even in the military. If management were merely giving orders, the job would be easy and could be performed by an automaton. In fact managers must use a variety of approaches and skills to effectuate their ends.

The first step in providing direction is to make clear one's intentions. But the job of selling may often require that the manager be circumspect in stating desires. Clear statements may be subject to attack by opponents. Or they may prematurely reveal an overall strategy. Yet if a manager wants to provide direction, at some stage the direction must be articulated. Furthermore, it must be made clear to numbers of individuals, depending upon the size of the organization and its scope.

Building successful relationships with subordinates is a complex undertaking. It is sometimes referred to as the ability to lead. Perhaps its most central component is the ability to get subordinates "to listen." Active listening requires subordinates who accept the manager's leadership. Sometimes this acceptance is referred to as the establishment of authority. Operative authority as distinct from formal authority means that subordinates really listen, rather than just politely nod their heads.

The basis for authority is usually organizational position. Most organizations have an hierarchical structure which defines authority within the organization. Organizationally based authority, however, may be strongly affected by professional and personal relationships. In human service organizations, professional considerations are particularly important in influencing authority relationships. A substantial proportion of the individuals working in human service organizations identify with one or more of the professions. Social workers, teachers and doctors are some of the more prominent professions within human service organizations. All of these professions lay claim to specialized bodies of knowledge and have a strong tradition of individual autonomy.

The basis of professional respect may be a common educational background. The possession of Masters in Social Work degrees is a bond for many human service managers. But the outward manifestation is only part of a larger source of identification with the profession which shares common values, perspectives and skills. Where the superficial bond of education is not present the common sense of professional respect must grow from day to day experience. Often individuals will have known each other within the larger organization before becoming part of the primary work group. This professional bond can be a potent force for the good.

It can also cause some conflict when two or more professional backgrounds are in competition. Thus in recent years the dominance of the social work profession over human service organizations has been challenged. In many government and not-for-profit organizations individuals with financial skills, or more general management backgrounds are challenging social workers for leadership positions.

Acceptance of authority within the professions is important. Thus, social workers may expect experience, education and recognition within their profession to translate into authority on the job. A non-social worker may have difficulty establishing authority over a social worker subordinate. A recent graduate of social work school may similarly have difficulty establishing authority over a graduate of ten years ago. Sensitivity to the role profession plays in defining authority relationships is important in understanding human service organizations.

All organizations, including human service organizations, find another element affecting authority, namely the personal attributes of the manager in his relationship to subordinates. Understanding the importance of winning the confidence of employees is a first step toward effective leadership. It means making an effort to develop rapport with individuals. Genuine personal respect for another individual is the beginning of any supervisory relationship.

If an individual has known another for a number of years or has professional relationships over a period of time, the authority relationship may be difficult to accept. The subordination required of the authority relationship may be resisted by the employee who has been personally acquainted or professionally associated with the supervisor for many years. If this person has been an equal on a personal basis, acceptance of the authority relationship may be more difficult. However, personal and professional relationships often reinforce the legitimacy of authority relationships. For example, if the supervisor is older than the subordinate and has higher professional status, authority will be strengthened. The establishment of an authority relationship is a difficult undertaking. In established bureaucracies, the position itself may have such clearly recognized status that the authority stems from the position. But in the long run the relationship between the superior and the subordinate will be characterized by a process of assertion and reassertion of role relationships. Getting others to listen involves a variety of strategies concerned with individuals and groups. It involves a flexibility on the part of the manager in adapting to different situations and a sensitivity to the needs of different employees. It requires an understanding of human psychology and how to motivate employees.

A number of studies of organizational behavior have pointed to the desire on the part of employees to have a greater sense of involvement in organizational decisionmaking. Particular individuals with a strong sense of professional expertise want to be part of the process that determines what decisions the organization will take. The use of MBO and similar systems to involve individuals in determining organization goals and fitting those goals to their individual objectives has been described above.

But apart from the formal process of goal setting, innumerable occasions occur within the work group when decisions must be made about alternative courses of action. While a manager should not ordinarily yield the ultimate responsibility for decisions, most managers find that involving subordinates in decisionmaking benefits the organization. It has a direct affect on their "listening" because they become committed to the goals which they have helped to formulate.

Involving subordinates in decisionmaking may take a variety of forms. It may involve polling their opinions singly or in groups. It may involve initiating discussion on issues which are to be decided. It may involve establishing task forces to develop recommendations. In fact, involving subordinates in decisionmaking is a pervasive attitude that affects a whole range of activities.

A number of investigators have identified willingness to involve subordinates as participants as a key dimension of leadership style. Leaders, it is said, may range from employing a solely directive approach, commanding what is to be done, to sharing decisionmaking at all levels, involving subordinates in a true spirit of participation. The need for involving subordinates in decisionmaking is particularly striking in many human service organizations. Particularly in organizations characterized by an ambiguity of goals, strong professionalism, and autonomous work situations, involvement and commitment of staff to organizational goals is critical to success. If participatory management is a design for involving staff in decisionmaking, it is also a design for committing staff to organizational goals. Individuals who have participated in decisions are likely to understand their rationale and be more committed to them than those who have only been ordered to perform.

Participatory management is linked to the human relations school of human motivation and the stress upon higher order motivations. If indeed individuals are motivated by self-actualization and they seek to gain a greater involvement in their work, participatory decisionmaking is an ideal approach.

While the movement toward participatory management has been strongly supported by many theorists, most prominently, perhaps, Douglas McGregor, Peter Drucker and Chris Argyris, its limitations should also be articulated. Participatory decisionmaking may complicate and slow the decisonmaking process. If handled poorly, it can generate and coalesce opposition to decisions that are taken.

In trying to understand the range of approaches that leaders use in relating to subordinates, a concept that is often used is that of leadership style. Leadership style is a means of differentiating patterns of behavior that are characteristic of different types of leaders under different circumstances. Perhaps the most extensive attention has been given to the concept of leadership style with respect to participation in decisionmaking.

One of the most frequently cited approaches to the differentiation of leadership style is that of Tannenbaum and Schmidt. They assert that leadership style may be viewed as a continuum depending upon the use of authority by the manager and the area of freedom allowed to subordinates. At one end of the spectrum, with high use of authority and low freedom, the manager makes the decision and announces it. At the other end of the spectrum, with low use of authority and high freedom for subordinates, the manager permits subordinates to function within limits defined by superiors.

Another popular approach to differentiating leadership styles is suggested by Blake and Mouton and has been incorporated in training exercises focusing on the "Managerial Grid." The grid plots leadership style according to two dimensions: attention to task and attention to people. The ideal leadership style is asssociated with a high orientation to both people and tasks.

Current thinking in management theory, while recognizing the usefulness of categorizing leadership style, emphasizes the need for adaptability. Fiedler's contingency theory stresses the need to adapt leadership style to the individuals being supervised and the situation in which action is being taken. Thus, while it is important for managers to understand their own leadership style, they should be able to adapt to different situations.

2. Motivating Individuals

Even the most self-centered of leaders would recognize that individuals perform better if they are motivated to do so. While any successful organization needs a comprehensive system of incentives to promote superior performance, the individual's attachment to the organization will be critical in determining his or her effort. Individuals who are committed to the organization and its goals will try harder.

In a sense, then, the first task of the effective leader is to build individual commitment. Managerial skills are needed to welcome and inspire individuals in the organization. For example, a charismatic leader will, by speech and bearing, inspire others to work for common goals. The ability to inspire should make itself felt in smaller meetings of the primary group and in one-to-one encounters as well as on the occasion of a public appearance.

To the extent that the manager can convince the subordinate by speech and action that his or her goals and the organization's are synonymous, the person will perform better. Good intentions, of course, are not the whole story, but they are the beginning of successful followership.

An understanding of the roots and sources of individual behavior is critical for effective management. Abraham Maslow's hierarchy of needs is a good place to begin. As each level of needs become satisfied, the individual focuses on the next level. Physiological needs such as hunger, sex and thirst command attention first. When these are satisfied safety needs such as security, stability, dependency, protection and the need for structure and order are addressed. At the next level, individuals strive for love and a sense of belongingness. Next come the esteem needs, including the desire for strength, achievement, mastery, competence, prestige, status, fame, glory, dignity and appreciation. When all these needs are met, the individual will develop an uneasiness or dissatisfaction unless he or she is doing what they are best suited for. The need to be true to one's own nature Maslow called the need for self-actualization. Maslow's approach, recognizing the variety of needs, is generally accepted, although the details of his hierarchy of needs may be criticized. It should be noted, however, that even Maslow recognized that the hierarchy of needs was not applicable to every individual. The hierarchy of needs has been used to bolster the views of those students of human behavior who reject the carrot-and-stick approach to understanding human motivation. They argue that even if at one time mankind was basically motivated by greed and fear, most workers today are reasonably secure and are more concerned with higher-level needs.

Herzberg, Mausner and Snyderman, in their classic study, Motivation to Work focused on the importance of higher level needs in job satisfaction. According to their study, positive job attitudes resulted from self-actualization. Performance of the task reinforced the individual's aspirations. On the other hand, the factors that related to avoidance of unhappiness were those involving the context of the job: supervision, interpersonal relations, physical working conditions, salary, benefits, job security and policies. These findings led the authors to suggest greater emphasis on structuring jobs to foster individual satisfaction and greater care in the selection of individuals for jobs.

Chris Argyris is another management expert who suggests that higher level needs motivate individuals and that these needs are often stymied by the structure of organizations. Argyris calls for the redesign of organizations to eliminate the constant loss of energy as individuals seek to adapt to the structure of organizations which frustrate their needs for self-actualization. Warren Bennis makes a similar plea in his call for planned organization change.

The theory of motivation, then, has moved beyond the carrot-and- stick approach to recognize a whole range of individual needs. Moreover, the problem of motivation is not solved by asking what can be done to motivate an individual, as if extra money or a smile or a pat on the back will suffice. Motivation is not a simple reaction to monetary or other incentives. A person's pattern of response is learned over the course of a life-time. To modify that response pattern is a laborious undertaking. In this sense, then, motivation requires both an understanding of the individual and an understanding of the organizational setting.

The manager must learn how to use rewards and punishments to encourage compliance with organizational goals. A skillful manager who, by force of personality can inspire individuals to high attainment is valuable, but a manager who knows how to use rewards and punishments will be more effective in the long run.

Managers find that the use of rewards in human service organizations is often constrained. Uniform pay policies militate against the use of pay incentives. Seniority rules constrain flexibility in job assignments. In human service organizations with active boards of directors there may be interference with rewards proposed by the executive director. In general, the flexibility in rewards, particularly where related to monetary incentives, is small when compared to profit-making institutions.

Perhaps the most common means of rewarding and punishing behavior is through praise and blame. Managers who have established their authority within the organization will be able to encourage employees by praise and discourage them with blame. Employees with new ideas are eager to receive praise and support in their implementation.

Suppose the manager of a community treatment facility wants to encourage a particular activity such as group counseling. Public and private praise of staff members who are responsible for conducting these sessions may encourage such activities. A manager of an income maintenance center, seeking to improve the ways in which staff relate to clients, praises the courteous treatment of clients by staff which she observes. A manager of a prime sponsor of employment and training programs encourages greater use of systematic evaluation efforts, by praising individuals undertaking such efforts. A manager seeks to discourage tardiness and absence by praising individuals with good attendance records.

But praise or blame of individuals by managers may be a time- consuming activity. Often a superior approach involves the structuring of a system of rewards which operates automatically, without the need for frequent personal intervention by the manager. Consider the case below.

The Vacationing Agency

Ms. Health has just taken over as head of Community Service, Inc., a public advocacy group in a large metropolitan area with a staff of close to 100 and a history of over 100 years. About ten years ago, the employee association became officially designated as a collective bargaining agent and formalized the leave policies which had developed over a period of fifty years. Those policies entitled employees to twenty days of vacation leave, five personal days, ten sick days, and unlimited unpaid leave each year.

During her first two weeks in office Ms. Health finds that each day one of her top deputies is absent. By contrast, in the organization in which she previously worked, she had a perfect attendance record, taking only one sick day in three years and never exceeding the two personal days allotted. She had, however, each year taken the allotted ten vacation days. Should Ms. Health be concerned with the absence of her top staff? What additional information should she obtain? What measures should she contemplate? What would constitute overreaction? Underreaction?

As she begins inquiring into the dimensions of the absentee problem she finds out that many employees do not report to work on time. How could she find out the dimensions of that problem and what actions should she contemplate?

While it is true that absence and lateness are two of the best indicators of organizational malaise, the incidence of absence and lateness are directly affected by the systems for allowing and controlling such practices. A manager experiencing problems with excessive lateness and absenteeism should be alerted to possible morale problems, but should also rethink the organizational policies leading to these difficulties. Who is rewarded more, those who are present or those who are absent? Do the incentives in the organization favor good attendance or poor attendance?

Many human service organizations have major problems of absenteeism and lateness that can have important impacts on productivity. These difficulties often result from systemic problems such as the high degree of professionalism and autonomy, the lack of controls over work, the human orientation which encourages personal development, the unclear nature of goals and the hesitancy to make specific work assignments and monitor them.

In analyzing absentee and lateness problems, attention should be directed first to general morale problems. Are employees unhappy with the work situation because of poor leadership, lack of goal definition or other causes. Secondly, are the incentives working to encourage attendance and promptness? Are the standards of attendance and promptness appropriate to the organizational operations?

The leave policies within Community Service, Inc. are clearly quite liberal. If the individual takes four full weeks of vacation, that would leave 48 work weeks in the year. Holidays affect 10 of those, and up to 15 could be affected by personal and sick days. Without taking any unpaid leave, the individuals would work full weeks in less than half of the total weeks in the year. Even so, it would appear that the deputies' absence is extraordinary and probably the indication of a morale problem.

Ms. Health must decide the extent to which the current leave practices are detracting from the operation of the organization. Perhaps individuals are not missed when they take leave, and in fact, their time on the job is so demanding that a liberal leave policy is justifiable. But what if Ms. Health decided that the organization was suffering from the liberal leave policy? What latitude would she have in making changes? Are there easy ways in which the leave policy might be changed to lower the amount of leave actually taken? Should she make changes directly or through a task force approach? How can she avoid lessening morale even further?

Probably any changes would have to be part of the collective bargaining arrangement and so would have to be included in the next contract. Meanwhile, could she institute methods for documenting sick leave and methods for tightening up on unpaid leave? What about tying unpaid leave to circumspect use of sick leave? Or would this just lead to additional abuse of sick leave? Should rules be instituted about how far in advance leaves must be planned? Should a different approach be taken entirely by making it clear that managers are responsible for high performance and that absenteeism detracts from performance and will be a consideration in reappointments and promotions? Do you think the collective bargaining agent might be willing to consolidate all leave to say 37 total leave days, with an additional provision for long-term sickness? Would this benefit the organization as a whole?

Altering the approach to sick leave is but a single example of how changes in the system of rewards can be changed to encourage behavior conducive to organizational operations. Most managers use rewards and punishments, but only a minority capitalize fully on their potential. In order to gain a greater understanding of the use of these techniques, we will now focus on them and consider what has come to be known as the theory of behavior modification.

3. Behavior Modification

The theory of behavior modification is rooted in the behaviorist school of psychology. Building upon the work of the Russian psychologist Ivan Pavlov, The behaviorists argued that all learned behavior resulted from objective phenomena. While Pavlov analyzed the conditioned reflex in terms of stimulus and response, the behaviorists extended a similar analysis to encompass all learned behavior resulting from environmentally observable stimuli and then observing that behavior might be affected by subsequent events. When a response to a situation is followed by a satisfying state of affairs, its likelihood of repetition is increased. When followed by an annoying state of affairs its likelihood of repetition is decreased. This statement is referred to as the "law of effect."

But it was B.F. Skinner who shifted attention away from behavior elicited by stimuli and emphasized the importance of learned responses, reorienting psychologists toward the importance of operant behavior. Operant behavior is behavior shaped, strengthened, maintained or weakened by its consequences, and it is this type of behavior that constitutes the great bulk of organizational behavior which managers seek to influence and change. Skinner's theories thus have considerable application to individual behavior in organizations.

According to Skinner, behavior is the result of prior environmental stimuli and cues and has consequences. By manipulating these cues and the consequences for the individual, behavior can be modified. Through past experience, organizational participants learn to associate specific consequences with various environmental settings. As a result individuals associate certain settings with certain consequences. Thus, if an individual associates his superior's office with punishment, a defensive reaction is apt to set in upon entering that office.

Consequences have varying effects upon behavior. If consequences strengthen replication of the behavior they are referred to as reinforcers. If they diminish replication, they are referred to as punishment. If they have no impact, they are neutral. Consequences are not necessarily the same for different individuals. However, it is true that, in general, managers know that certain consequences, such as praise and higher pay, are likely to reinforce behavior, while scolding and failure to grant raises function as punishment. Effective manipulation of contingencies requires a detailed understanding of the individual and the individual's reaction to contingencies.

The theory of behavior modification provides a potentially powerful tool to the manager. It suggests that by manipulating contingencies, the manager can affect the behavior of individuals in the work unit. If the manager knows what kind of behavior to encourage, behavior modification provides a particular technique for reinforcing that behavior.

It also suggests that the importance of systematic, consistent manipulation of contingencies is critical. A good deal of the manager's conduct of the job involves interaction with staff. By providing reinforcement and punishment, the manager is manipulating the contingencies that affect subordinate behavior. The manager may often be unaware that slight smiles or slight frowns can be taken as reinforcing or punishing. But a large part of the manager's job is shaping behavior and even if the manager is unaware, the effects will remain.

The theory of behavior modification provides an approach to bringing about changes in individual performance. It suggests that first the desired behaviors should be identified and a preliminary reading should be made of the frequency with which they occur. Then the contingencies associated with that behavior should be identified. A method should be developed to ensure that in the future when the correct behavior occurs, reinforcing contingencies will be associated with it, and if desired, punishing contingencies associated with failure to emit the desired behavior. Finally, after a time lapse the frequency of the desired behavior should again be tested. Luthans and Kreitner suggest a series of sequential steps to be followed in the process of behavior modification: (1) identify behavioral performance problems, (2) chart the frequency of target behavior, (3) identify existing behavioral contingencies through functional analysis, (4a) develop contingency intervention strategy, (4b) apply appropriate contingency intervention strategy, (4c) chart frequency of resulting behavior, (4d) maintain desirable behavior, and (5) evaluate process.

The actual use of such an approach, of course, depends upon the situation in question. The manipulation of reinforcing and punishing contingencies is really not a new idea for managers. What is special about behavior modification is the systematic approach which it suggests and the potency which it attributes to the manipulation of contingencies.

In truth, managers have always manipulated contingencies, and like other individuals, provide a great deal of praise and blame in attempting to get subordinates to do what they would like them to do. Praise and blame are well-known as reinforcing and punishing contingencies. In fact, if a manager cannot rely upon the effectiveness of praise and blame, his ability to function as a manager will be severely undermined. The basic authority of a manager and the ability to command are directly dependent upon this ability to praise and blame. Unfortunately, some managers emphasize praise and blame too much and as a result emphasize a command view of management. We have already discussed the importance of participatory approaches in management, particularly within human service organizations.

The theory of positive reinforcement also suggests a decided advantage for reinforcing over punishing contingencies. The positive reinforcement of a desired behavior is preferable. Punishing contingencies do result in a lessening of certain behaviors, but after punishment is discontinued the behaviors often appear once more.

Praise and blame become important secondary contingencies. For them to operate successfully, they must be used consistently and they must be carefully tied to the existing environmental cues. Since behavior is often complex it may not be readily apparent what behavior is anticipated and what the relationship between the contingency and behavior is. An important part of management requires that not only contingencies be used, but that their relationship to environmental cues be made explicit. Where these environmental clues consist of spoken messages, clarity in expression is critical to the link between cue, behavior and consequence.

While the use of praise and blame by the manager can be effective in bringing about behavior modification, it requires the presence of the manager to decide when to give praise and blame. It has the added disadvantage of requiring close supervision of the subordinate and frequent intervention. Close supervision, however, is not only time consuming, but runs the risk of antagonizing subordinates. Individuals who have a need for autonomy may rebel against such supervision. In such cases, the use of self- administered feedback may be preferable.

4. Self-Administered Feedback

The use of self-administered systems of reinforcement provides periodic feedback directly to individuals about their own performance. In some cases the design of such a system is simple. For example, if an individual is processing a given number of applications in a given period of time, the rate of processing can be periodically relayed to the individual. In fact, the manager can get the same reports on a periodic basis and can review the results with the employee.

An example of such an intervention is reported in an adult psychiatric treatment unit in a medium-sized hospital. After studying the performance of mental health technicians, it was decided that efforts would be made to increase three target behaviors: a) the completion of group therapy sessions; b) the completion of one-on-one therapy sessions, and c) the completion of assigned daily routine duties. At the end of each week an inter-office memo was posted which listed each technician's name and the frequency of target behaviors for the previous week. Accelerations occurred for all eight subjects across all three target behaviors.

Self-assessment techniques, can also be a powerful stimulus to behavior modification. They are one of the principle reasons that the more general strategy of providing feedback to individuals on goal attainment is a useful technique. Feedback of actual attainment provides a contingency for the reinforcement of behavior. Too often individuals are asked to perform in a certain way or to avoid certain behaviors, but are given no feedback on whether or not they have accomplished what they were asked to do. Feedback provided in the correct form serves as a reinforcing contingency. In order for feedback to be most effective it should go directly to the individual whose behavior is being modified; it should be promptly related to the actual performance; it should be reinforcing; it should not include extraneous and confusing information.

This view of how to improve individual performance is based upon a view of organizational behavior which emphasizes learning in an organizational setting. It applies general learning principles to organizational settings and places the emphasis on reinforcing desired behaviors. The critical element is determining what the reinforcers are and then associating them with the desired responses. While such methods are sometimes criticized as being overly mechanistic, they have proven to be useful in a large variety of circumstances.

Regarding the question of what the reinforcers are in a human services environment, it can be said that within human service organizations many intrinsic rewards exist. The motivation for working in human service organizations is often a desire to help people. Many of the workers are professionals oriented toward broad social goals. With successful use of participatory techniques, self-feedback can be a powerful reinforcer.

The theory of behavior modification suggests that monetary incentives may be less important than are sometimes supposed. While monetary rewards can be reinforcers, many other reinforcing contingencies exist. Once a reinforcer has been identified, much more attention needs to be focused on the repetition of its use, and its proximity to the behavior that is to be reinforced. The behavioral orientation focuses on identifying the desired behaviors, identifying reinforcing contingencies, and structuring a system of reinforcement. Its potential application to human services organizations is vast.

One of the obstacles to the use of behavior modification is the difficulty of changing human behavior, particularly the behavior of adults in responsible positions. Indeed, this objection to behavior modification is true of any approach to improving individual performance. It may be difficult to alter the behavior of individuals who are set in their ways, have functioned in their positions over long periods of time, and believe that they are in a position to counsel others, rather than to receive counseling. Particularly at higher levels, the obstacles to behavior modification may be formidable. Contact with individuals may be irregular and the behaviors may be non-routine, making a system of regular feedback difficult to implement. But behavior modification should be used where possible. Good managers have always practiced behavior modification in some form. Today all managers should understand its principles and apply it to the everyday management job.

The critical importance of feedback in the modification of behavior suggests that the process of communication is central to organizational interaction, a topic to which we next turn our attention.

Selected Bibliography

Argyris, Chris. *Personality and Organization*. New York: Harper and Row, 1957.

Bennis, Warren. *Changing Organizations*. New York: McGraw-Hill, 1966.

Berne, Eric. *Games People Play*. New York: Grove Press, 1964.

Blake, Robert and Mouton, Jane. *The Managerial Grid*. Houston, Texas: Gulf Publishing, 1964.

Budde, James. *Measuring Performance in Human Service Systems*. New York: AMACOM, 1979.

Callahan, Carol and Carrera, Joan. *Income Maintenance Supervision: On the Firing Line.* Washington, D.C.: Social Security Administration, Office of Family Assistance, 1979.

Cherniss, Cary. *Staff Burnout, Job Stress in the Human Services.* Beverly Hills: Sage, 1980.

Deegan, Arthur X. *Coaching: A Management Skill for Improving Individual Performance.* Reading, Massachusetts: Addison-Wesley, 1979.

Drucker, Peter. *The Practice of Management.* New York: Harper and Brothers, 1954.

Fiedler, Fred. *A Theory of Leadership Effectivenes.* New York: McGraw-Hill Book Co., 1967.

Herzberg, Frederick et al. *Motivation to Work.* New York: John Wiley, 1959.

Luthans, F. and Kreitner, R. *Organizational Behavior Modification.* Glenview, Ill.: Scott Foresman and Co., 1975.

Maslow, Abraham. *Motivation and Personality.* New York: Harper and Row, 1970.

McGregor, Douglas. *The Human Side of Enterprise.* New York: McGraw-Hill, 1960.

Sayles, Leonard. *Leadership: What Effective Managers Really Do . . . And How They Do It.* New York: McGraw-Hill, 1979.

Skinner, B. F. *Contingencies of Reinforcement.* New York: Appleton-Century Crofts, 1969.

Tannenbaum, R. and Schmidt, W.H., *"How to Choose a Leadership Pattern,"* Harvard Business Review, 36 (1958) 95-101.

Chapter 6.

Communications

1. The Centrality of Communications

While traditional conceptions of the managerial job often focused on decisionmaking and providing direction through authoritative pronouncements, contemporary studies of managerial behavior indicate that a good deal of the manager's interactions involve transmitting and receiving information within the organization. The manager becomes a "linking pin" in the organization and a center of communications.

This view of managerial activity may be sobering, but it also provides a more realistic basis for understanding what managers really do. It also emphasizes the importance of understanding communications and developing communication skills. In order to provide direction in attaining organizational goals, the manager must communicate with other organizational members. In fact, the manager's success depends upon the communications process within the organization. This process determines the ways in which direction is perceived, interpreted and acted upon. Similarly the manager depends upon communications channels for obtaining updated information about organizational operations.

The extent to which information and information processing generally are critical to effective management cannot be overemphasized. Henry Mintzberg, based upon his important study of executives, has characterized the manager as the organization's nerve center. Chester Barnard in the classic work, *The Functions of the Executive*, stressed the centrality of communications: ". . . the function of executives is to serve as channels of communication. . . ." Indeed, more and more, students of managerial behavior stress the importance of the manager as communicator. The classic command view of management is giving way to a view of management which stresses the role of information processor. In almost every contact with others and in working alone, the manager finds that he is receiving, transmitting and processing information.

81

Communications are especially important in human service organizations. Any visitor to an income maintenance center or health facility will be struck by the proportion of resources that are spent on gathering, recording and transmitting information. In fact the production and channeling of information is a major preoccupation of most human service managers.

Mintzberg's study of the interaction patterns of executives found that they spend much of their time in informational activities both in responding to written inquiries and in verbal interaction. Such activities as receiving and transmitting reference data, reports, news of events, and new ideas dominate written communications. Similarly most oral contacts involve passing along information, receiving briefings, and taking tours. The manager is an information processor.

The relationship between effective management and communication is reinforced by the unique access of the manager to both external and internal information. Mintzberg's findings from direct observation are very similar to Barnard's earlier findings, based largely upon participant observation.

Mintzberg distinguished three managerial roles involving communication: those of monitor, disseminator and spokesman. The role of monitor involves obtaining information about organizational activities, including changes, problems and opportunities occurring within the organization. As disseminator, the manager transmits both external and internal information to the organization. Finally, in the role of spokesman, the manager transmits information about the organization into the environment. This environment may include other units within the same organization, superiors within the hierarchy, including the board of directors, and the various publics, including trade organizations, peers, government agencies, customers, the press and suppliers.

It is the manager's task to ensure that adequate communication exists within the organization and between the organization and the outside world. This involves a judgement about the mission of the work unit and the kinds of information that are necessary for successful operation. It also involves an assessment of the formal and informal communication patterns within the organization. Where necessary, the manager should be ready to redirect communication patterns to increase their usefulness to the organization.

Most organizations develop mechanisms for facilitating information flow. Periodic staff meetings are a common mechanism for institutionalizing the flow of information. Many organizations maintain newsletters. Written requirements of all kinds abound in organizations, including documentation of cases histories, weekly updates and regular reports. The use of data processing has allowed for detailed monitoring of individual cases and the generation of summary reports for management. But the regularized information flows that become part of the organizational procedures are not sufficient by themselves. Every organization is also subject to informal non-scheduled information exchanges that are part of the process of interaction. These informal information flows are a critical source of information for managers. In fact, often they are more important than the regularized and documented information exchanges. Understanding the differences in the use of informal and formal channels of communication is important to managers.

Many managerial problems can be solved by more effective communications. The manager who finds that the work group is not responding to direction should examine the way in which direction is communicated. If individual performance is not reaching anticipated levels, it may reflect a failure of feedback mechanisms to provide information to the individual about failed performance. Low work group morale may reflect poor communications among work group members.

The process of communication may be conceptualized as an exchange of information among two or more individuals. The initiator of the message is usually referred to as the sender and the one for whom the message is intended is referred to as the receiver. The message, which contains the information that is transmitted must be communicated through some language, such as a written English, spoken French or sign language. The process by which the sender translates the message into the language is called encoding, while the process by which the receiver interprets the language is called decoding.

The simple process of communication from one sender to one receiver involves a complex set of processes by which thoughts are translated into language, transmitted and then translated by the receiver. The clear communication of the message requires accurate encoding by the sender and decoding by the receiver. It requires active involvement of both individuals. Communications is a two-way process.

This simple model of two-way communication from sender to receiver is complicated in the real world by the multiplicity of messages and the number of individuals involved. Information and its transfer are part of the everyday exchange among individuals and involve personal as well as work-related matters. Individuals ordinarily alternate in sending and receiving messages except in such stylized formats as lectures, where the sender may deliver a formal presentation for a period of more than one hour.

2. The Elemental Skills

Because of the central role of the manager in organizational communications, the manager must pay special attention to the mastery of communication skills. These include both sending and receiving skills. Ordinarily the sending skills receive the greatest attention, but the importance of receiving skills is increasingly recognized.

Messages are ordinarily communicated through written memos or oral presentations. The form of the messages is also important. The words used, the oral expressions, the punctuation and the pauses, are used to embellish the meaning of the actual words. The intonation in oral messages or body language can be more important than the words themselves. Sometimes we refer to body language as a separate language although ordinarily it forms part of the message itself.

Written and spoken English are not the only language in which messages are sent. Messages can be sent in "foreign languages" or in other languages such as sign language or mathematical notation. Perhaps not so obvious are the specialized usages which are appropriate only in certain circumstances. Business memos may use a certain style of expression. Within a particular agency certain forms and modes of expression may predominate.

Speaking

For managers, oral communication clearly predominates over written communication. Thus its mastery is most important. In fact, the ability to present a cogent point of view may be one of the most important attributes of the successful manager. Speaking abilities are developed over a long period of time and the manager who has developed these abilities is indeed fortunate. The effective speaker, one who can express a message clearly and compellingly, is likely to be successful at the more complex tasks of testifying before public bodies, running meetings, participating in conferences and conducting interviews.

Speaking skills can be learned and improved and should be given particular attention by the upwardly mobile manager. Some specific guidelines may be useful.

Guidelines for Public Speaking

1. Decide exactly what you want to say. The first step in communicating a message is deciding what you want to communicate. Don't try to communicate too much. Often speakers go on at great length searching for some particular point they want to make. Such "exploratory" prose may be appropriate in certain specialized circumstances, for example, where a participant is not yet present at a critical meeting and there is a need to stall for time. Most of the time, however, people want to hear your message stated clearly and succinctly. A few moments of thought before beginning your

remarks can clarify in your own mind what you wish to communicate.

2. Organize your presentation. In order to have impact, verbal presentations must be carefully organized. If those listening do not receive the message in a relatively short period they will miss it. Usually a verbal presentation has three parts: the introduction, the narrative and the summary.

3. Get the attention of your audience. Since verbal communication occurs so quickly, it is important that you have the attention of the audience and that they are prepared for your remarks. When delivering formal presentations, this problem may assume considerable importance. Often speakers will precede their information with attention-getting devices such as jokes, or statements intended to shock or surprise the listener.

4. State the message in language the audience will understand. Where the point is abstract, be sure to use relevant examples. Having prepared the audience for the message, make sure the language that is used is appropriate to the audience. Formal and informal occasions require different styles. Large and small groups require different styles. Audiences with higher and lower levels of education require different styles. Professional and lay audiences require different styles. The purpose of communication is to get your message across to your audience in language appropriate to that audience.

5. Reinforce your message through repetition. Never assume in oral communication that your message has been communicated if it has been made once. Always try to obtain feedback from your audience to see if they have understood your point. After presenting an explanation, summarize your main point where it is appropriate.

These guidelines can be used in evaluating presentations. Try them out on presentations of others. Try to model your own style after that of others who measure up to high standards. Don't be ashamed to attend workshops on improving speaking skills. Take the opportunity to practice your skills when possible.

Listening

In learning communication skills, attention is usually focused on sending messages with little attention to receiving messages. This is reinforced by the tendency to view management from the command perspective. Since the manager is the commander, the skills most needed are those of written and spoken English so that directions can be transmitted. But as our model of management emphasizes the role of communicator and intermediary, the importance of two-way communication between the manager and the subordinate is emphasized. Two-way communication involves a succession of messages where individuals alternate in sending and receiving roles. In fact the roles become blurred as the receiver responds to the message by sending messages in return. The importance of being able to receive messages then takes on an equal importance in facilitating the mutual exchange of information which is at the heart of effective management.

To those who think carefully about the manager's role, the need to obtain feedback should be clear. The manager must be skilled in receiving information as well as transmitting it. The first step in effective listening is recognizing the importance of listening. Listening provides important information for the manager but it also helps build the commitment of individuals to organizational goals. By active listening to subordinates' suggestions, the manager reinforces the worth of that subordinate. Be patient in listening to others. The manager's instincts are to provide direction and cut short the statements of the subordinate. While the manager should redirect discussion when it goes astray, patience in listening to the subordinate will be rewarded by greater attention on the part of the subordinate.

Listen objectively by providing the sender a fair chance to explain. Listen actively by being attentive and demonstrating through facial and body expression that listening is continuing. Avoid distractions. Where questions are appropriate they should be used, but they should not be used to disrupt the main flow of the presentation. Check up on your understanding by paraphrasing and repeating what you hear to make sure you are hearing right.

Listening, like speaking and writing, is a skill which can be learned and improved by practice. Check yourself when you are listening by going back over the last paragraph and seeing how good your listening score is. Try to get feedback from others as to how they perceive your listening skills. Pay attention to listening. It is just as important as speaking.

Writing

While the majority of interactions for most managers involve oral rather than written communication, written communications play an important part in most organizations. In presenting written ideas, similar principles to those of speaking apply. Written communication differs from oral communication in its permanence. Be extra careful in your use of words because there is a lasting record. Be precise, because you will probably not be available for clarifying imprecisions. Be brief, because most people do not like to spend time reading long memos.

The permanent and more formal aspects of written communication make them the preferred method for important occasions. The written memorandum becomes the official record of interviews and the agenda and minutes of meetings become important in terms of establishing a written record. Most formal directives and official actions are communicated through written documents. Thus, although oral communication skills are more frequently used by managers, written skills can have a special importance. An important difference in written communications is that a manager may rely upon others to help. Many secretaries and assistants help compensate for the shortcomings of managers. Yet written skills can be learned, and managers who can write well have a prized ability.

In undertaking written communications three important dimensions that should be kept in mind are tone, clarity and explicitness. Tone is perhaps the most immediate factor in determining the reception by the reader. It reveals the mental and emotional attitude of the writer and signals the reader as to how the message should be taken. Tone can be colored by fear, dislike, jealousy and anxiety. Ordinarily the writer strives to communicate a professional serious tone. However, sometimes humor or even anger is appropriate. The writer should always check to make sure that the tone which is transmitted is the tone that is intended. Emotion can sometimes be transmitted which is counterproductive in achieving the purpose of the communication.

Clarity is the central guiding principal of all communication. The purpose of communication is to make a message understood by the audience. Attention to clarity is easy. But achieving clarity is a sometimes difficult undertaking which depends upon carefully developed skill.

The final aspect, explicitness, both demonstrates to the receiver that the message is intended for this particular receiver and ensures that the message tells exactly what is needed for this particular purpose. Explicitness keeps the message focused on its direct purpose. The main forms of written communication include the official document containing a regulation, the brief query or response, often of an official sort, and the report on some particular issue. Many managers go through their careers without drafting regulations or preparing reports. All managers at one time or another must commit to writing a request or a response to a request.

The main focus of written communications is the memorandum which is a concise form of communications and is used to make requests, provide information or inform others about decisions that have been made.

In order to inform, written commuications uses words, sentences and paragraphs. Their usage should be carefully designed to promote that clarity which is essential to all communications. The best communication is the most direct. Written communications should be brief, simple, and avoid jargon.

The memorandum or memo is the most frequently used communication between members of an organization. It is preferred over oral communication where a record is needed or where oral communication may be more time consuming or ineffective. Most organizations adopt standard forms for memos, which contain the following elements: 1. Receiver, usually preceded by the word, "To"; 2. Sender, usually preceded by the word, "From"; 3. Subject, often preceded by the phrase, "Re"; 4. Date; 5. Agency from which memo is being sent.

An effective memo is direct and concise. It should explain why a message is being sent, who and what are involved, where and when events are to take place and how actions are to be performed. In writing memos some additional guidelines can be suggested for achieving the intended effect.

Guidelines For Effective Memos

1. Be candid: Explain honestly and sincerely what is meant.
2. Be considerate: Consider the impact of the phrasing on the feelings of the receiver.
3. Be calm: Avoid unnecessary emotional language.
4. Be clear: Phrase things without elaborate and unnecessary phrases.
5. Be concise: Don't use unnecessary words.
6. Be correct: Strive for accuracy, especially in dates and details.
7. Be complete: Provide all essential details.

In writing memos, special attention should also be given to the purpose of the memo. Is it simply a request for information or is it requesting a difficult decision and response? Is it intended to be persuasive? Is it announcing good news or bad news? The purpose of the memo should always be in the mind of the writer. The basic skills of speaking, writing and listening are critical to the success of any manager. Their manifestations occur in the progression of day-to-day interactions that make up the manager's daily routine. While these interactions are tremendously varied, ranging in duration, place, and number of individuals present, some of these interactions are particularly important because of their repetition within the daily routine. Three types of interactions will be considered below, one focusing on face-to-face contact with a single individual in what may be termed an "interview" situation, the second a group situation in which a meeting is being conducted, and the third the techniques of team building. All of these situations require effective speaking and listening skills and to some extent writing skills. They will be discussed in turn.

3. Coaching and Other Interviewing Techniques

Many managerial activities involve one-on-one situations in which the manager is face-to-face with a subordinate or other individual. Face-to-face interactions often involve the exchange of information toward some specific objective. Interactions which are particularly frequent for managers involve assisting, evaluating and selecting subordinates. While many of the skills of effective communication are needed in all these situations, certain approaches, strategies and skills are associated with particular purposes. Special importance may be attached to situations involving assisting, evaluating and selecting subordinates. In fact, general principles governing these relationships have been developed and have been formalized in interviewing skills focused on coaching, appraisal and selection. At this stage, the coaching interview is particularly important because of its frequency and centrality in understanding the interactions between managers and subordinates.

The importance of the coaching interview as a tool of effective management cannot be over-emphasized. Its purpose is to provide support and direction to subordinates. The manager who can skillfully handle the coaching interview has mastered an important aspect of organizational life.

The central idea behind the coaching interview is to provide a climate in which the subordinate is relaxed and willing to accept direction from the manager. The purpose and approach in providing direction should be well thought out ahead of time and should be as positive and supportive as possible. In order to provide effective coaching, the manager must have a good understanding of the subordinate and the subordinate's motivation. The overall approach should be one of helping the subordinate to overcome the obstacles which are standing in the way of accomplishing the given tasks.

The coaching interview may be initiated by the manager or the subordinate. It may occur on the spur of the moment or be formally initiated. In fact the most effective coaching occurs when there is mutual recognition of the need to do better. The manager, however, bears ultimate responsibility for initiating coaching interviews when they are necessary and appropriate.

The initiation of the interview is perhaps the most critical stage. The way in which the interview is scheduled is critical in establishing the right atmosphere to allow for effective problem resolution. It is important that in the initiation there is a mutual recognition of the need for interchange about the common problem. Both the subordinate and manager should perceive that something is not going well and that organizational needs are not being met. While the most sought after situation is one in which the subordinate recognizes a problem and comes to the manager, the ultimate responsibility for locating inadequate performance is the manager's. Where the manager must point out to the subordinate the need for a coaching interview, it should be done in a non-threatening way. In fact, it may often be possible to initiate such an interview on the spot. The designation of a future time for the meeting may make it more formal and threatening to the employee. Sometimes such formality is necessary for the process. This is particularly true if a major difficulty has surfaced which could lead to formal sanctions or other disciplinary action. In this case the coaching interview takes on a warning function.

The method of initiation is critical in promoting an atmosphere conducive to effective coaching. Coaching is a developmental activity. The point is to help the individual learn to overcome a specific situation, and more general problems. The way to accomplish this task is to establish a learning environmonent. The individual should not be castigated, but an atmosphere of mutual examination of a problem should be established. It should be recognized that a punitive atmosphere is inappropriate. The problem is as much the manager's as the subordinate's. They are in this thing together.

The focus of the interview is to surface the problem that is identified and to explore it in the context of the organization's operation. While it may be that the individual has made a mistake, the focus should be on understanding what has happened and how the problem that has arisen can be successfully resolved. If the correct atmosphere has been established, the problem should be surfaced easily. If a punitive atmosphere has been established, most likely the employee will react defensively and surfacing the problem will be difficult.

Once the problem has been surfaced and discussed, a resolution should be sought. Again the emphasis should be mutuality in exploring options and a hesitancy to lay blame on the employee. The problem will be resolved through mutual effort and measures and the employee should see the manager's role as supportive, rather than condemnatory. This pattern of support which will result in the long run is necessary to establish an effective manager-subordinate interaction. If necessary, future meetings may be set to discuss the problem or future opportunities should be explored.

An important skill in the coaching interview, as indeed in all interviews, is eliciting information. A conducive atmosphere is important. In addition, questions should be formulated in a manner to illuminate problems rather than to introduce extraneous issues. Questions asked in this manner are sometimes a means to fact-finding. Either relatively open-ended questions which allow for a great deal of latitude in answering or more focused or closed questions may be used. They both have their place. The former stand greater danger of being misinterpreted and taking away from the problem identification. On the other hand, open-ended questions may be useful where a problem is potentially difficult and the individual may be resistent to acknowledging a personal role in the problem.

To direct the interview to information exchange, the interviewer should ask questions which are directed toward obtaining specific information. In formulating questions, the interviewer should try to be brief. If possible questions should be less than 10 words and avoid judgmental terminology.

Present action words first, so that the receiver focuses on the required response. Words to be included are list, describe, explain, and tell. Avoid questions which require only a yes or no answer or two answers. These questions do not provide very much information and respondents may easily avoid the more unpleasant question, or actually miss one of the two questions.

The use of specific questions should relate to a more general strategy in managing the flow of information in the interview. These strategies include:

1. *Tracking.* Tracking involves asking a series of questions about a given topic to fully explore a particular line of inquiry. Example: "Describe what you did when the client first entered the room. What did you do next? What happened after that?. . . . Explain how you closed the interview."

2. *Probing.* Probing refers to the use of follow-up to collect additional in-depth information not elicited by the initial question. Probing questions are used in the process of tracking. Example: "Describe what you did when the client first entered the room. Say more about that. Tell me what your reasons were for behaving that way."

3. *Illustrating.* Illustrating refers to giving examples to help the supervisee understand your question or point: "You don't understand why I say you don't make appropriate use of help. Let me give you an example. You were told that the report was not written satisfactorily. However, you did not take Mr. Allen's offer to help you improve your writing skills."

4. *Summarizing.* Summarizing involves tying together the information that the supervisee has given. This helps both the supervisor and supervisee keep track of what has been covered and what remains to be dealt with. Example: "Let's review the decisions which we reached today. We decided that you would hire an assistant, that you would set up a training program for the counselors, that I would review the budget. . . ."

5. *Blocking.* Blocking refers to cutting short off-focus responses in order to prevent the interview from going off in direction that is not helpful. Example: In discussing the sloppy work which the supervisee is submit-

ting, the supervisee responds by saying, "No one else in the agency types their reports." The supervisor responds by saying, "Let's just talk about your reports."

6. *Pacing.* Pacing refers to managing time during the interview so that all important information is gathered.

7. *Silence.* Most individuals have difficulty managing silence. They respond by talking. Silence can have many meanings. It can provide an opportunity for individuals to privately reflect on what has previously been said or about a statement made or a question posed. Silence may, on the other hand, point up a misunderstanding or a disagreement. It may be the result of confusion or a way of blocking or defending oneself. It may be the defense of a person who is unwilling to communicate or it may be a reflection on an answer which is more acceptable than the one response made spontaneously. Unless the interviewer is sure of his ground, he should avoid extensive silences. However, when appropriate, silence can be an invaluable tool.

8. *Restatement.* A restatement provides the supervisee with an echo, to encourage the supervisee to go on speaking, examining, looking deeper. There are four basic types of restatement: a. restating exactly; b. restating exactly, changing only the pronoun; c. restating in summary fashion; d. restating part of what has been said, the part that is most significant and worth having the supervisee hear again.

9. *Clarification.* The interviewer remains very close to what her partner has expressed by simplifying it to make it clearer. The interviewer in her own words tries to clarify for the interviewee what the latter has had difficulty in expressing clearly.

The coaching interview is one tool in counseling subordinates. Properly used, it can greatly facilitate one-to-one interactions. Developing staff in the broadest sense, an extension of the coaching interview, is a critical managerial skill which will be treated in the next chapter.

4. Conducting Meetings

Of course most managers devote a substantial portion of their efforts to group situations where two or more subordinates or others are involved. A large share of these encounters, particularly in human service organizations, involve scheduled and unscheduled meetings. The manager, of course, has particular responsibilities for the conduct of meetings.

Scheduled meetings are planned well in advance, although sometimes meetings may be called on short notice. Meetings in fact are distinguished from other encounters in part because they are arranged beforehand and are more formal. Meetings are an occasion for calling attention to particular problems. In fact, the prerogative to call meetings may be one of the most important and sought after powers in an organization. Calling a meeting becomes an expression of authority and the manager should recognize the fact that by calling a meeting, others are in fact being prevented from engaging in other activities. Of course, in some organizations, where individuals have little to do, the occasion for a meeting may be a great joy. In fact, the hesitancy of individuals to attend meetings may be an indication of a healthy, dynamic organization where individuals have other demands on their time.

Any meeting then must be viewed as an organizational event of particular significance. The manager calling the meeting must understand its relationship to other organizational needs and treat it as an encounter among mature individuals. Meetings have a potential for teambuilding within the organization and dealing with one of the manager's most important needs: to maintain contact with subordinates on a personal level. Meetings also have the potential for coalescing opposition to the manager and challenging managerial authority.

Because of the potential of meetings for good and bad, it is important that they not be treated frivolously. The managers should have a clear idea why a meeting is being called and its likely outcomes. Individuals attending the meeting should know ahead of time what the purpose of the meeting is and should leave with a sense of having accomplished that purpose.

Knowing when to call meetings and when to handle matters in different ways is a critical management skill and admits of no easy rules. It is helpful in considering this issue, however, to distinguish between periodic meetings such as weekly staff meetings, meant to enhance the regular flow of organizational communications, and meetings called for a particular purpose. In planning and executing periodic meetings the focus should be on balancing the needs for organizational communications against the time that such meetings require. Most organizations provide for periodic, often weekly staff meetings to allow for a regular exchange of information among work group members. Often such meetings are held at the beginning of the week, such as Monday mornings. Other meetings may be held to resolve specific issues, to exchange information where more than two individuals are involved and to facilitate group communications and team building. These meetings should be scheduled as needed.

The initiation of the meeting is the first step and involves a decision as to the necessity of a meeting, the purpose of the meeting and who should attend the meeting. Often this process involves several or all of those attending the meeting. For example, a work group will ordinarily jointly decide to hold periodic meetings at a time of mutual convenience. An individual encountering difficulties will arrange to meet with a superior to discuss the matter. A group of individuals finding a problem involving overlapping responsibilities will arrange to meet to resolve their confusion. Managers have a special responsibility to initiate meetings when they are needed to facilitate work group activity or the resolution of difficult problems. Ordinarily a manager will take responsibility for initiating a meeting by designating a particular time and place. Where individuals of equal status in the organization are involved, the obligation for initiating and housing the meeting will require explicit agreement. Similarly a joint decision may be necessary as to who will chair the meeting.

The manager or chosen initiator will have the responsibility for informing the attendees of the site for the meeting, arranging an agenda and conducting the meeting. Sometimes the site is subject to negotiation, particularly if status concerns intrude over where to locate the meeting.

The agenda may present greater difficulties. An agenda is basically a list of items to be discussed at the meeting arranged in sequential fashion. More elaborate agendas may match items with individuals responsible for initial presentations and may allocate a given amount of time to particular items.

Whenever possible, an agenda should be distributed prior to the meeting so that the attendees know ahead of time what the meeting is about. This will facilitate their preparation and ensure that they will bring the relevant materials and any personnel required. It also allows for prior discussion about the agenda to ensure that everyone is meeting about the same topic.

Sometimes it is not possible to prepare an agenda ahead of time. In this case an agenda should be prepared so that at the beginning of the meeting it can be agreed upon. In some informal meetings or in those where the agenda is perfectly clear, an agenda may not be necessary. The agenda should be concise and clear and should be reviewed at the beginning of the meeting so that everyone knows what is to be covered and what sequence is to be followed. Changes may be made at the beginning of the meeting to facilitate the requests of individual members at the meeting.

Once an agenda has been agreed upon, it is the task of the individual coordinating the meeting to guide the group through the agenda in a timely fashion. Of course, the cooperation of individual members is required.

Individuals may in fact move the meeting along themselves, when appropriate, by suggesting to the chair sufficient time has been devoted to a particular item. The chair may use discretion in extending discussion of particular items. If it appears that the agenda will not be completed, usually an appeal to the group is made to change the agenda because of the need for extended discussion of an important item.

The skills needed in conducting a meeting and moving a group through an agenda are similar to the skills needed more generally in group facilitation. The manager must be fair with everybody and yet remind the group when it must move on to other items or make particular decisions. The meeting coordinator, or chairperson, must be devoted to the agenda and ensure that the agenda is kept. Most meetings have mixed purposes in exchanging information, building group cohesion and taking specific actions. Individuals may assume a variety of functions within the meeting, including: 1) providing information; 2) receiving information; 3) clarifying information; 4) expressing a point of view; 5) bolstering a point of view; 6) opposing a point of view; and 7) mediating between competing points of view. Skills in pursuing these multiple purposes are important for managers.

Managers in human service organizations have a particular need for skill in initiating and conducting meetings. Because of the high level of professional training within these organizations and their orientation to dealing with individual difficulties, a tendency exists to require frequent formal communications and documentation for actions taken. Also because status considerations are important, calling and attending meetings often become sought after as marks of status. Also, because human service organizations allow a great deal of individual autonomy, meetings serve the purpose of reminding individuals of common goals.

5. Team Building

Managers need skills in one-to-one communication, in explaining tasks, developing confidence, providing counseling and receiving feedback about tasks that have been accomplished. They also need group skills in running meetings, inspiring dedication and achieving coordination among individuals. A basic part of this ability is to gain acceptance as a leader. Formal designation as work group leader by no means ensures that the members of the group will listen carefully, and move in accepted directions. Respect and actual authority must be gained over time.

While the manager must be attentive to motivating individuals, the primary work group as a whole is the object of most attention. Since the primary work group is the filter for a preponderance of the manager's effort, its ability to effectuate managerial initiatives is critical. In addition to working with the members of the work group on an individual basis, the manager must focus attention on the coordination of their activities. The manager must ensure that the primary work group as a whole is working toward common organizational goals and that their efforts are mutually reinforcing, rather than at odds.

The most salient medium for achieving work group coordination is the periodic "staff" meeting at which the work group members coalesce to discuss issues and receive direction. The conduct of such meetings becomes central to the effective management of the work group. While they are an important form in which the manager asserts and reinforces authority relationships, they also provide invaluable feedback to primary group members about what other members are doing. They also provide an excellent context in which to coordinate individual efforts and ensure they are reinforcing each other rather than working at cross-purposes. The ways in which the manager mediates among individuals and encourages them to work together can provide a supportive background for coordinated activities.

These formal meetings, however, should be the beginning and not the end of work group coordination. The manager should use other opportunities to bring individuals together for collaboration in common activities. The ability to generate group cohesion within the primary work group is an important determinant of managerial success.

Team building within human service organizations can be particularly difficult. The strong professional orientation of staff, coupled with a tendency to isolation in the work setting militate against strong team efforts. Yet efforts can be taken to counteract these negative factors. Many mental health centers, for example, have adopted a team approach to service delivery which places individuals within a group context. Training situations may be modified to allow for team teaching. Other approaches can be developed.

Ad hoc measures can also help build team bonds. Task forces can be established to bring individuals together or subcommittees can function on a regular basis for establishing coordination in a particular area.

Work Group Coordination

Perhaps no task is more central to management than the establishment of a system of coordination, and espirit de corps within the primary work group. In all the manager's interactions this goal should be remembered. The manager's interactions with staff present the opportunity for establishing this team spirit and reinforcing cooperative undertakings.

Sometimes, however, special efforts need to be undertaken outside of the regular course of business to bolster work group coordination. Social events may be helpful or more formal training efforts may be undertaken. Such training efforts often involve an outside consultant who can facilitate interaction within the group and help bring submerged problems to the surface. The processes of communication that operate in the organization are critical in achieving work group coordination. The importance of the manager as group facilitator should be noted, whether in a formal meeting, or otherwise.

Sometimes supplementary efforts must be undertaken to establish work group coordination. They may include special meetings devoted to group processes, formal training sessions involving outsiders or special training for individuals outside of the organizational context. Special group sessions ordinarily provide a context in which possible sources of group tension can be aired. They provide for interchange among members to air problems and help improve the regular group communication processes. A skilled neutral individual, brought in as an organizational consultant, can facilitate interchange and help the organization to strengthen its own processes for communication and problem solving.

Sometimes the difficulties in group interaction may result from an individual who has weak communication skills. Managers, of course, have an especial responsibility to take the lead in this area. Where individuals seek to build their own skills, a variety of mechanisms are available through outside organizations which specialize in training. One of the most well-known and well-established programs is run by the National Training Lab. It usually involves 2-3 weeks of training in a special environment to improve the group skills of participants.

Team building focused on the primary work group is an important aspect of organization building, the subject of the next chapter.

Selected Bibliography

Barnard, Chester. *The Functions of the Executive.* Cambridge: Harvard University Press, 1938.

Deegan, Arthur X. *Coaching: A Management Skill for Improving Individual Performance.* Reading, Massachusetts: Addison-Wesley, 1979.

Goldhaber, Gerald. *Organizational Communications.* Dubuque, Iowa: William C. Brown, 1974.

Golembiewski, Robert T. *Behavior and Organization: O+M and the Small Group.* Chicago: Rand McNally, 1962.

Huseman, Richard, Hahiff, James, and Hatfield, John. *Interpersonal Communications in the Organization.* Boston: Holbrook, 1976.

Improving Your Written Communications. New York: Preston Publishing Company, Inc., 1963.

Maier, Norman et al. *The Role Play Technique.* La Jolla, California: University Associates, Inc., 1975.

Mintzberg, Henry. *The Nature of Managerial Work.* New York: Harper, 1973.

Pfeiffer, J. William and Jones, John E. *A Handbook of Structured Experiences for Human Relations Training.* La Jolla, California: University Associates Press, 1972-81.

Rendero, Thomasino. *Communicating with Subordinates.* New York: American Management Association, 1973.

Chapter 7.

Organization Building

While improving individual performance on a daily basis is a central goal of management, longer range concerns focus on improving organizational performance. In attempting to build a high performance organization, the human service manager is confronted by such obstacles as lack of discretion in the selection of staff, lack of sophistication in choosing among potential staff, lack of skills of individuals for current or future positions and inadequate coordination.

Suppose you have just been asked to establish a day care facility in conjunction with an industrial plant to serve 50 children in a suburban area. Furthermore, you are given a fixed budget which calls for yourself as director, and two full-time staff and one part-time secretary. How would you recruit applicants for such an undertaking? What type of selection process would you design? What qualities would you seek in your new employees? While most human service managers are confronted with ongoing organizations, from time to time they are confronted with vacancies or new positions that must be filled. How should they go about filling those positions?

Suppose after one year of operation the day care center is not fulfilling the expectations of management. You are asked to prepare a report analyzing your accomplishments and shortcomings, including an evaluation of the performance of individual staff members. On what basis would you evaluate your staff and decide who to retain? How would you decide if individual performance could be improve through staff development? How would you decide if the operation of the group was inadequate and whether there was a need for organization development measures?

1. Staff Selection and Termination

The situation described above is unusual for human service managers. Usually they operate in organizations in which most members have already been selected. Yet most managers do select some new employees. In making such selections, how can a manager optimize the chances for success?

The selection of staff is difficult at best. Yet it is a critical managerial prerogative. The manager who is able to select astutely can build an effective organization over time. This involves an intricate process of weighing a variety of sources of information about the expertise and organizational abilities of the individual. Unfortunately the indicators of these qualities are not always readily available. In obtaining information on potential employees a range of sources should be tapped. The most reliable source of information is direct on-the-job observation. Such a perspective allows the manager to see the employee in action, using expertise and functioning in an organizational setting. Where prior observation is not available a try-out process may be advisable. Such a try-out approach is suggested by contemporary theories of effective leadership which stress the contingent nature of the manager-subordinate relationship.

In focusing upon the importance of building a managerial team and in orchestrating a complex process of interaction among a number of individuals, once again the try-out process is recommended whenever possible. That try-out process may involve efforts at providing direction, monitoring and development on the part of the manager. The investment in a member of your managerial team is going to be of overwhelming importance to you. It is probably unrealistic to believe that such a decision can be made on the basis of available information at the time of the initial decision even where such information includes all of the types mentioned above. Unfortunately direct observation during a tryout period is often impossible and so such substitutes as interviews and recommendations from other employers must be used.

The use of interviews in staff selection is widespread. But the results of this process may be very difficult to interpret. Interviews may give deceptive impressions about individuals and may register more about an individuals's ease and mastery of brief verbal encounters than actual on-the-job performance. Skill in selection interviewing can be a critical skill for managers in high turnover organizations. While many of the approaches used in other interview situations may be applicable, selection interviewing has some special characteristics. The problems of deception and individual bias need particular attention.

Recommendations are another source of information about potential applicants, but unless those providing references are very well-known to the manager, the judgment may not be reliable. References may have a vested interest in encouraging the individual to depart or the level of information about the individual may be low.

A more sophisticated process known as the assessment center which combines interviewing and testing with exercises measuring group skills has been successfully used to assess managerial talent. But this process may be expensive and is not ordinarily accessible to individual managers without a general organizational decision to commit substantial resources to the process.

It is probably easier to use indirect approaches such as interviews and references when focusing on technical abilities than on organizational abilities. Since managerial skills fall largely into the latter area, they are more difficult to judge without the benefits of direct observation. They may often involve such personal characteristics as resilience to stress, high energy level and ability to cope with ambiguity and contradiction.

In judging the ability of individuals to function within the defined organizational context, the individual's relationship to the manager making the selection is important to consider. For example, a manager will be more concerned about personal compatability in considering a staff assistant who will be in constant contact than a subordinate manager who may be seen intermittently. The manager may also want to consider the issue of personal loyalty in the selection of staff. In many bureaucracies, particularly at the higher levels, intense competition abounds among the individual managers. The loyalty of staff to the particular agendas and personal goals of the individual manager may be critical in such situations. It is not unusual for high level managers, particularly in the competitive and exposed public sector to rank loyalty above technical or organizational ability in staff assistants.

Limitations on Staff Selection

In the staffing area, the limitations on human service managers are striking. Human service organizations that are subject to state and local civil service systems have the most detailed requirements for selection and termination. These constraints affect all aspects of staffing because they establish a framework in which the choice over staff is severely limited. In such a context, direction, monitoring and development become even more critical, yet they often do not receive the attention required. In not-for-profit organizations which carry out many direct social services the strictures on selection and termination may be considerably reduced. However, these organizations often depend upon government or private funding sources which may themselves place constraints on the selection and termination of personnel. Furthermore, the ties of the organization to the community may result in a conservative bias against firing employees. In fact, retention of employees who are not performing adequately may be encouraged by the "helping" ideology of the organization. Organizational tolerance for inadequate performance may be justified as contributing to the overall organizational goals. The human service manager must, at the beginning, understand and test the constraints on his or her authority to hire and fire. For these powers are at the basis of the staffing function.

The development and structuring of effective staff relationships which over time will bring about organizational goals through the attainment of individual objectives is critical. The importance of developing a team approach is at the heart of the staffing problem. No manager can accomplish much alone. The creation of an effective management team requires that the manager select, direct, monitor, develop and terminate staff over a period of time and promote these activities within the larger unit. At times the constraints may be great. But the ability to carry out this task is the most important single element in determining organizational effectiveness.

Merit system principles in the civil service require that entry into the organization be based upon a competitive examination, ordinarily in writing. While originally the merit system was conceived as a counterweight to political patronage in job selection and promotion, the constraints it places today upon managerial discretion are formidable. Unless a manager is creating a new unit the lack of discretion may be overwhelming. And even where a new unit is created, the civil service system will require that individuals selected be from examination lists, and that transfers be honored as recognized by union contracts offering positions to those with the greatest seniority. Given the strictures of the system, the attempt to recruit individuals from other units may meet with extreme resistance. In not-for-profit organizations the formal constraints are less onerous. But informal constraints may be considerable.

The manager in a human service organization will often feel as if the struggle to increase discretion in staffing is a losing one. Yet in order to maintain a balanced perspective, it is important to remember that in all organizations constraints on hiring exist. In a family-run business, relatives have special rights. In large corporations, elaborate bureaucratic rules exist to govern selection. But it is probably true that managers in human service organizations have an especial challenge to enlarge their area of discretion.

The ability to select new people for an organization depends upon vacancies within the organization. Vacancies may exist or may be created by reassignments either of a voluntary or involuntary nature, departures from the organization or the creation of new positions. Since human service organizations are often under pressure to reduce expenditures, unfilled positions may exist. A new manager may demand the right to make new apointments to vacant positions as a requirement of accepting the new position. Sometimes, of course, where budget constraints are insuperable, such a demand can not be met. A manager may find that employees undertake voluntary transfers or may be encouraged to leave. Termination of employees for insubordination or incompetence is a final possibility. The ability to undertake such actions, however, particularly within a civil service context is severely limited. It may involve extensive organizational resources in terms of legal and managerial attendance at hearings. But when used wisely this can be an effective means of creating vacancies while also encouraging existing employees to work to capacity.

All too often, however, in human service organizations, the creation of vacancies is only the beginning. The organization and sometimes the political executive must authorize the filling of vacancies. And, often, an elaborate process must be carried out. Particularly at the lower levels, the filling of vacancies is based upon ranked lists resulting from written examinations. The one-in- three rule is common in such situations, requiring that the manager appoint one of three highest scoring applicants.

Deviations from this and other civil service norms are sometimes possible. Exempt positions may be created which are freed from this rule. A common practice is to relax the requirement that individuals be selected in rank order of their appearance on a list. The rule of three allows for the selection of the most suitable from among those achieving the highest scores. Some believe that the rule of three should be extended to a rule of ten, to allow for greater selection authority. In other situations, a qualifying examination has replaced the ranked order exam, so that the manager may select from among those who demonstrate minimal qualifications. Oral examinations are being used to substitute for written examinations.

The pressures upon managers to select from a particular list have led to informal procedures to subvert the civil service system. A common practice is to create new titles or appoint individuals to titles for which no lists exist. Individuals become "provisional" appointees pending the offering of an examination. Such examinations may be years in coming or they may never come. When they do come, incumbents may have special advantages.

Human service managers operating outside of the civil service system are relieved of responsibilities for appointments from lists, but they may find other constraints such as lists of recommendations arising from the board of trustees or other sources. They too, like human service managers operating within the government, must first find the vacancies to make the selection. It should be clear that the opportunity to organize new units and the ability to increase one's discretion in selection are highly sought after prerogatives.

After Selection

Once an individual has been selected to join your organization, the process of direction, monitoring and development takes place and, in some instances, actions to effectuate termination. Direction has been discussed above in the section on leadership and so will not be considered here, though its place within a total approach to staffing is clear. Monitoring has also been discussed and particular attention was given to the role of feedback in providing a basis for behavior modification. Another aspect of monitoring which has received considerable attention in recent years is the systematic periodic appraisal of staff.

Many organizations have instituted performance appraisal systems requiring periodic sessions between superior and subordinate managers to set objectives and assess the extent to which these objectives have been reached. This process can be an important means of reinforcing a common direction. It can also be used as the basis for a fair and objective system of termination. An appraisal system, also, offers considerable potential for abuse if it is poorly and inconsistently administered.

On the other hand, a formal appraisal system may lead to fear and timidity rather than openness and motivation. It is probably accurate to say that a poorly-run organization will not be helped by a formal appraisal system, while an organization that is well-run may benefit from such a system. It requires a minimum of sophistication about setting objectives, evaluating them and tying them to individual performance.

The ultimate sanction in an appraisal system is removal from office. Often this step is difficult to consummate in human service organizations. Government agencies have strong protections for employees past the probationary period (usually 6 months in duration). Thus removal from office is infrequent. Even in human service organizations which function outside the civil service, removal is often difficult. Community based organizations run by local boards may have built-in roadblocks to the removal of individuals. And the ethic of human service organizations themselves militates against removal from office.

Yet the ultimate sanction is ordinarily available to managers if they want to use it. While removal proceedings should be undertaken with a realistic view of their costs in terms of time and money, they should not be dismissed out of hand. The threat of removal when backed up by concrete actions can be a powerful tool and the actual removal of individuals can often be a boon to organization operation.

While removal from office is often difficult in human service organizations, transfers in assignment are more common. Reassignment may be a perfect strategy for the individual manager who can thereby remove an obstacle to organizational operation. The problem, of course, is that the individual may then proceed to adversely affect another organizational subunit to which the individual is transferred. Where the performance of an individual indicates such a pattern, every effort should be made to remove the individual from the organization.

Given the limitations upon human service organizations in hiring and firing employees, the skills of direction, monitoring and development take on a particular significance. Since getting rid of an individual is so difficult, the manager very often must accept current staff and try to move that staff in a sensible direction.

2. Staff Development and Training

Staff development, particularly at the managerial level is an area that has been neglected by human service organizations. This is particularly unfortunate since the constraints upon selection are so great. A manager most often inherits an organization and its employees. Staff development may be the only way to effectuate real changes in organizational performance.

Scepticism of staff development in human service organizations stems from several sources. The constraints imposed by merit system principles make it appear that staff development activities will not affect career patterns unless these efforts are directed toward promotional exams. The lack of discretionary monies and the attempts to reduce costs often lead to downgrading staff development which is looked upon as suspect or of doubtless utility. There is also a fear in human service organizations that individuals benefiting from staff development will seek higher paying jobs elsewhere.

Staff development has a variety of meanings and a variety of manifestations. It is a critical management function, though sometimes it is perceived as an isolated responsibility of an office of staff development which conducts dull sessions about professional responsibility or some relatedly unimportant topic. To the goal-oriented manager, staff development is an important and critical tool in bolstering organizational productivity. For in most organizations a major limitation upon goal attainment is staff capability.

Staff development, in its broadest conception, is meant to assist individuals operating within the organization to become better at their current and future jobs. It should be part of a comprehensive and coordinated human resource strategy aimed at improving the quality of the workforce. In a human service agency staff development should find ready and natural support. After all, don't human service professionals seek to improve people and their conditions as part of their everyday jobs? Shouldn't efforts at developing staff be second nature? They aren't always.

Perhaps the greatest obstacle to effective staff development is the lack of organizational perspective and focus. A staff development program presupposes organizational goals and ways of measuring staff inadequacies in the pursuit of those goals. But human service organizations often are not clear about their goals. Clarity about organizational goals, however, is only the beginning. Individuals must understand their own roles in relationship to organizational goals. That is why it is important for individuals to establish personal objectives relating to organizational goals. Once individuals have established their objectives, they can begin to understand what efforts should be made to improve their abilities to carry out those objectives. The beginning of staff development lies with the individual perception of need. Of course individual need must be harmonized with organizationally perceived needs to improve individual staff.

Staff development begins at the top of any organization. The executives must understand their own needs for development and the needs of subordinates as well as other individuals in the organization. In large organizations, an individual or office is given responsibility for staff development efforts. Often that office falls within the personnel department or the broader and increasingly common human resources department. The danger in a differentiated staff development office is that the training function becomes separated from management and hence the imperatives of the organization. In many large organizations, including human service organizations, a differentiated staff development office comes into conflict with top management over the needs, directions and resources to be devoted to these activities. Often top managers view programs conceived and run by the staff development office as of questionable value, especially when it takes the subordinate away from on the job.

Staff development serves a variety of organizational purposes related to making individuals more effective in organizational operations. These purposes include:

Current Staffing Enhancement. In any organization a need exists for the upgrading of current staff so that they can better perform their current jobs. Secretaries may need more practice on typewriters and word processors. Keyboard operators may need greater proficiency at the keyboard. Managers may need additional platform skills. An important priority of staff development should provide better skills so that individuals may perform better in their current positions.

Orientation of New Staff. Most organizations have a turnover of staff. New individuals enter the organization and others are promoted within the organization. An important function of staff development offices in larger organizations is to provide orientation to new jobholders. In small organizations, the individual manager is usually responsible for orientation.

New Procedures and Systems. Organizations are constantly introducing new procedures and systems. In human service organizations governmental regulations change constantly. Many of these changes may be handled through written memoranda and materials. A staff development office may provide valuable consultation to management on the best way to introduce such changes. They may also provide the skills for introducing such materials, whether in oral or written form.

Organizational Improvement. From time to time managers see the need to undertake improvements in the operation of the organization. Attention may be directed to communications, processes for goal-setting and accountability. The staff development office may help in these efforts. In other situations, an outside expert may be retained.

Upgrading Individual Skills. All organizations must look to the future as well as the present. Development activities should therefore be directed toward the goals of the organization over a long period of time. This involves, in the first instance, planning for jobs which open up when individuals leave and the creation of new job positions. Often an organization seeks to place into new positions individuals already working within the organization. A carefully designed training program can ensure a supply of individuals with the skills needed for future job openings. An added benefit of such a career-oriented program is the enhanced commitment of individuals who perceive an organizational interest in their personal and career development. Of course such training should be related to the actual needs of the organization.

An organization should also be ready to face the fact that training and development may result in the loss of individuals who cannot be satisfied within the organization or who see opportunities outside the organization. While such a loss of individuals should be carefully examined, it may actually be consistent with attracting a motivated high quality work force.

Given the needs of organizations to enhance staff abilities, orient new staff, establish new procedures, improve organizational operations and upgrade individual skills, how can these goals be met? In most organizations the bulk of staff development activity is carried out by ongoing supervision. A large part of effective supervision is improving the operation of the work unit and bolstering the individuals in that work unit. The medium for accomplishing these development goals are the one-to-one coaching session in which the supervisor provides guidance to the subordinate on an individual basis and the group meeting in which the supervisor works with the entire work unit or subgroups of the staff. These activities are described in the preceding chapter. Sometimes a supervisor will organize special training sessions for the work group or arrange for other developmental efforts. These are the beginnings of the differentiated activities which come to be known as staff development activities. In understanding the role and function of these activities it is important to recognize that they should supplement the role of the manager as staff developer. Unless the developmental activities are related to the job situation and reinforced by the field supervisor it is unlikely that they will have significant impacts upon the individual or the organizational unit.

Closely related to staff development through active supervision is staff development through job rotation. One way to develop an individual's skills and knowledge is through a systematic program of job rotation. Organizations, grooming future managers through internship programs, often provide an opportunity for new employees to serve in several different positions to obtain a variety of experience within the organization. Many large corporations also maintain a policy of job rotation at the middle and higher levels of management to expose individuals to a variety of company operations and to ensure a distribution of talent among the various program areas.

Another offspring of supervisory oversight as a path to development is on-the-job training. In industrial organizations, a large proportion of the training for assembly line workers takes place on the job site. The foreman, or first line supervisor, ordinarily takes a major role in this activity. The special characteristic of on-the-job training is that a formal program is worked out, which usually serves as both an orientation to the organization and skill development for the worker who is gaining experience.

Very often organizations find that on-the-job training can be expensive because it ties up productive equipment and provides practice in all aspects of the job, even those which are not necessarily the most difficult. Where these constraints exist, off-the-job training may take place. Many large corporations now run schools of their own with regularly scheduled classes to provide classroom instruction. Classroom instruction is used rather widely to train higher level employees, including managers and professional level staff.

A step beyond classroom instruction developed and run internally is the use of outside consultants to assist in development activities. Many organizations will hire a consultant to focus on organizational improvement. Measures such as changes in organization procedures, or special training sessions to increase communications or focus on organizational development may be undertaken. Consultants may also be retained to provide special courses for building individual skills in a variety of areas.

Finally an organization may subsidize classroom instruction outside of the organizational setting for individuals whose development is not sufficiently enhanced by internal devices. Classroom instruction outside of the unit usually focuses on upgrading current staff capabilities or preparing individuals for future responsibilities. Where the enhancement of individual abilities is not closely related to existing job needs, the organization may not assume the full cost of classroom instruction. Arrangements for organizational subsidies for instruction outside of regular work hours are common and partial subsidies may be given where the link between the classroom instruction and current job responsibilities is tenuous. Some organizations, on the other hand, take an active role in encouraging staff development of all kinds, and are willing to cover the cost of education and training which is not directly job related.

3. Planning for Staff Development

Since staff development is a critical function of management it should be included in the organizational planning process. Every manager should include development efforts in both organizational and personal planning processes.

In addition to the individual plans that managers develop for themselves and their subordinates, organizations often require overall staff development plans. Some organizations have an individual or group of individuals who are designated as staff development specialists and assume this responsibility. In other organizations staff development will fall within the broader responsibilities of a personnel officer. In small organizations staff development will be the responsibility of a special assistant to the director or the director. An organizational staff development plan should flow directly from the organizational goals, both short-term and long-term. For example, if new automated systems are being implemented, training and development should focus on developing the capabilities of staff to work with these new systems. If poor communication is identified as an organizational weakness, training should be directed at improving organization communications. If eligibility determinations are inaccurate training and development should focus on improving their accuracy.

The allocation of resources for staff development should be directly related to organizational needs. These needs include immediate and long-range goals. Too often in human service organizations, even when staff development is explicitly addressed, it focuses on the needs of the moment rather than the future. In part this reflects the uncertainty of the environment in which human service organizations find it difficult to predict and plan for the future. But care should be taken to include future projections, even if tentative, in a staff development plan.

The plan itself should derive both from overall organizational goals and the individually expressed needs of individuals in the organization. Since the staff development office is clearly a support function, its leadership should make an extra effort to ensure that its goals and approaches are always serving their constituency, the line managers. All training activities should be evaluated on an ongoing basis.

In producing an annual staff development plan, which focuses on inservice and external training activities, the staff development unit should survey the entire organization. Particular attention should be given to top management. A mechanism should be developed for the unit to meet on a regular basis with top line managers to ensure that training is serving the needs of the major organizational units.

In large organizations the decentralization of the staff development function may be advisable. Rather than maintaining one centralized staff, individual units may have staff development officers responsible for working with the line managers. Such an approach ensures that training will be directly related to organizational function. Training and development can also serve a centralizing function in large decentralized organizations. Common programs in which individuals from different subunits are brought together for common instruction is an ideal way to build group cohesion.

Planning for staff development should be a regular part of organizational activity, linked closely to organizational planning. It should be incorporated into the periodic planning of organizational goals and individual objectives. When the individual manager meets with subordinates, usually on a quarterly basis, to assess individual progress toward annual objectives, staff development should be a part of this process. From the beginning, the staff member should be made aware of the need to incorporate staff development plans into the annual objectives that are established. Staff development objectives should flow from the needs of the annual objectives. They should represent additional developmental needs which are related directly to the attainment of annual objectives. In fact, these annual and quarterly conferences represent an important part of the staff development process, as the manager attempts to encourage the subordinate to accept new responsibilities and develop individual abilities to operate more effectively on the job.

Since this process of objective-setting should stretch the capabilities of the employee, it should incorporate the need for new, more highly developed skills. The manager should accept personal responsibility for coaching the employee and assisting the employee in obtaining in-service or external training. A critical element in the motivation of many employees is encouraging him or her to develop into positions with greater responsibility. The individual is much more likely to accept new responsibilities if a mechanism exists for obtaining support in this endeavor. This is an important role that staff development, properly planned, can play.

Decisions about the training mode, whether to provide training internally or externally and in what format and length, should be guided by the staff development specialist. But the active participation of the line managers and those being trained should be sought. In-house training is often preferable both for ensuring that training will be job-related and for minimizing costs. But the purposes and costs of training should be constantly kept in mind and external training should be used when the purposes or costs justify such decisions. One of the dangers in allowing the staff development unit to decide these questions is that there may be organizational incentives to train in-house even where external training will be cheaper and more effective. To minimize this problem, responsibility should be divided for the administration of internal programs and deciding whether to use internal or external trainers.

Specific strategies should be developed to reach a limited number of organizational goals. These strategies should indicate the staff development approaches and resources needed to implement the approaches. Particular attention should be given to the loss of on-the-job time of staff who may be involved in training efforts. Too often this lost resource is not considered in the costs of training and may in fact outweigh other costs. For example, it may cost only $200 to have a consultant train 100 individuals for a half day each. The costs in staff time may well be 50 times that amount.

It is important that the particular development mode chosen, whether one-on-one coaching, job reassignment, on-the-job training, external courses, or some other alternative be appropriate to the goals. The choice of the proper mix of these options in part depends upon an understanding of the staff development function. Professional expertise can be useful in making such decisions, although management and subject matter experts should be closely involved. The best mode for introductory computer instruction depends in part upon the knowledge needed, the level of the staff, the expected level of performance, and the number of individuals who need the training. In some cases the option to select is obvious. In others, it is more difficult.

If an individual needs to learn a particular programming language which nobody else needs, a commercially offered course is the best option. If 20 new supervisors are beginning their jobs and no one in the organization can conduct supervisory training, an outside contract might be developed. If 20 new supervisors need to be trained every six months, it would probably be worthwhile to have someone from the organization assume the training function, even if only on an ad hoc basis.

The potential of coaching, job reassignment and on-site training as staff development strategies are enormous and often considerably less expensive than classroom training which takes individuals off the job. Yet few organizations take the time and effort to emphasize the importance of these modes or develop their managers' abilities to pursue these types of development effort.

Offsite training is sometimes approved too readily, without an adequate understanding of the payback to the organization. On the other hand, such training can be used effectively to build morale, reward individual performance and encourage even better performance. The ability of individuals to leave their job situations and be exposed to a new situation, even at a considerable distance from the organization, can result in considerable benefit to the organization.

One of the critical issues in staff development is the extent to which the organization should encourage individual development. Many organizations require that training be job-related and discourage support for individual development. While the importance of relating staff development to organizational needs has been stressed above, it is also important to take a broad perspective in viewing individual development. Human service organizations, with their emphasis on improving people, should be more sensitive than other organizations to the legitimate aspirations of employees for personal development. Indeed, any organization has a vested interest in encouraging its staff to improve themselves and develop their abilities broadly. This includes the ability to prepare individuals for more demanding jobs within the organization, but should also include general abilities which might, indeed, result in the loss of the individual to the organization. The problem is that given limited organizational resources, decisions must be made on how best to spend available resources.

One of the most controversial questions is the extent to which human service organizations should support employees in undertaking undergraduate and graduate degree programs. Particularly for organizations that are interested in developing staff to assume more responsible positions within the organization, the encouragement of degree programs may be justifiable. Some organizations provide partial subsidies for such programs. And if the courses can be directly related to current or future positions, total reimbursement may be available. A similar policy may be adopted with respect to released time. Where the program is directly related to a current or future job, at least some released time may be given as an incentive toward personal improvement. An organization which has a developing, improving staff is one which itself has the opportunity for development and dynamism. It may even be said that the human service organization has a particular need for investment in its own staff — both as a way of emphasizing its investment in human improvement and as a way of staying ahead in a rapidly changing world. The organization whose members are enthusiastic, aggressive, and ready for change is much more likely to be successful in the long run in the ever changing world of human services.

One of the best ways of protecting against poor investment in staff development is evaluating the impact of staff development in a systematic way. Do individuals who engage in staff development benefit from their involvement? Do their superiors think they do? Do their subordinates? Is it possible to attribute changes in organizational performance to training in spite of the difficulty of separating training effects from other organizational factors? The area of training evaluation is a complex one in which the services of an expert can be invaluable. It is part of the larger field of program evaluation which is considered in Chapter 12.

4. Organizational Development

Staff development planning attempts to focus individual efforts on organizational goals. By strengthening the skills of individuals, their contributions to the organization are made more valuable. Sometimes staff development focuses more on the interrelationships among individuals than on their individual skills. These activities may be referred to as organizational development. Managers have always recognized the need to take a broad view of organizational activity and make organizational changes to improve performance. Increasingly today, a manager's responsibilities for organizational development are becoming more explicit.

A poignant example of organizational level change strategies is the use of reorganization. Ever since organizations have been in existence, managers have initiated changes in the structure of organizations to improve performance. Individuals are given different responsibilities or the configuration of responsibilities and roles are themselves changed. Recently, however, the practice of planned change within organizations has taken on a growing sophistication. Often the term "organization development" is used to describe the set of techniques that are associated with planned change in organizations.

Organization development has developed out of an understanding of organizational behavior which includes the complexity of organizational life and the importance of communications to effective organizational operation. It emphasizes the interactions between the organization and the environment and the need to consider this environment in effectuating change in organizations. It uses the tools that are available and recognizes the need to pursue planned, consistent strategies in effecting change.

The organizational development approach emphasizes action training and research as an approach to planned change. It is particularly indebted to Kurt Lewin and Carl Rogers for their early research and theory. Lewin emphasized the dynamic setting of organizations proposing the force-field as a construct for conceptualizing the competing forces acting on individuals and organizations. The change process, according to Lewin, reinforces those factors favoring change while neutralizing those factors opposing change. Carl Rogers is associated with the human relations school of organizational behavior which emphasizes the drive of human beings for self-enhancement. Organizational change will result through participative leadership as individuals are brought to understand the ways in which they can move toward greater self-enhancement.

The breadth of approaches to organizational development is wide. Invariably there is a heavy emphasis on rational planning, gathering data about actual organizational operation and sharing information throughout the organization. Often an outside intervenor or consultant is involved in the process. The importance of following an explicit procedure cannot be overemphasized, but specific steps may vary according to the model followed and the circumstances of the particular intervention. One model is described below.

Suggested Steps in Action Training and Research*

1. *Orientation:* During this phase the intervenor discusses the general approach and values with the organization leadership. The emphasis on individual enhancement and information-sharing should be emphasized and the trust between the intervenor and the client must be developed.

2. *Contract Setting:* This formalizes the relationship between the intervenor and the client by establishing resources available, ground rules for the use of the data, and an expression of willingness on the part of the client to utilize the findings to the extent possible.

3. *Reconnaissance:* Through the use of such data collection techniques as group meetings, observation, interviews and questionnaires, the intervenor, sometimes with the assistance of the client, will gather information about the perceived problems, solutions and opportunities that exist within the organization.

4. *Problem and Opportunity Identification:* The data collected during reconnaissance are classified and reduced to a manageable number for inclusion in a questionnaire, usually distributed throughout the organization.

5. *Aspirations:* Based upon the problems and opportunities that have been identified, a range of possible options needs to be defined. This can be accomplished in a group session with the relevant individuals.

6. *Analysis:* A number of analytic techniques are available for deciding on the options for action, such as force field analysis introduced by Kurt Lewin.

7. *Experimentation:* Changes agreed to by the group are now initiated on a "trial" basis. They may be tried for a limited time on an organization-wide basis or within a subunit of the organization. Those implementing the change will have been involved in the various previous stages.

---

* Adapted from Neely Gardner. "Action Training and Research." *Public Administration Review*, 1974, vol. 34, pp. 106-115.

8. *Results Analysis:* At the conclusion of the trial period, the results are analyzed and a decision is made whether to implement changes on a long-term basis.
9. *Program Design:* Based upon the trial program, a new program is designed for implementation on an organization-wide basis. The program is then implemented and evaluated to ensure that it is having the desired effects.

Organization development methods are still being perfected, but they represent a major advance. They emphasize the complexity of undertaking organizational change and the need for facilitating communications as a method for improving organizational performance. While an outside intervenor can be extremely useful in many situations, the principles of organizational development should become part of the manager's everyday routine. Organization development emphasizes the importance of communications, the use of formal data collection techniques, and the need for participation in adapting organizational operations to the ever-changing environment.

Selected Bibliography

Bennis, Warren. *Changing Organizations.* New York: McGraw-Hill, 1966.

Brager, George and Holloway, Stephen. *Changing Human Service Organizations.* New York: The Free Press, 1978.

Byers, Kenneth, ed. *Employee Training and Development in the Public Service.* Chicago: Public Personnel Association, 1970.

Denora, Charles. *Establishing a Training Function.* Englewood Cliffs, New Jersey: Educational Technology Publications, 1971.

Freyer, Douglas, Feinberg, Mortimer, and Zalkind, Sheldon. *Developing People in Industry.* New York: Harper & Brothers, 1956.

Gardner, Neely. "Action Training and Research," *Public Administration Review,* 1974, Vol. 34, pp. 106-115.

Hersey, Paul and Blanchard, Kenneth. *Management of Organizational Behavior.* Englewood Cliffs, New Jersey: Prentice-Hall, 1977.

House, Robert. *Management Development: Design, Evaluation and Implementation.* Ann Arbor: The University of Michigan, Bureau of Industrial Relations, 1963.

Lewin, Kurt. *Field Theory in Social Science.* New York: Harper and Row, 1951.

Meyer, Carol H. *Staff Development in Public Welfare Agencies.* New York: Columbia University Press, 1966.

Nadler, David. *Feedback and Organization Development: Using Data-Based Methods.* Reading, Massachusetts: Addison-Wesley, 1977.

Chapter 8.

Representation and Resources

1. The Representational Role

The scope of managerial behavior includes providing direction, monitoring subordinate behavior, and representing the work unit in the larger system. Representation is critical to the success and survival of the work unit. It involves the manager in coordinating the work unit's activities with other units within the organization and with external organizations. The way in which this representational role is played is critical not only for articulating with other units, but for survival within the organization. The manager is the link between the work unit and the larger organization as well as the external environment.

Since human service organizations are concerned with caring for and improving individuals, they often need to articulate with other organizations that are affecting the same individuals. Rarely is all assistance of one sort centralized in one organization. In fact, some human service organizations primarily refer individuals to other organizations for services. The variety and number of human service organizations in urban areas can be staggering. In fact, considerable attention is now being given to developing systematic computerized referral networks to provide the best information to individuals seeking assistance.

The movement to achieve greater integration of human services is a byproduct of this proliferation of human service organizations. State and local governments have made efforts to achieve greater coordination among human service agencies by creating local and state super-agencies consolidating separate agencies. The Vermont State Human Services Agency is one prominent example. The New York City Human Resources Administration is another.

While efforts at providing integrated human service agencies are helpful, the achievement of effective service integration is the responsibility of line management in all human service agencies. It is easy to be caught up in the competitiveness of different individual organizations which provide overlapping services, but effective human service managers will seek to integrate services for the recipient so that they have the greatest possible impact. The range of activities that managers engage in to further these integrative processes falls within the representational role. They include participating in formal coordinating groups and meeting with other managers to insure that relationships among organizations are working smoothly.

The performance of this linking function has important implications for the ability of the organizational unit to survive and prosper. The perception of the unit's efficacy in large part is determined by its interactions with other units. Internal efficiency must be translated into external perceptions of efficacy. This involves, of course, not only the opinions of superiors within the organization, but those of other key individuals in the external environment, particularly those who control the flow of outside resources.

Human service organizations, both governmental and non-governmental, find they are dependent on a variety of government officials. They are also dependent upon others who influence government policy, legislators, public opinion leaders, their own constituencies, and employee organizations.

Understanding the ways in which these individuals and institutions interact to affect the fate of the unit is important, perhaps the most important knowledge that an individual human service manager needs. This knowledge enables the manager to develop the contacts and strategies which will help ensure organizational survival.

The influence of federal policy in any particular program cluster will differ, but the major actors will be analogous. The initiation of new federal legislation often begins in the White House, as it did during the period of the Great Society under President Lyndon Johnson. President Reagan has demonstrated the power of the presidency to curtail human service programs.

In developing legislation, the President will rely upon staff operating within the White House as well as staff within the agencies. Often major interest groups are invited into the process to attempt to resolve any possible conflicts beforehand. And of course members of both the House of Representatives and Senate are drawn into the process of developing legislation. Once legislation has been adopted in a specific area, the Congress will take the initiative itself. Within the Congress legislation falls within the jurisdiction of particular committees and subcommittees which are organized on a permanent basis. The heads of these committees and subcommittees are very influential and when they wish to lead in the design of legislation and in the management of the legislative process, they are not ordinarily challenged.

In areas that have been defined by legislation, the agencies and congressional committees tend to take the lead with the presidential staff falling into the background except in situations of especial interest to the President. Agencies are not only active in the legislative process but exercise continuing regulatory authority. Interest groups maintain active links with both the bureaucracy and the Congress. At the Federal level many of the individuals involved in the delivery of services are represented through interest groups. These include state and local governmental officials.

Once legislation has been enacted a subsidiary process takes place in which appropriations are made for specific fiscal years. This appropriation process in dominated in the Senate by the Finance Committee, the Budget Committee, and the Appropriations Committee and in the House by the Ways and Means Committee, the Budget Committee and the Appropriations Committee.

The institutions which impinge upon the manager can be classified as executive, judicial, legislative, and non-governmental. They operate at national, state and local levels.

Executive agencies include elected officials and their staffs such as presidents, governors, mayors and county executives. These individuals and their associated budget offices have a critical role in approving agency budgets. President Reagan's sweeping changes in the levels and types of support for the human services in the development of the fiscal 1982 budget are a continuing reminder of the power of the executive. Governors and mayors, too, have much to say about where public resources will be spent. From the perspective of the manager of a service delivery organization functioning at the local level, the elected executives and their staffs may seem far away, although their influence may be directly felt.

Most service delivery organizations will relate to local agencies in the first instance, but they may also find fairly frequent interactions with state and Federal agencies. Agencies which are dependent upon direct grants from Federal or state agencies, of course, will interact more frequently with those levels. At the Federal level, the Departments of Health and Human Services, Education, and Labor are the major sources of funds for human service programs. At the state level, agency structures vary considerably so that it is difficult to generalize. All states have a major agency responsibility for welfare and a varying combination of other services. State education agencies are also common. Employment and training funds are for the most part administered by locally based prime sponsors, though in small states the prime sponsors may be the states themselves and the new *Jobs Partnership Act of 1982* will result in greater overall state authority. In other respects, the variety of local agencies is great too. Boards of Education are almost universally in charge of elementary and secondary education. Counties often are responsible for welfare programs. Health services are usually institutionally based.

While the greatest number of interactions are with the executive branch, the legislative branch of government can also have profound effects upon the human services, particularly in making budgetary choices. In the United States Congress, the Senate Human Resources Committee and the House Education and Labor Committee handle a large proportion of legislation in the human services. However, a number of other committees are involved in specific programs, such as the Agriculture Committees in the Food Stamp program. The committee systems in the state legislatures vary considerably and often the legislative leadership is very strong. At the local level the variety is even greater. Counties tend to have a larger role in welfare, so that county legislative units, such as the Board of Supervisors, tend to be involved. In large cities the city council may also play a role.

Judicial intervention in the human services tends to result from the interpretation of Federal and state constitutional guarantees as requiring a certain distribution of services. The courts have intervened often in educational matters, with the two most poignant issues being desegregation of schools and state intervention in funding as a means of reducing inequality in the statewide distribution of resources. Both Federal and state courts have been involved in hearing these suits.

Non-governmental actors in the human service system include interest groups, foundations, corporations and community groups. Interest groups work to influence the operation of the political system, usually through affecting the decisions of public officials. Specialized interest groups such as unions and recipient groups are particularly important in the human services. The American Federation of Teachers has been very effective in increasing expenditures for public education. The American Association of Retired Persons, in addition to performing a range of social welfare functions, has also been a powerful force on behalf of the elderly.

Foundations are another source of direction for the human services. They take an active role in bringing about change in the nature of human services and supporting particular projects of assistance. The Ford Foundation is one of the most prominent which has had a particular interest in education. Their efforts on behalf of school decentralization during the 1960s were both well-known and controversial.

Corporations perform a range of philanthropic activities to help people and support institutions. They are important contributors toward the United Way and other charitable community efforts. Also, through such organizations as the Chambers of Commerce, they take positions on national, state and local legislation, often urging decreased funding for human service programs.

Community groups have always been with us, but their number and variety increased dramatically during the 1960s and 1970s as they assumed a variety of service and advocacy roles. They often are an outlet for the activities of wealthier members of society who seek to assist the less fortunate. Since the 1960s, however, community-based groups, such as neighborhood organizations within the larger cities, have seen considerable growth in membership among middle class and working people.

In dealing with this variety of external groups and intraorganizational forces, the manager as representative must blend strong communications and bargaining skills. To the extent that representation is aimed at projecting a certain image of accomplishment, it involves oral and written communication skills, discussed in greater detail in Chapter 6 above. To the extent that representation seeks to obtain resources, it involves bargaining. The techniques of bargaining are important to any manager, but to human service managers especially

2. Bargaining Techniques

Representational tasks involve lateral contacts outside the work group, rather than contacts with subordinates. Where subordinate relationships are guided by well-defined authority relationships, lateral interactions are more ambiguous. Organizational loyalty and command authority are minimized. The basis for lateral relationships is exchange. The individual on the other side must believe that the interactions are providing some tangible benefits either immediately or in the future.

Of course, even lateral relationships may be characterized by common goals, collegiality and the exchange of value. The director of one nursing home may ask the director of another to borrow forms that they both use. Or the director of one drug care facility may refer an individual to another center where treatment is better suited to his needs. Where the director seeks to have regulations changed or interpreted differently, or tries to have the reimbursement rates changed, or seeks to protect a position in a public budget, the exchange relationship dominates.

In these cases, the exchange is for value. The manager is seeking to gain some favor or some special consideration from another individual who may ask for something of value in return. The reason that elected political leaders are often effective as ombudsmen, assisting individuals to get better treatment from administrative agencies, is that the agencies know they will need those elected leaders at budget time. The representational role often involves exchange with political leaders.

When the representational role involves the request for resources, particularly within the same specific context as passing legislation or adopting a budget, the importance of power considerations is great. Managers of human service organizations, since they depend for their units' survival on the public budgeting process, have a propensity for becoming involved in bargaining situations while engaged in the representational role. They also tend to spend a very large proportion of their time in this role in order to secure their future funding.

The effective exercise of power involves considerable knowledge of the processes as well as the individuals and circumstances of a particular situation. In order to exercise power, an individual must both have power and know how to use it. Thus, to the extent that managers engage in those aspects of the representational role requiring power, they must spend time developing and conserving it. Of course, the effective use of power is important, too. Since human service managers, especially those in higher positions in the public sector, spend a considerable portion of their time seeking resources, political power and its effective use often becomes of overwhelming importance. That is why it sometimes seems as if politics and its exercise far outweigh the other managerial qualities necessary in effectively guiding the internal aspects of work group activity.

In dealing with political leaders as well as carrying on other lateral relationships in the representational role, the ability to bargain effectively is critical. In order to be effective at bargaining, a manager must know what power is, how to develop power, how to conserve power, and how to use power. The manager must also develop a reservoir of power. While the ability to bargain effectively is a skill developed over time and is enhanced by ongoing relationships with individuals, some rules for effective bargaining can be suggested.

Rules for Effective Bargaining

1. *Bargain From Strength.* The best position to bargain from is one where you have already developed the power to get what you want. Power is influence over people; it is developed over time. The source of power is the ability to command loyalty from people. If political leaders are backing you, or if their constituents are backing you, or if the individuals you are bargaining with owe you favors, you have the best chance of getting what you want. Threats are always a last resort.
2. *Present Your Desires In A Positive Light.* If possible, try to show the immediate benefits of your position for the individual whom you are trying to convince by articulating good reasons for your position.

3. *Avoid Forcing Choices On Your Opponent.* To the extent possible, the best bargain is one that never has to be struck. If your position can be presented in a non-confrontational way, do it. You might be able to win without expending any real resources.

4. *Set A Value.* When an indirect approach does not work, set a value on what you are trying to achieve. What is it worth to you to have your adversary agree to your position?

5. *Be Willing To Compromise.* If your opponent is unable or unwilling to go along with all of your request, a compromise may be reached. Sometimes splitting the difference is necessary through give and take where an intermediate position can be agreed to. Sometimes a concession on an unrelated matter will get you what you want.

6. *Accept Defeat.* Sometimes your deal will not be accepted, but don't let that bother you. Credibility has been established so that the next time you will be able to get what you want.

The flexibility exercised by a good bargainer is in stark contrast to the rigidity of ideological purists, or those who think they don't have to bargain. The heart of effective bargaining is really the ability to compromise. An imaginative and flexible approach to arriving at compromises is an unusually helpful asset for the human service manager.

3. Influencing Governmental Decisionmakers

Almost every human service manager will spend some portion of time attempting to influence government decisionmakers. These decisionmakers determine to a large extent the resources devoted to particular functions and programs of government which translate into support for individual service delivery organizations. Of special importance is the annual budget process which determines the future existence of human service organizations. To defend a unit, a manager must know how to influence government decisions, when to influence decisions, and have power to attain the ends sought.

Government decisions are made by individuals or groups of individuals, based on the information available to them and in response to pressures brought to bear on them. The first rule of influencing government decisions is to know the decisionmakers and cultivate ongoing relationships with them. In this way, when a decision is made, the manager will be in a position to enter into a dialogue with the decisionmaker. Actually this rule applies equally well to both lateral relationships and superior relationships. The second rule is to provide information to decisionmakers on an ongoing basis about your organization which will reflect favorably. Of course, the manager must provide accurate information to the decisionmaker to develop trust. Finally, exchange relationships must be developed so that decisionmakers may be influenced when the need arises.

In fact, human service organizations, particularly larger ones, or in some cases specially designated lobbying associations, spend a good deal of time observing governmental processes to determine when to intervene. Of particular interest to human service organizations are the processes by which legislation is passed and funds are appropriated. The memorandum below is adapted from the files of a large city multi-service agency and illustrates the careful monitoring of pending Federal legislation. The outcome of legislation will often determine the level of resources available to human service organizations.

This attached description of the legislative history of one bill which originated in the House of Representatives HR 3434 provided an agency with knowledge about when intervention will be most effective. In this particular instance, the agency head chose to testify in Washington on behalf of several sections of the proposed legislation, at the appropriate time. An excerpt of the presentation follows the legislative memorandum.

MEMORANDUM
TO: HEAD
    OFFICE OF SERVICES PLANNING

FROM: STAFF ASSOCIATE
    OFFICE OF SERVICES PLANNING

SUBJECT: STATUS OF H.R. 3434

5/13/79   I contacted the Public Assistance Sub-committee of the House Ways and Means Committee regarding H.R. 3434. When it was reported out of committee on May 10, it was suggested that a rule be added to prohibit amendments from the floor when the bill comes up for debate. The rule to prohibit amendments now goes before the Rules Committee which has the final decision to prohibit amendments from the floor. There has been no decision from the Rules Committee as of 5/18/79.
6/13/79   The bill is before the House Appropriations Committee which has 15 days (from 6/4/79) to review and discuss it. On 6/25/79 the bill will be sent to the Rules Committee, where rules on the bill will be set. Voting by the full House should take place on or about 6/25/79.
6/19/79   H.R. 3434 was assigned to the House Appropriations Committee to review Section 401-B, public assistance payments to territorial jurisdictions; the Committee plans to review H.R. 3434 on June 20, 1979, 10:00 AM.

6/26/79   H.R. 3434 was favorably reported in the House Appropriations Committee on June 25, 1979. On June 26, H.R. 3434 was reported out of Appropriations and sent back to the Rules Committee for a ruling as to whether or not amendments to the Bill can be made when it comes up for vote by the full House. Congress will be in recess from 6/30 through 7/8/79; no action is expected until after this recess.

7/17/79   Today the Rules Committee reviewed H.R. 3434; the result was a *modified closed rule.* When the Bill comes before the full House: 1. Only the Ways and Means Committee members can make amendments to the Bill; 2. Two hours will be allotted for debate. The Bill should come up for debate very soon; however, Congress will recess on August 3, 1979. H.R. 3434 may come up for debate either before or after the recess.

7/31/79   House Sub-committee on Public Assistance advised that H.R. 3434 will come up for debate by the full House on *August 1, 1979.*

8/2/79   H.R. 3434 was passed by the full House today; the vote was 401-2. One amendment was added, Title IV-B's ceiling will not be an entitlement as proposed. Funds for Title IV-B will be appropriated at the end of each Federal Fiscal Year.

9/25/79   I contacted the Senate Finance Committee who advised that H.R. 3434, S.1184 and S.966 will be reviewed in executive session by the full Committee on Thursday, 10/27/79. Recommendations on the Bills will be made for full Senate vote.

9/28/79   The Senate Finance Committee, in executive session, ordered H.R. 3434 out, on 9/27/79, with the following amendments: (1) *Ceiling* for FY 80 3$2.7 billion, FY 81—$2.9, FY 82—$3.0, FY 83—$3.1, FY 84—$3.2, FY 85 3$3.3. At this point it is not clear if the $200 million for Day Care Services will be included in the ceiling. We will receive clarification on this by 10/1/79. (2) *Title XX Training Funds*— for FY 1980, a 4% cap will be imposed. States can claim 4% of actual expenditures for FY 1979 or FY 1980, whichever amount is greater. 3.*Title IV-B, Child Welfare*—Provisions outlined in the amended S.966 (Cranston/Moynihan) have been incorporated into H.R. 3434. We will receive clarification on this section by 10/1/79.

Based on the work of the legislative office, the Administrator decided to offer public testimony before the Senate Finance Committee. Testimony before legislative hearings requires effective oral presentation skills. The ability to make effective oral presentations is of immense importance to higher level government officials for just this reason. Ordinarily the oral presentation is based upon a written document. In making such a presentation, brevity and persuasiveness are critical. Examine the excerpted speech below to assess how well it accomplished the communication task it sets forth.

Testimony Before the U.S. Senate, Committee on Finance, Subcommittee on Public Assistance

Mr. Chairman, Members of the Subcommittee:

I am the Administrator of the City Human Services Agency. I welcome the opportunity to comment on the three bills the Subcommittee is considering tonight, S. 1184, S. 966, as amended, and S. 1661. Taken together, they are vitally important to the lives of many citizens of my city as well as children and families throughout the United States. I would like to say, first, that we enthusiastically support the goals of each of these bills: Title XX remains unique among federal legislative accomplishments in its comprehensiveness and the flexibility it allows localities in funding social services; the proposed Child Welfare bill, S. 966, as amended, reflects our long time emphasis on prevention and reunification as well as foster care services; and S. 1661 represents, in my opinion, an extremely important Federal initiative in the area of adoption assistance.

As you know, my city has always been generous in its commitment to providing for the needs of the economically disadvantaged. The ceiling on social services expenditures, which has created fiscal stress in many localities, has thus been especially damaging to us ever since it was first imposed in 1972. During years when inflation has skyrocketed and my city's needy population has grown, we have actually received steadily less Federal assistance for essential social services.

In the next fiscal year, my city will spend millions of dollars to provide such services as protection, adoption, and foster care for children, home care for disabled adults, family planning, shelter for battered women, senior citizens programs, and day care, all of them eligible for funding under Title XX. Yet we will receive from the federal government less than one-fifth of our total expenditures. In the category of services to children, the Federal Title XX share is less than 5 percent.

One strategy we have used to cover such drastic shortfalls in the past has been to transfer many programs, such as foster care and home care, to other funding streams. This is clearly not an adequate solution over the long term, however, and is becoming more troublesome with each passing year. Nearly all of those alternative sources require a susbstantially greater local share than Title XX. This fact, combined with inflation, the city's fiscal situation, and expanding caseloads, puts us in the painful position of falling further and further behind: Not only can we not meet the growing needs of our poor and dependent residents, but we are facing cuts in the current levels of essential services. Meanwhile, my city's taxpayers are forced to assume more than their fair share of the country's social services costs.

My city is further harmed by the current Title XX allocation formula, which distributes funds based on absolute population figures. In fact, while our overall population has declined by 7.8 percent since 1970, the numbers of those living below the poverty level actually has risen by more than 9 percent. Furthermore, the nationwide proportion of persons below the poverty level in 1978 was 11.5 percent, while in my city that figure was 21 percent.

I am appealing today for an increase in the Title XX ceiling over the fiscal year 1979 level that will both ensure that we can continue to provide some minimum standard of services to the poor people of my City and serve as a clear signal that the Federal government is not, in this economically troubled period, turning its back on those most in need. I also wish to express my support for a revised Title XX allocation formula that is more responsive to the true demographics of poverty in this country.

Beyond that, I would like to address two other specific provisions of the bill. First, my city strongly opposes the imposition of a cap on 1980 Title XX training funds based on our 1978 expenditures. Such a formula would have the effect of cutting in half our current budget for Title XX training, a measure that would be particularly devastating for our day care programs. Besides the impact on their existing training, the ceiling would have other implications as well: HEW is proposing new training requirements that would place expanded responsibilities on the individual day care center. Unfortunately, no new HEW training funds will be available for this effort. Should the ceiling be implemented, the day care centers will be unable to comply with existing requirements, let alone new ones. For these reasons, I would urge that the Subcommittee recommend instead either a cap based on 5 percent of the State's fiscal year 1978 Title XX appropriation or a hold-harmless on the 1979 Title XX training expenditures.

And second, we support enthusiastically S. 1184's provisions for planning and allocations over more than one year at a time. Those of us who have had direct experience with the uncertainties and anxieties of year-to-year funding can affirm that these provisions would allow for better long-range planning and, ultimately, better programs.

Effective communication and conscientious lobbying are only the beginning of effective influence over governmental decisionmaking. In the final analysis, with myriad competing influences converging upon the decisionmaker, the ability to bargain with the decisionmaker is critical. In fact, the power relations among political and administrative personnel are often dominant in decisionmaking. That is why the accretion of political power in the broadest sense is sought by individuals who head human service organizations. A hospital which serves the community well will probably be supported by the community. By providing services and being responsible to individual requests, particularly those of influential individuals, the human service organization gathers power.

But power must be jealously guarded and not foolishly expended. The human service manager must understand how to bargain: when to press a point, when to delay, when to compromise, and when to stand firm. Some human service managers spend most of their time attempting to influence governmental decisionmakers. In large public agencies, of course, top managers tend to spend much of their time in this way. This problem, incidentally, is not unique to the human services, but is true of large bureaucracies generally. The difference in human service organizations is that, while at the top of business organizations consumer demands and market strategy take priority, the human service manager ordinarily focuses on political strategy to gain support among elected executives and legislators who in the final analysis determine agency budgets.

4. Public and Community Relations

Although the pervasive influence of government is felt by many organizations in society, the level of involvement with government is especially high for human service managers. The representation function demands considerable time from many human service managers. This means that they have less time to devote to other competing functions. It is one reason for the tendency in human service organizations for the director or top-level manager to have a deputy who will be responsible for internal operations. The top manager may spend so much time away from the organization that it is impossible to function without a full-time "inside" manager.

While private industrial and commercial organizations depend upon the general public for their support, they generate support through public relations and marketing units. Only in unusual circumstances do top corporate officials deal with public groups. Human service managers invariably become involved in budgetary processes and public controversies about the level of support for their programs. In fact, at the higher levels of operation, the human service manager expends most effort convincing the public and the political leaders of the usefulness of the organization's activities. The human service manager must have a carefully thought out public and community relations campaign. Such a campaign, of course, must be designed from the perspective of the organization in question.

Human service organizations today face extraordinary challenges nationally and locally to justify their expenditures. It is fashionable to criticize the inefficiencies of public programs and human service programs in particular. In economically difficult times, the ordinary citizen is not eager to spend tax dollars to support others, even if they are the needy.

Reports of misuse of government programs in the human services have contributed to the reluctance of the average citizen. Certain egregious examples are often cited, for example, the woman on welfare who is separately registered at several different locations, has a business on the side and drives a new Cadillac to work. Similarly, the press carries stories of doctors who receive excessive reimbursement under government financed health programs. A more difficult problem to handle is the fact that human service programs frequently operate in difficult areas. Their success may be uncertain at best and even where they succeed, the documentation of their success may be difficult. Citizens tend to merge all these criticisms of human service programs and remain skeptical of their efficacy.

Because of this vulnerable position, human service managers need to promote their successes and respond to criticisms. The public must have a realistic, balanced view of their operations. Human service programs, probably more than most, need good press to survive and prosper. General public and community relations require attention to the media and contact with the community. The manager of a human service organization should define the organization's constituency and get to know the important leaders within that constituency. Efforts should be made to maintain contact with other managers of similar organizations and to form coalitions that will gain broad acceptance of their common cause.

The need for attention to public and community relations extends beyond the manager to other members of the organization. One of the great assets of human service organizations is their frequent contact with the public because of the type of services they provide. By sensitizing the individuals who have daily contact with people about the need for projecting a helpful image, public relations can be greatly facilitated.

Clientele groups deserve special attention. By serving their clientele groups well, the organization can build a supportive active constituency. Clientele groups are natural allies in attaining greater visibility for programs and in gathering public support. By building ties with them, the human service manager can do much to further the agency's cause. Satisfied clientele groups, if well organized, can provide important political support. The difficulty that many human service organizations experience results from the relative political impotence of their constituency.

In an important book examining social programs, *State of Welfare*, Gilbert Steiner emphasized the relative success of programs geared to veterans as opposed to those focusing on women who have been abandoned by their husbands and are forced to raise children by themselves. Steiner observes that the power of the veterans groups in providing organized political power is an important ingredient of the success of their human service oriented programs. During the late 1960s, in fact, an organization of welfare recipients, the National Welfare Rights Organization, gained prominence in drawing attention to the needs of welfare mothers.

Schools are another human service organization that has worked closely with organized clientele groups. Parent associations, organized on a school, region, state, and national basis, have supported budgetary allocations for public education strongly and consistently. Over the years this support has aided in the maintenance and expansion of government expenditures for education. Another feature of the education lobby has been the prominence of professional organizations, particularly the organized teachers. Teachers' unions and professional associations have taken an active political role in supporting expenditures for education. They are perhaps the most sophisticated and well organized human service professionals in the political arena. They often become involved in political campaigns to further their interests.

The support of clientele and professional groups can be of immeasurable assistance in influencing political leaders. This support can be critical in the budget process and in securing resources more generally. New grant programs can be established with the support of political leaders. Special facilities may be provided. The opportunities and occasions for using the support of political leaders on behalf of human service programs are almost limitless. Many human service programs owe their support and prosperity to political leaders who have adopted these programs and nurtured them. Rosalyn Carter's support of mental health programs was well-known. Lyndon Johnson's support of the myriad Great Society programs, and education programs in particular, was critical in gaining their acceptance. President Roosevelt's support of Social Security is still remembered by many grateful older Americans.

5. Obtaining Resources

Effective representation in human service organizations, as should be evident from the discussion above, is a prerequisite for adequate levels of resource acquisition. In fact, for those human service managers who are responsible for resource acquisition, representation will be a major, if not overriding, concern. Since most private sector organizations sell their products and services in the marketplace, resource acquisition is part of the sales and marketing aspect of organizational life. A good part of the resources of most private sector organizations are devoted to these needs. Each type of human service organization, public, not-for-profit, or proprietary, organizes itself for resource acquisition differently.

An abiding characteristic of human service organizations is the extent to which they use alternatives to marketing and sales for obtaining financial support. The reasons for this are complex. They are related to the fact that the most needy often have the least resources and to the belief that services such as education, health care and welfare should be provided on the basis of need, not ability to pay.

The mix of support for human services in the United States is quite distinctive. This is true even when compared to England and France, two countries similar to the United States in their level of industrialization. The result is a variety of funding mixes that support individual organizations, which may be public, not-for-profit or proprietary in character.

Public organizations include regular city, state and Federal agencies and special government agencies such as school districts or state hospitals. Their funding is part of the regular government budget process. Not-for-profit organizations, including most hospitals, nursing homes, parochial schools, and many community organizations, are organized to perform public services, often by religious or fraternal organizations. They ordinarily receive support from a variety of sources, including government agencies, foundations, and the fees of those who use the services. Proprietary organizations are similar to other profit-making institutions. They provide services such as health care and schooling through direct user payments. Since they often serve the needy, they become dependent upon government subsidy in the form of third-party payments or direct grants.

In taking a broad perspective on resource acquisition for human service organizations, several different kinds of processes can be identified: 1) Regular Budget Support; 2) Special Grants; 3) Individual Contributions; and 4) User Fees. The most reliable source is regular budget support which emanates from within the organizational hierarchy. Human service managers who head units within larger organizations are most familiar with this source of support. This is the funding source most familiar to most managers who, in fact, may be oblivious to the actual source of funds for the larger organization. A request must generally be made on an annual basis for funds to support operations for the coming fiscal year.

Managers who are directly responsible for securing the total organization's resources are more likely to be familiar with other sources. Many human service organizations depend on recurrent sources of revenue which are committed by some outside organization on an annual basis. The two most prominent sources of such funds are the government and United Way. Many not-for-profit organizations depend upon such regular contributions to support a major portion of their budget. They often also have other means of support. Many human service organizations are being helped to move in new directions by obtaining special grants from the government, foundations or other sources. Ordinarily special grants are for carefully delineated efforts of an innovative sort which have a limited life. Private contributions are another important source for many human service organizations, especially those which restrict their support to individuals in great need. Sometimes individual benefactors establish charities. In other cases extensive canvassing or direct mail campaigns are used to raise monies. User fees, which most private organizations depend upon entirely, are used to varying degrees in human service organizations. Hospitals, schools and nursing homes all charge fees and some of these institutions are organized on a profit making basis. The next chapter will discuss in detail each of these techniques for generating resources.

Selected Bibliography

Anderson, James. *Public Policy-Making*. New York: Praeger, 1975.

Bachrach, Peter and Baratz, Morton S. *Power and Poverty*. New York: Oxford University Press, 1970.

Gates, Bruce L. *Social Program Administration, The Implementation of Social Policy*. Englewood Cliffs, New Jersey: Prentice-Hall, 1980.

Haveman, Robert H. *A Decade of Federal Antipoverty Programs*. New York: Academic Press, Inc., 1977.

Lindblom, Charles and Braybrooke, David. *A Strategy of Decisions*. New York: Free Press, 1963.

Lowi, Theodore and Stone, Alan. *Nationalized Government: Public Policies in America*. Beverly Hills: Sage Publications, 1978.

Rosengren, William R. and Lefton, Mark. *Organizations and Clients*. Columbus, Ohio: Charles Merrill, 1970.

Sayles, Leonard. *Managerial Behavior*. New York: McGraw-Hill, 1964.

Steiner, Gilbert. *State of Welfare*. Washington, D.C: The Brookings Institution, 1971.

Sundquist, James. *Making Federalism Work*. Washington, D.C.: The Brookings Institution, 1969.

Williams, Walter. *Government by Agency*. New York: Academic Press, 1980.

Chapter 9.

Resource Acquisition

1. Planning for Resource Acquisition

The manager of a human service organization must understand the mix of resources that are the basis of the organization's operations. This mix will be reflected in planning both for the acquistion and use of resources. The focus of these planning efforts is the budget process. The acquisition of resources is detailed in the revenue budget and the use of resources is detailed in the expenditure budget. The budget process aims at balancing revenues against anticipated expenditures. Organizations which do not balance their budgets in the long run become bankrupt and defunct. One notable exception is the Federal government. Because of its ability to borrow monies and its unique fiscal role, the Federal government is not governed by the same rules as other organizations. Continuing deficit budgets, however, do create considerable consternation among political leaders. Some observers predict that unless a balanced Federal budget is achieved, the nation itself will become bankrupt.

In profit-making institutions, revenue is generated mostly through sales of products and services in the open market. In not-for-profit and government agencies, the bulk of human service agencies, most revenues come from government sources, although private grants, and fees for services generate additional revenue. The variety of government sources of revenue for a single agency can be great, as is indicated below.

As can be seen the organization receives support from three levels of government, the Federal, state and county; the United Way; special contracts; and user fees from the cafeteria. Reliance on government, foundation and third-party reimbursement has greatly complicated the day-to-day management of human service organizations. When an organization has raised its funds through direct charitable solicitation, efforts focus on the preparation of an annual report to describe its activities to its supporters. The paperwork generated by funding agencies on the other hand can

Revenue Sources of A Residential Care Facility for Mentally Retarded Persons

Sources	%Total
State Office of Developmental Disabilities	39
State Office of Vocational Rehabilitation	21
State Education Department	12
County Department of Mental Health	3
Medicaid and Other Fees	9
United Way	4
Contracts and Cafeteria	10
United States Department of Health and Human Services	2

be voluminous. In addition, the need to comply with myriad procedures and regulations requires vast commitments of resources and particular attention by management. Lateral relations with funding agencies, elected officials and the public generally take a large portion of the time of top executives. Constant requests are made for justification of spending and operating procedures and compliance with specific procedures. Many human service organizations in specific areas like child care, long term care for the elderly and hospitals find the need to create their own associations to relieve executives of some of the need for dealing with funding agencies. These organizations also allow for a coordinated effort to influence policies which are adopted to regulate them.

As government has become more deeply involved in human services, there has been a tendency toward greater regulation. The relationships among human service agencies and the mechanisms for establishing accountability and ensuring efficiency are currently developing. Their uncertainty makes the representational role even more central than it might otherwise be.

More and more, organizations that formerly concerned themselves with providing services and thought little about the revenue aspects of their operations are confronted with the need to plan for revenue acquisition. The development of such a plan will ordinarily be based upon the previous year's experience in obtaining direct budgeted funds, special grants, recurrent grants, user fees and private contributions. For government agencies the focus is ordinarily on budgeted funds with some attention to grants which may derive from other levels. From the point of view of most managers below the executive, the task of resource acquisition focuses on the internal organizational processes for requesting and obtaining funds.

When human service organizations are a part of the government, they submit their annual requests for funds in conjunction with standard procedures for government agencies. Six months or more prior to the adoption of the budget by the legislature, the agency will submit its proposed budget for the next fiscal year to the budget office of the chief executive. Ordinarily, this budget request is based upon the previous year's budget, taking into account changes in costs and the scope of services to be performed. It is the job of the budget examiner, the budget director and the chief executive to scrutinize each request and based upon existing priorities, to allocate available funds.

The Federal government's fiscal year runs from October 1 to the following September 30. State and local governments often have fiscal years beginning and ending earlier. Not-for-profit and proprietary organizations generally follow the calendar year, January 1–December 31.

A marked distinction exists between the budget procedures for government agencies and those for not-for-profit and proprietary agencies. Government units submit proposals within their agencies up the hierarchy. Eventually the budget request becomes part of a larger request which becomes part of the executive budget submitted by the local state or Federal executive to the legislature which ultimately adopts the budget. In not-for-profit and proprietary agencies, the budget is submitted by departments to the executive director, who then submits the budget to the board of directors for approval.

Budgets submitted by government, not-for-profit and proprietary agencies are contingent upon revenues from independent sources. For example, most social service programs are funded mainly by the Federal and state governments. A budget request by the city social service agency to the city executive would include a request for the city's share of social service funds, which would in turn generate state and Federal funds. Typically, Federal employment and training monies have funded the entire cost of the city agency responsible for administering that program. They have also funded many projects included as part of the budget of not-for-profit agencies.

The proliferation of grant programs in the human services has greatly complicated the budget process of human service organizations. It has also greatly enhanced the ability of those agencies to diversify their funding. In the process, the entrepreneurial ability of human service managers has become more important than ever. The ability to persuade others of a program's merits has become an important attribute of successful managers. The multiple revenue sources of a small agency were set forth above. Now consider the expenditures for separate programs. As indicated below these funds may support diverse programs.

Expenses of A Residential Care Facility for Mentally Retarded Persons

Activities	% of Total
Work Training Center	54
Community Residence	6
Day Training Center	15
Developmental Disabilities Center	15
Recreation	4
Clinic	6

While public funds have become a major source of revenue for human service organizations, many agencies continue to rely upon private foundations, private individuals and fees generated by the users of their services, either directly or through third party reimbursement. Increasingly as they attempt to diversify human service organizations are developing varied expenditure patterns. The need for a human service managers to gain competency in the various aspects of budgeting is only limited by their abilities to delegate responsibility to technically proficient staff.

2. The Budget Submission

In public agencies, since resource acquisition is typically reserved for the highest level managers and specialized staffs, most middle managers are only familiar with internal organizational budget processes aimed at justifying and controlling expenditures. They submit a projected budget to their supervisor for their organizational unit and forget that in many organizations managers must also indicate the resources likely to be generated.

The head of the organization usually oversees the process of budgeting and at some stage becomes involved in the acquisition of funds. While some human service organizations operate like private sector organizations, surviving on fees generated from services, most supplement fees with other sources.

In the typical public agency providing human services, the budget is prepared and presented to the agency head who in turn submits the proposal to the president, governor, mayor, or other responsible official. In all but the smallest jurisdictions, the elected executive relies upon a professional budget staff for recommendations about spending plans. Spending, of course, reflects the willingness and ability of the executive to raise funds from available sources.

The specific details of the Federal, state and local budget processes need not concern us here. It will suffice to outline the major steps that occur in the preparation of the budget for a given fiscal year.

Steps in Budget Preparation

Step 1. Announcement by the Office of the Budget of a due date for Agency budgets for the next fiscal year.

Step 2. Organization of, Agency Process, Requests to Subunits for anticipated budget needs.

Step 3 Submission of Unit Budgets to Agency.

Step 4. Submission of Agency Budget to Office of Management and Budget.

Step 5. Submission of Draft Budget to Executive, usually based upon revisions by budget staff after consultation with agencies.

Step 6. Preparation and submission of Executive Budget to Legislature.

Step 7. Legislative Hearings on Budget.

Step 8. Reconciliation of Differences Between Executive and Legislature.

Step 9. Adoption of Budget by Legislature.

Step 10. Approval of Budget by Executive.

Step 11. Revision of Agency Budget Requests based upon Executive and Legislative changes and establishment of Operating Budgets for upcoming Fiscal Year.

Step 12. Beginning of the Fiscal Year.

To the operating manager, the initial step in the budget process is the submission of the unit budget with accompanying justification. At whatever level of the budget process, whether in a public agency or not-for-profit agency, managers are required to prepare a budget submission document. While the format of the document will differ from agency to agency and from level to level, depending on the detail required and the overall approach to budgeting being used, the basic purpose of the document remains the same: to set forth the level of funding requested and relate it to the level of services provided. The document, of course, should explain why a given level of resources is needed.

Below you will find an abbreviated budget submission made by the Department of Health and Human Services (HHS) through President Carter for Fiscal Year 1981. As you will see, the document submission was made in January 1980, almost nine months prior to its actual implementation. This submission was part of the President's total budget submission. The occasion of a budget submission from the elected executive to the legislature is a particularly significant moment. For many agency executives, it represents the culmination of many months of work and the continuation of a struggle to obtain resources for needed programs. It also represents the most public aspect of the budget process and the prelude to the formal adoption of the budget by the legislature.

The budget of HHS is, of course, particularly important for understanding human service management, since a major portion of Federal funding for the human services is contained within it. As you look over the HHS proposed budget for Fiscal Year 1981, consider some of the issues about the budget process, along with some of the issues about the substance of the HHS budget which have so great an impact on the entire human service field.

What is the magnitude of the budget? How does it compare to the budget of other Federal departments? How does this submission stand up against previous submissions? What factors affect the level of funding?

What priorities were reflected in this budget? Were these priorities presented in a framework likely to encourage Congressional support? In the light of the small amount of discretionary programs as compared to entitlements, what measures would be most important in limiting the level of spending?

Department of Health and Human Services Fiscal Year 1981 Budget (Billions)

	1979 Actual	1980 Estimate	1981 President's Budget
Budget Authority	$171.8	$194.8	$222.9
Outlays	$169.4	$193.3	$219.3

The 1981 HHS budget and legislative program reflects the Department's continued commitment to: provide basic, sustaining assistance to the aged, disabled, and poor; protect and enhance the health of all citizens; provide basic medical and social services to the most vulnerable groups of the population; and reduce or control the rate of growth in the cost of human services without reducing the quality or quantity of needed services.

HHS outlays are expected to increase by 13.5 percent between FY 1980 and 1981, compared to a 9.3 percent increase for the Federal budget as a whole. HHS will continue to comprise a growing share of Federal budget outlays, rising from 34.3 percent in 1980 to 35.6 percent in 1981. HHS also is expected to account for 50 percent of the increase in total Federal outlays, up from 34 percent in 1980.

Approximately 95 percent of projected HHS outlays are devoted to programs which confer entitlements on people who meet statutory eligibility requirements for benefits from Social Security, SSI, AFDC, Medicare and Medicaid. Outlays for entitlement programs are expected to grow by 13.9 percent in 1981 as compared to 1980, and 98 percent of the outlay increase in the HHS budget is for entitlement programs.

Outlays for discretionary programs in the aggregate are expected to increase by $0.5 billion (5 percent) while budget authority will increase by $0.7 billion (6.4 percent).

Budget Highlights

1. *Entitlement Programs:* The President has submitted a budget for 1981 that provides essentially full service levels for Social Security. No significant benefit reductions are proposed. The budget includes $199 billion in income support and medical entitlement benefits for the most vulnerable groups in our population. Altogether, 1.6 million additional persons would receive Social Security, cash assistance, and Medicare than in 1980.

2. *Health:* Primary health care services for the underserved are expected to be funded at $1.8 billion in FY 1981, an increase of nearly $200 million, including a 14% increase for Community Health Centers; a 62% increase for the National Health Service Corps; enhanced funding for Indian health services and Maternal and Child Health programs; a legislative proposal to mandate Medicaid coverage to comprehensive services provided in primary care clinics, at a cost of $52 million; and a related proposal to increase by more than 50% Federal funding for Medicaid programs in Puerto Rico and the territories, at a cost of $18 million.

3. *Children:* In addition to the substantial new resources to be devoted to the pending Child Health Assurance Program, the budget increases funding for children participating in the Head Start program.

4. *Aging:* An increase of $62 million is provided for Older American Act programs, including funding for 410,000 daily meals and enhanced social and community services.

5. *Refugees:* Major increases are provided in 1980 and 1981 to meet the needs of new immigrants from Indochina and other areas. Funding for refugee programs rises from $235 million in 1979 to $524 million in 1980 (+$289 million) and $598 million in 1981 (+$74 million).

6. *Management and Legislative Savings:* The fiscal year 1981 budget reflects the Department's continued commitment to eliminate excess costs, program abuses and administrative inefficiencies. Total administrative, regulatory, and legislative savings are projected at $4.0 billion.

HHS Budget by Agency (In Millions)			
	1979	1980	1981
Public Health Service			
Budget Authority	$ 7,679	$ 8,181	$ 8,553
Outlays	6,929	7,439	7,768
Health Care Financing Administration			
Budget Authority	44,997	50,566	61,518
Outlays	41,655	47,821	53,250
Social Security Administration			
Budget Authority	114,039	130,719	147,247
Outlays	115,807	132,791	152,860
Office of Human Development Services			
Budget Authority	4,909	5,161	5,406
Outlays	4,836	5,038	5,223
Departmental Management			
Budget Authority	242	251	259
Outlays	164	256	266
Offsetting Receipts			
Budget Authority	-35	-32	-34
Outlays	-35	-32	-34
Total HHS			
Budget Authority	171,831	194,846	222,949
Outlays	169,356	193,313	219,333

Can you guess from the limited excerpt above what the strategy of the budget submission was? What kinds of strategies are important generally in preparing a budget submission? A budgeting document has two different audiences. One is decisionmakers who will survey the document and make decisions about what to include and what not to include. In dealing with superiors, those preparing the budget documents often have a lot of information about their preferences. Often the individual in a decision-making role will have initiated the budget process with a statement of organizational priorities. Clearly the strategy is to show how the priorities of the top management can be reflected in the budget that is submitted. The budget document should also be designed to appeal to the public and to possible constituencies. Programs that benefit strong constituencies or that meet especially appealing needs should be emphasized.

A budget document should also indicate the continuing effectiveness of ongoing programs. By demonstrating continuing effectiveness, the agency builds a record justifying additional support. The agency with strong credibility is likely to continue to win additional resources.

Often the format of the budget request is dictated by the overall format of the budget process. Budget processes that are largely incremental emphasize connections with the previous year. Budgets adopting particular formats like PPB (Planning, Programming, Budgeting) and ZBB (Zero Base Budgeting) may require special attention to detailed justifications of all programs.

The art of preparing successful budget requests requires wide- ranging knowledge and good skills. In order to be successful, these must be combined with sound strategy and political acumen.

3. Special Grants

An important source of funds for human service agencies, particularly for those starting out or taking new directions, is special grants. Sometimes special grants become a source of recurrent support; sometimes they last only a short period of time. Grants are made ordinarily to carry out specific purposes. They may be long- or short-term in duration. In order to understand what grants are, how to apply for them, and how to monitor them, both recipient and donor points of view must be taken into consideration.

Donors, whether the government, foundations, corporations or individuals make grants to start new and worthwhile programs in particular areas. Since the human services are an area of such great need, a broad range of grant programs exist. Grants are ordinarily for a fixed, limited period of time. They are generally not meant to be a source of permanent support. In some cases they may, however, be semi-permanent, for example, when United Way supports a rehabilitation facility over a number of years. Grants vary tremendously in their amounts, purposes, regulations, and eligibility. Some are open to anyone who wants to apply. Some are narrowly restricted to a certain group of organizations or individuals.

Since grants are a supplementary source of resources, they are a constant lure to managers of human service agencies who find it hard to support all the services they would like to supply. The central task for the effective manager is to decide what types of new services might be provided and to find sources for obtaining grants. In under taking grant development activities, the manager must be constantly aware of the investment necessary to locate grants, apply for them, administer them, and run the new programs established. Where these costs are low, the possible return to the organization is more easily justified. Where the costs of applying for and administering grants is high, the manager should be wary of applying for them. Unfortunately, because of the usefulness of grants in stimulating the development of human services, some managers on their own or through pressures on their superiors may spend an inordinate amount of time to apply for and administer grants with little return to the organization.

As mentioned above, grants are almost always intended to fund a specifically designed project which fits within guidelines determined by the funding agency. Since ordinarily a grant application must be made, often on forms supplied by the grantor, understanding the elements of a good application are critical to the manager and help delineate the types of considerations that determine whether a grant application will be successful.

The Elements of a Grant Application

1. The *Introduction* is intended to alert the grantor to who is making the proposal and what the proposal is about. Usually it will contain a formal cover letter in which an individual in authority formally submits the proposal and a proposal summary which provides an overview of what is being proposed. The introduction will also provide some overall rationale for the project.

2. The *Problem Statement* fully explores the reason for the project and how it will address the needs of the organization, the target group it is aimed at, and the priorities of the funding sources. It is helpful to have preliminary discussions with representatives of the funding source to ensure that the project description is presented in the correct way.

3. The *Program Objectives* follow from the problem statement. They state concisely and clearly what the purpose of the project is in terms of what it will accomplish. Whenever possible, objectives should be stated in a form which will lend themselves to evaluation.

4. The *Activities/Methods/Procedures* are the description of how the project objectives will be met. They are in effect what is being proposed to meet the problem identified above.

5. The *Evaluation* is the procedure for determining if the objectives have in fact been met. Sometimes a process evaluation is included which focuses on the quality of the activities.

6. It is ordinarily important to include a plan for *Future Funding*. Since projects are ordinarily of limited duration, the funding source is very interested in knowing that mechanisms exist for continuing them into the future, when special support is withdrawn.

7. The *Budget* is a statement of the resources that will be needed to carry out the activities. Often a budget justification is included to explain how these resources will be used and why they were requested at the given levels.
8. The *Capability Statement* is a general discussion of the ability of the applicant organization to carry out this project and projects of this sort.

It is often useful to include biographical data on the proposed project staff and descriptions of similar projects already undertaken by the applicant.

Of equal importance to knowing how to apply for grants is knowing where to apply. No easy answer can be given. Ordinarily when managers spend time within an organization, they find out what regular sources of funding are available. Attendance at professional meetings, reviewing professional publications and newspapers, and speaking to colleagues in the field are good ways of locating funding sources. Since competition for funding is often high, the ability to learn early when new funds are becoming available may be critical.

For the new manager unfamiliar with an area, it may be worthwhile to attend specialized grantsmanship seminars which focus on the particular area of interest. Since the funding sources vary so widely, a general seminar will probably not be too useful in supplying leads, though it may be helpful in general strategy considerations. Almost every major government agency has some funds available for grants. Of course, the agencies that handle the areas in which the service delivery organization is operating are the most logical for attention. For further help, the *Catalog of Federal Domestic Assistance* may be consulted. To keep abreast of new opportunities, particularly special governmental funding open to competitive bid, the *Federal Register* and *Commerce and Business Daily* are helpful. In competitive situations, because of the short lead time for proposal preparation, often as short as 3-6 weeks, daily scanning of these publications may be necessary, a task best left to an office specializing in grant procurement. For help in locating the more than 25,000 foundations and finding out about them, the Foundation Center in New York City is a great resource. It provides a number of services to assist would-be grant applicants. An excellent practice is to approach foundations directly; most have an office for this purpose. It is also a good idea to cultivate colleagues who may be able to provide direct access to the subtle and ever-changing foundation world.

Some human service organizations, hospitals and educational institutions, for example, have relied heavily upon individual contributions to sustain a portion of their budget. Colleges, in recognition of the acceptance of contributions, often recruit their presidents with a view to their fundraising potential. The total resources currently contributed by individuals are not insignificant. In 1978 Americans gave nearly $40 billion to 500,000 private education, medical, religious, cultural, civic, and social welfare institutions. Almost half went to religious organizations. Other major recipients included hospitals and health, education, social welfare, and arts and humanities. Over 80% of these funds originated with individuals (including bequests); about 5% derived from foundations and an additional 5% derived from corporations.

The role of individual gifts in the total budget picture for a specific organization must be carefully considered. Campaigns may be launched for specific purposes, for example, to raise money for a building, or as part of an annual campaign to gather general organizational support. In undertaking fundraising campaigns, important considerations must be given to the actual costs of the campaign and the likely returns to the organization. Where a built-in group of supporters is available, such as a group of alumni, the prospects of significant individual contributions may be great.

In undertaking individual solicitations, whether through telephone contacts or direct mail, careful attention should be given to costs and benefits. A professional fund raiser should be consulted. Of course, some organizations are large enough to secure their own fundraising staff. Others will assign fundraising as one among several responsibilities to a top-level executive.

While every not-for-profit organization can apply for tax-exempt status under section 501(c)(3) of the United States Internal Revenue Code, which allows individuals to deduct contributions for income tax purposes and thereby facilitates the receipt of individual gifts, the decision to undertake a concentrated campaign to gather individual gifts must be carefully made and executed with care and diligence. The genesis of a solicitation campaign is the development of a rationale for support. Since the organization will be competing with approximately 500,000 tax-exempt organizations in the United States, the basis for a fundraising drive must be carefully stated. Ordinarily such a statement points out how the need will achieve an overriding social purpose, such as the eradication of a particular disease. The specific goals sought should be achievable within the means of the organization proposing to meet them. In the development of such a statement it is often useful to involve the constituency of the organization. This achieves the additional purpose of involving individuals who may take an active part in the solicitation of funds.

A basic ingredient in the success of any organization's fundraising is the quality of leadership within the organization and on the board of trustees. The community perception of the organization will be critical in establishing a favorable attitude toward a fundraising campaign. Competent leadership which has developed a reputation for successful service to the community is most likely to find fundraising successful. Individual staff members who have credibility within the community are very valuable.

Of potentially great assistance in the fundraising drive is the board of directors. To the extent that this board is composed of well-known and well-respected individuals, the task of fundraising will be greatly facilitated.

The trick of a successful campaign is to target the individuals and groups most likely to support the fundraising campaign and approach them in an effective manner. Particularly where fundraising is a periodic organizational activity, the systematic development of a list of individuals and groups with information about their giving habits and prospects is critical. These gift sources become a valuable element in the overall campaign.

Of course, the organization of the fundraising campaign involves the development of a plan and the assignment of individual responsibilities. Organizations which depend upon individual contributions for ongoing revenue will typically have a development director or other individual who is responsible for periodic fundraising campaigns. But the top management, too, is typically involved in fundraising efforts, particularly in contacting potentially large donors. Development offices range in size from a few individuals to as many as 100 individuals. In smaller organizations the manager may serve as the chief fundraiser.

The tasks of the development officer are varied. They require an individual with excellent administrative skills as well as the ability to work well with outsiders and to articulate the organizational case. They are, if you will, the salespersons of the not-for-profit organization. The development officer must cultivate internal organizational ties with individuals who can be helpful in convincing contributors. And, naturally, the development office must maintain contacts with potential contributors. A background in public relations is helpful, and strong communications skills are required.

The close relationship between developmental activities and public relations results in the combination of both functions in many organizations. An organization which cultivates a good public image through favorable publicity of its accomplishments has gone a long way toward easing its job of fundraising. Yet many not-for-profit institutions have traditionally eschewed public relations as crass and unbecoming to a quality institution. This attitude is giving way to one which understands the pervasive importance of effective public relations to an organization dependent on the largesse of the public.

One of the central concerns of managers responsible for developing and approving fundraising campaigns is limiting their cost. The old adage that you must invest money to make money applies equally to fundraising. The costs of staff, whether they be regular members of the staff or outside consultants, can be high. Incidental expenses for direct mail and telephones can be considerable. An organization must carefully consider what resources it is willing to expend on fundraising. It must also be understood that the first campaign is likely to be the most costly since it involves design and startup costs. Most organizations expect that a fundraising campaign will not cost more than 15% of the revenue generated. This figure may be low for initial campaigns and may not fully include all staff time and contributed time. One very common technique is to use contributed time and the time of staff that do not have a major impact on other organizational activities.

4. Marketing the Human Services

While most managers of human service organizations are heavily involved in selling their organizations to the general public and political leaders as well as other agency personnel, marketing services directly to users has not been emphasized. This has resulted because, by and large, human service programs have provided services free or at reduced rates to the needy.

Today the marketing of human services to those served is becoming of increasing importance. This has resulted on the one hand from the proliferation of human service programs, often competing for the same clientele. Where government funding follows the client, the institution may be in a competitive situation with other institutions. The growth of the not-for-profit sector and the cutback of governmental grant programs has also forced human service organizations to focus more attention on raising money from fees paid by consumers. Even in areas which have traditionally been immune from such market pressures, such as elementary and secondary education, pressures exist for moving toward more of a market orientation.

Marketing is a concept which applies to all organizations that interact in a complex world and enter into exchange relationships with other organizations. A market is a group of people who have resources that they might conceivably exchange for some benefit to them. Service organizations are those that provide services to clients for fees, but ordinarily they are subsidized by donors so that their services are offered below actual costs. These publics, the donors and the clients become the major points of reference in determining the direction of the organization.

A thorough going marketing orientation is relatively new even to many business organizations which not long ago emphasized production and sales. The marketing orientation stresses the interrelationship with the consumer through the regulation of demand. The marketer must understand how to deal with a variety of demand inadequacies, including negative, nonexistent, latent, faltering, irregular, full, overfull and unwholesome demand.

The process of marketing includes two parts: market structure analysis and consumer analysis. In market structure analysis, the first step is to define the market, those who have an active or potential interest in the product or service. Then, within that large group a division into homogeneous parts is made, which is labelled market segmentation. Finally, market positioning takes place in which the organization chooses which segments of the market to focus on. Organizations seek to measure four attributes of the target markets they choose to serve: their needs, perceptions, preferences, and satisfaction.

Preferences are usually measured through direct questioning, projective tests and simulation exercises. Perception is guaged by image which is measured through unstructured interviews, object sorting, multidimensional scaling, item lists, and semantic differentials. Preferences and satisfaction are measured on the basis of survey research, using interviewing and written questionnaires. A number of analytic techniques have been developed, including the use of standard scales and such statistical techniques as multidimensional scaling.

Of special significance is the market survey. On the basis of these surveys, decisions can be made about further services to be offered and likely responses to them. In gathering systematic survey data, it is ordinarily impossible to gather information from everyone who might be served. Often information can be gathered from current recipients by means of a regular survey procedure. Another common approach is to select a sample from a larger group and obtain data from that sample. The trick in this approach, however, is to select a sample group which reflects accurately the larger group. In other words, a representative sample of the total population must be selected. A number of procedures exists for selecting such groups and ensuring their representative qualities. The survey technique can be particularly useful when new services are contemplated by a human service organization. It can allow for reaching new populations and finding out their needs and their willingness to pay for particular services.

A critical aspect of effective marketing is pricing. Once a potential need for service and a willingness of consumers to pay for the service has been identified a price must be set. Arriving at this price is, however, a difficult task. If a price is set too high, the service may not sell. If it is set too low, it may not be worth providing. Pricing is a trial and error procedure, one which benefits from experience and a clear concept of the priorities to be addressed in pricing.

Among the competing goals which pricing strategy may seek to attain are: maximizing revenue, recovering costs, encouraging consumer use of service, and discouraging consumer use of service. In practice, these goals are ordinarily met by three simplified approaches to setting prices: 1) charging what the service actually costs, based upon available cost data; 2) charging what people are willing to pay, based upon market considerations; 3) charging what the competition is charging. Adjustments and readjustments of these procedures are often needed. In not-for-profit agencies, an additional complicating factor may be an unwillingness to generate too much revenue in a given year. Many organizations are unwilling to attain too large a surplus in any particular year, since they are not supposed to make a profit. In addition, some recurrent contributors may reduce their shares.

The marketing perspective, while related to the human service organization's need to build support, is a distinctive departure for many managers. It is an extension of the exchange relationships with recipients that currently exist, but is sufficiently new to justify special attention. It requires a new perspective, but one which promises increased control over the organization's future, increased autonomy, and increased service to recipients.

Selected Bibliography

Budgeting, A Guide for United Ways and Not-for-Profit Human Service Organizations. Alexandria, Virginia: United Way of America, December, 1975.

Burkhead, Jesse. *Government Budgeting.* New York: John Wiley, 1956.

Herron, Douglas. *Marketing Management for Social Service Agencies.* Columbus, Ohio: The Association of Professional YMCA Directors, 1978.

Kotler, Philip. *Marketing for Nonprofit Organizations.* Englewood Cliffs, New Jersey: Prentice-Hall, 1975.

Sharkansky, Ira. *Spending in the American States. Chicago: Rand McNally, 1968.*

Wildavsky, Aaron. *The Politics of the Budgetary Process.* Boston: Little, Brown & Co., 1964.

Chapter 10.

Resource Control

1. Managerial Control of Resources

The management control process consists of a range of informal and formal activities. It uses memoranda, meetings, conversations and signals such as body language, as well as more formal information systems. The focus of managerial control processes are on the inputs and outputs of the organization. First, decisions are made as to what outputs and inputs ought to be; then records are maintained as to what they actually are; and subsequently reports are prepared to compare actual outputs and inputs to those that were planned. This formal process may be divided into: programming, budgeting, operating and reporting.

In the programming phase, decisions are made as to what resources will be expended in what programs. Where possible, anticipated benefits are compared to expected costs. But even in profit-making businesses this is not always possible. In the budgeting phase, a plan expressed in monetary terms is proposed for some given time period, usually one year. Program decisions are expressed in terms of organizational units and set forth in dollar amounts based upon a process of negotiation between their managers and priority setting central staff. Expected outputs are associated with estimated input resources. During the period of actual operations, records of resources consumed and outputs achieved are kept, both according to program and organizational unit. Finally accounting information, along with a variety of other information, is summarized, analyzed and reported to appropriate managers. Action to improve performance is taken.

Many of the weaknesses associated with planning and control in not-for-profit agencies can be attributed to the poor implementation of one or more of these phases. Ironically, in not-for-profits, where the need for management control is even greater than in profit making institutions which can rely to some extent on the market's invisible hand, management planning and control has tended to lag. This lag may be attributed to a number of factors associated with the developments of information and accounting procedures that have occurred in the twentieth century. A basic factor complicating the situation in the not-for-profit sector was the failure up until the mid-70's to adopt accrual accounting which made it virtually impossible to develop effective cost accounting systems which are tied into the basic debit and credit of accounting records. Similarly, standard cost approaches which are built upon cost accounting were not available. In addition, the line item budget and its emphasis on large object classifications within agencies for fiduciary purposes, have discouraged the use of budgetary control approaches. In addition, variable costing and break-even analysis, responsibility accounting, and effective cost allocation to programs have not been successfully introduced.

While the budget process may be viewed as part of a larger managerial effort directed at gaining and allocating resources for the organization, budgeting has another important dimension. The budget may be viewed as a mechanism to control the use of resources. The budget, in fact, lies at the heart of the planning and control process of the organization. A budget is ordinarily prepared on an annual basis and sets forth a plan for the acquisition and use of resources. In governing resource utilization, the budget becomes the basis of the management control function. Management control is sometimes defined as: The process by which managers assure that resources are obtained and used effectively and efficiently in the accomplishment of the organization's objectives.

The development of the budget is a process of planning to obtain and use resources. In the execution of the budget, resources are obtained and expended. Control is exercised to ensure that these resources are expended for the purposes that have been agreed upon during the adoption of the budget. The Office of the Budget at the executive level and line managers operating through their budget offices are responsible for adhering to budget guidelines.

At the higher levels in the organization the budget execution process is one of managerial control. As the budget process moves toward the middle and lower levels of the organization, it becomes involved with what is often referred to as operational control: the process of assuring that specific tasks are carried out effectively and efficiently. Particular attention at this level, of course, is focused on fiscal responsibility. Managers are required to stay within their budgets; the execution process is intended to ensure that they, in fact, do. The budget process at the operational level will be discussed below.

The processes for setting organizational goals were described in Chapter 2. Management by Objectives (MBO) is sometimes used to establish annual organization goals. Usually the director or agency head is responsible for designing and implementing such a process. But these goals remain abstract until translated into operational terms. An integral part of the budget process is translating these organizational goals into operational imperatives. The budget process translates goal statements into specific resources, reflected in money spent for materials, supplies and personnel.

In traditional budgeting systems these resource decision are stated in terms of organizational units and resources. These units have mission statements and goals. So, for example, if a new program is to be established for providing care to infants and their mothers in poverty areas, the budget would indicate that within a particular division a new unit would be created consisting of a Director and three part-time nurses, with funds obtained from a Federal grant and foundation resources. The budget explains what the financial resources are that will be directed toward the operation of specific organizational units.

The process of budgeting is time-consuming and intertwined with politics. This is true especially within governmental budgeting. The budget represents the allocation of resources, so that budgetary changes often affect competing groups and individuals. Budget decisions involve choices in the use of resources affecting real people. The result is a thoroughly political process.

In order to manage the conflict inherent in such a process, certain overall principles seem to operate. The budget is incremental in nature. Changes from the existing allocation of resources are undertaken slowly. The process of bargaining tends to minimize change from the status quo. There is a general recognition that agencies and units will receive their "fair share" of new appropriations.

The drawback of the incremental nature of this highly political system is the slow pace of change. Many programs may be continued which are not effective or not as effective as they should be. Budgeting systems which focus on organizational units make it difficult to change programmatic direction. In order to reorient the budget toward programs and purposes, approaches such as Planning, Programming, Budgeting (PPB) and Zero-Based Budgeting (ZBB) have been introduced.

Perhaps the approach that has received the most attention and controversy is the Planning-Programming-Budgeting System (PPBS) which was introduced into the Johnson Administration after its use in the Defense Department under Secretary of Defense Robert McNamara. This system explicitly expanded the budgeting system into a system for planning and control by requiring that budget submissions be divided into specific programs associated wtih goals and objectives. For each program, the resource requirements are described along with the purposes, goals, and objectives to be attained. Budget submissions are also expected to pose alternatives and analyze the relative ability of each alternative to attain stated objectives which are matched with associated costs. Difficulties have arisen with such comprehensive approaches to budgeting, which can be time-consuming and overstructured, especially in an environment that is rapidly changing.

Under President Carter, Zero-Base Budgeting (ZBB) came into vogue. ZBB requires that every aspect of a budget be thoroughly justified. It attempts to avoid the consequences of incrementalism by requiring that each and every program be thoroughly defended. The problems with this approach to budgeting are similar to those with PPBS. It requires an enormous amount of extra work by both those preparing budget requests and those examining them. It is unrealistic to think that each year every single program can be scrutinized in every detail. The resulting overload on the budget system either results in paralysis or a *pro forma* process which yields little of substantive value.

While the development of comprehensive systems of budgeting are considered warily by operating officials, the importance of linking resources to purposes is almost universally accepted. Almost every level of government has some way of making this explicit linkage, and boards of directors of not-for-profit organizations require that linkage as a matter of course. Top management finds that the budget process provides a regular, systematic method of managerial control. Periodic budget reports allow for a review of expenditure patterns and at the same time questions can be asked about the results of those expenditures. Budget staffs provide top executives with an ideal source of expertise to assist in the control function.

The effectiveness of the budget process as a management review process depends upon the extent to which resources are realistically linked with purposes and the extent to which performance indicators can be associated with those purposes to allow for a useful assessment of achievement. The development and use of performance indicators is described in detail below in Chapter 12.

The budget process should not be oversold, however. While it does provide a regular and periodic mechanism for exercising control in organizations by top management, it should be complemented by other information gathering techniques. Sometimes projects merit continuous monitoring through extended field visits. Sometimes special studies are needed to monitor the progress of new programs. The mechanisms and modes of managerial surveillance are many. The need is for a variety of methods. Budgetary processes hold a central place in managerial control, and they should be used to the fullest extent.

2. Operational Budgeting

While the importance of the budget for managerial control is clear at the higher levels of the organization, in the middle and lower levels of the organization its use as a tool of operational control dominates.

Once a budget had been approved by the legitimate authority, the legislature or board of directors, it must be implemented. This requires an expenditure plan, sometimes developed on a quarterly basis, detailing what expenditures can be made. Often after a budget is finally adopted, the initial expenditure plan will need to be revised to reflect changes which have been made in overall expenditures. Indeed, throughout the year, additional changes may be made in overall expenditure targets which will necessitate changes in specific expenditure categories.

This process of changing an operational budget is often referred to as the budget modification process. A budget modification is a deviation from the fiscal plan approved at an earlier stage. The need for modification depends upon the level of detail contained in the budget. If the level of detail is great, the power of budget control is great. Where centralized budget offices are established, they will often favor detailed schedules which increase their authority to approve changes made by the agency. Of course, the trade-off is a slowing down of the bureaucratic process. One of the continuing difficulties faced by human service agencies which are part of larger municipal or state agencies is the need to obtain approval before action. A detailed budget with attendant modification procedures can cause considerable delay in bureaucratic processes.

The importance of maintaining a system of control to ensure that budgeted items are not exceeded is highlighted during times of fiscal crisis. When dealing with enormous budgets, the uncertainties of revenues and expenditures can be susbstantial. It is critical that periodic checks be made to ensure that actual expenditures do not exceed actual revenues. Remember, a budget is only a plan for showing how much expected revenues will be spent. Management must ensure that the plan is followed.

Basic fiscal accountability to ensure that an organization's expenditures do not exceed an organization's revenues is a central responsibility of top management. Within the Federal government this responsibility is incorporated into the *Federal Anti-Deficiency Act*. It gives agency heads the responsibility for obligations and the integrity of the budget control system and gives the agency budget officer the responsibility for insuring that money is not overobligated. A person knowingly and willfully violating the apportionments is subject to fine and imprisonment. Those violating the apportionments without knowledge are subject to administrative discipline, including reprimand, suspension from duty without pay, and removal from office. Indeed, within any organization failure to carry out these basic fiscal responsibilities will ordinarily result in reprimand or dismissal.

While the fiscal accountability of top management is clear, accountability of lower level managers will vary. Often fiscal accountability for balancing budgets is limited to a small number of managers. Units carrying out this obligation are sometimes referred to as responsibility centers. As lower levels of management become involved in the budget process, the connection between revenues and expenditures will weaken. Thus an individual manager might have responsibility for generating a certain amount of revenue, while another might have responsibility for monitoring expenditures. Clarification of these responsibilities is a prerequisite to effective fiscal management.

An important distinction that is often made in budgets is that between expenditures for personnel services and those for other than personnel services. Within human service agencies and government in particular the expenditures for personnel services tend to be high. The ratio of staff salaries to total expenditures reflects the labor intensive nature of the services. Particularly within government, attempts at limiting expenditures often will focus, therefore, on personnel services. When the executive for any jurisdiction, whether local, state, or federal, finds that expenditures are exceeding desired levels, a hiring freeze may be imposed or the number of positions allocated to an agency may be lowered after the budget has been approved. In order to insure adherence to these limits, a system of position control may be instituted. Such a system may result in considerable savings and is in effect a supplementary system of budget control, focusing on personnel. All agencies are then required to demonstrate that they have not exceeded their position allocations before new individuals are approved for placement on payroll.

The system of fiscal control breaks up large budget categories into smaller subunits and allocates monies to them. Within government this process is often referred to as the allotment process, whereby the agency head provides authority to operating officials to incur obligations within prescribed amounts for specified time periods. The bases of allotments can be organizational units, activities, geographical location or object classification, depending upon management needs.

A central component of a budget control system is periodic reports that are generated to provide a summary of individual transactions. These reports may be on a daily, weekly, monthly, quarterly and annual basis. They summarize transactions recorded by the accounting system. It becomes the responsibility of managers and budget officers at each successive level to ensure that in the categories for which they are responsible expenditure limits are not exceeded.

The degree of complexity of such a system, of course, depends upon the amount of money and the size of the organization. One of the difficulties encountered by large human service organizations is the volume of transactions. For example, the New York City Human Resources Administration had a budget for fiscal year 1982 of $3.2 billion and employed over 20,000 people. In order to maintain control over expenditures and revenues, extensive systems are needed.

3. The Accounting System

A system of budget control requires detailed knowledge of individual transactions that are occurring, including all receipts, obligations, and disbursements. This information is accumulated by the accounting system.

A fiscal control system keeps track of actual revenue and actual expenditures to ensure that a budgetary imbalance does not occur. While individual managers, budget officers and, in some cases, personnel officers are responsible for ensuring that the budget is followed, they all depend upon the financial reporting system to provide the information they need. The accounting system records financial transactions of an agency, summarizing, reporting, interpreting, and analyzing the data for a range of users. Transactions which are included within the accounting system include both decisions to commit or obligate funds and the actual passing of funds both to and from the organization. The integrity of this information is a prerequisite to effective fiscal control of all funds, property and other assets. It also can be used to support a variety of analytic functions deriving from cost accounting principles.

Accounting in not-for-profit agencies differs in basic concept from accounting in business organizations. The primary objective of business organizations is to earn a profit. The financial statements emphasize the points where resources are earned and used. They emphasize earnings as a measure of achievement and net resources consumed. In business organizations the accrual based accounting systems are common in which revenues are recorded when earned and expenditures are recorded as soon as they result in liabilities for benefits received regardless of when each is exchanged.

In some profit making enterprises, the cash or modified accrual basis of accounting is used. The cash basis focuses on the points at which cash is received and disbursed. In the modified accrual basis, revenues are recognized in the accounting period in which they become measureable and available to finance expenditures. Expenditures except for interest or long term debt are recorded when the related liabilities are incurred.

In not-for-profit enterprises, however, since the objective is to provide socially desirable services, the emphasis is placed on showing the inflows and outflows of spendable resources. Cash or modified accrual based systems are typically used. Governmental units prefer the modified accrual basis, which does not distinguish between capital and revenue expenditures and does not recognize depreciation of fixed assets. The focus again is on inflow and outflows of appropriatable resources.

Government accounting occurs within the framework of the *Governmental Accounting and Financial Reporting Principles* contained in Statement 1 issued by the National Council on Government Accounting. These principles require that accounting procedures adhere to legal requirements except when in conflict with GAAP and operate within authorized budgets. The basic entity within which the recording of transactions occurs is referred to as a fund, thus government accounting is often labelled fund accounting. Other principles describe the types of funds that may be used, when revenues may be included in the funds, and when expenditures must be recorded.

In implementing a successful government accounting system, certain norms are followed. The organization of the accounting system must be consistent with and in sufficient detail to articulate with the budget system. Accounting procedures should be flexible, but within a consistent uniform whole. Perhaps the most distinctive aspect of government accounting is the use of separated funds. A fund is a sum of money set aside for a particular purpose and accounted for separately from the other monies of government. The purpose of fund accounting is to assure that monies are spent only for the purposes intended. Within the U.S. Social Security System, for example, separate funds operate for Old Age Survivors Insurance, Disability and Medicare. Monies generated by taxes for these purposes cannot be spent for other purposes. Ordinarily when grants are made for specified projects, they must be deposited in special funds and used only for that purpose. The different types of funds include the general, special revenue, debt service, capital projects, enterprise, trust or agency, internal service and special assessment.

A number of different types of statements can be used to register the actual revenues and expenditures. Such statements are issued on a monthly, quarterly, and annual basis. Sometimes they may be issued on a daily or weekly basis. The purpose of the statement is to indicate the assets or monies available in the fund and the claims against the fund, indicating the deficit or balance resulting. Of course, this is a significant departure from business accounting which focuses on the enterprise unit. The major principles of government accounting are set forth below.

Government Accounting and Financial Reporting Principles, Summary Statement*

Accounting and Reporting Capabilities

1. A governmental accounting system must make it possible both: (a) to present fairly and with full disclosure the financial position and results of financial operations of the funds and account groups of the governmental unit in conformity with generally accepted accounting priniciples; and (b) to determine and demonstrate compliance with finance-related legal and contractual provisions.

Fund Accounting Systems

2. Governmental accounting systems should be organized and operated on a fund basis. A fund is defined as a fiscal and accounting entity with a self-balancing set of accounts recording case and other financial resources, together with all related liabilities and residual equities or balances, and changes therein, which are segregated for the purpose of carrying on specified activities or attaining certain objecties in accordance with special regulations, restrictions, or limitations.

Types of Funds

3. The following types of funds should be used by state and local governments:

(A) Governmental Funds

(1) The General Fund—to account for all financial resources except those required to be accounted for in another fund.

(2) Special Revenue Funds—to account for the proceeds of specific revenue sources (other than special assessments, expendable trusts, or for major capital projects) that are legally restricted to expenditure for specific purposes.

(3) Capital Projects Funds—to account for financial resources to be used for the acquisition or construction of major capital facilities (other than those financed by proprietary funds, Special Assessment Funds, and Trust Funds).

(4) Debt Service Funds—to account for the accumulation of resources for, and the payment of, general long-term debt principal and interest.

(5) Special Assessment Funds—to account for the financing of public improvements or services deemed to benefit the properties against which special assessments are levied.

---

*Reproduced with permission from the National Council on Governmental Accounting Statement 1, Governmental Accounting and Financial Reporting Principles (Chicago: Municipal Finance Officers Association of the United States and Canada, 1979). Copyright 1979 by the Municipal Finance Officers Association of the United States and Canada.

(B) Proprietary Funds

(6) Enterprise Funds—to account for operations (a) that are financed and operated in a manner similar to private business enterprises—where the intent of the governing body is that the costs (expenses, including depreciation) of providing goods or services to the general public on a continuing basis be financed or recovered primarily through user charges; or (b) where the governing body has decided that period determination of revenues earned, expenses incurred, and/or net income is appropriate for capital maintenance, public policy, management control, accountability, or other purposes.

(7) Internal Service Funds—to account for the financing of goods or services provided by one department or agency to other departments or agencies of the governmental unit, or to other governmental units, on a cost-reimbursement basis.

(C) Fiduciary Funds

(8) Trust and Agency Funds—to account for assets held by a governmental unit in a trustee capacity or as an agent for individuals, private organizations, other governmental units, and/or other funds. These include (a) Expendable Trust Funds, (b) Nonexpendable Trust Funds, (c) Pension Trust Funds, and (d) Agency Funds.

Number of Funds

4. Governmental units should establish and maintain those funds required by law and sound financial administration. Only the minimum number of funds consistent with legal and operating requirements should be established, however, since unnecessary funds result in inflexibility, undue complexity, and inefficient financial administration.

Accounting for Fixed Assets and Long-Term Liabilities

5. A clear distinction should be made between (a) fund fixed assets and general fixed assets and (b) fund long-term liabilities and general long-term debt.

   a. Fixed assets related to specific proprietary funds or Trust Funds should be accounted for through those funds. All other fixed assets of a governmental unit should be accounted for through the General Fixed Assets Account Group.

   b. Long-term liabilities of proprietary funds, Special Assessment Funds, and Trust Funds should be accounted for through those funds. All other unmatured general long-term liabilities of the governmental unit should be accounted for through the General Long-Term Debt Account Group.

Valuation of Fixed Assets

6. Fixed assets should be accounted for at cost or, if the cost is not practicably determinable, at estimated cost. Donated fixed assets

should be recorded at their estimated fair value at the time received.

Depreciation of Fixed Assets

7. a. Depreciation of general fixed assets should not be recorded in the accounts of governmental funds. Depreciation of general fixed assets may be recorded in cost accounting systems or calculated for cost finding analyses; and accumulated depreciation may be recorded in the General Fixed Assets Account Group.

   b. Depreciation of fixed assets accounted for in a proprietary fund should be recorded in the accounts of that fund. Depreciation is also recognized in those Trust Funds where expenses, net income, and/or capital maintenance are measured.

Accrual Basis in Governmental Accounting

8. The modified accrual or accrual basis of accounting, as appropriate, should be utilized in measuring financial position and operating results.

   a. Governmental fund revenues and expenditures should be recognized on the modified accrual basis. Revenues should be recognized in the accounting period in which they become available and measurable. Expenditures should be recognized in the accounting period in which the fund liability is incurred, if measurable, except for unmatured interest on general long-term debt and on special assessment indebtedness secured by interest-bearing special assessment levies, which should be recognized when due.

   b. Proprietary fund revenues and expenses should be recognized on the accrual basis. Revenues should be recognized in the accounting period in which they are earned and become measurable; expenses should be recognized in the period incurred, if measurable.

   c. Fiduciary fund revenues and expenses or expenditures (as appropriate) should be recognized on the basis consistent with the fund's accounting measurement objective. Nonexpendable Trust and Pension Trust Funds should be accounted for on the accrual basis. Expendable Trust Funds should be accounted for on the modified accrual basis. Agency Fund assets and liabilities should be accounted for on the modified accrual basis.

   d. Transfers should be recognized in the accounting period in which the interfund receivable and payable arise.

Budgeting, Budgetary Control, and Budgetary Reporting

9. a. An annual budget(s) should be adopted by every governmental unit.

b. The accounting system should provide the basis for appropriate budgetary control.

c. Budgetary comparisons should be included in the appropriate financial statements and schedules for governmental funds for which an annual budget has been adopted.

Transfer, Revenue, Expenditure, and Expense Account Classification

10. a. Interfund transfers and proceeds of general long-term debt issues should be classified separately from fund revenues and expenditures or expenses.

b. Governmental fund revenues should be classified by fund and source. Expenditures should be classified by fund, function (or program), organization unit, activity, character, and principal classes of objects.

c. Proprietary fund revenues and expenses should be classified in essentially the same manner as those of similar business organizations, functions, or activities.

Common Terminology and Classification

11. A common terminology and classification should be used consistently throughout the budget, the accounts, and the financial reports of each fund.

12. a. Appropriate interim financial statements and reports of financial position, operating results, and other pertinent information should be prepared to facilitate management control of financial operations, legislative oversight, and, where necessary or desired, for external reporting purposes.

b. A comprehensive annual financial report covering all funds and account groups of the governmental unit—including appropriate combined, combining, and individual fund statements; notes to the financial statements; schedules; narrative explanations; and statistical tables—should be prepared and published.

c. General purpose financial statements may be issued separately from the comprehensive annual financial report. Such statements should include the basic financial statements and notes to the financial statements that are essential to fair presentation of financial position and operating results (and changes in financial position of proprietary funds and similar Trust Funds).

The *Summary Statement* emphasizes the importance of consistency and full disclosure. Changes in resources and obligations must be recognized when they occur. Financial data must be presented consistently from period to period, using the same forms and including the same items. All significant financial facts must be disclosed. The financial statement must include a summary of accounting policies, including measurement bases, restrictions on assets, contingencies, commitments not recognized in the body of the statement, changes in accounting principles and subsequent events.

While the Principles of Governmental Accounting are designed to insure accuracy in reports to outsiders, the managerial importance of accurate cost accounting should not be forgotten. A particularly critical use of accounting information relates to the ever-tightening policies for third party payments. They often require documentation that the costs alleged actually cover the reimbursed services. The accounting system may have to be adapted to generate such data. To the extent that accounting information is recorded in sufficient detail to refer to specific identifiable programs, the potential for comparing the relative costs of different programs is great. Such benefit/cost analyses are a valuable tool in program evaluation efforts.

4. Relating Benefits to Costs

In many human service programs, the question arises as to whether the outcomes of the program justify its costs. In other words, what is the relationship between the program and its real-world effects. Consider a community health facility. When are the expenditures for the facility justified in terms of the effects that it has on the health of the local community? Or consider a special educational program for disadvantaged youth. Under what circumstances are the expenditures for the program justified?

The costs of programs are important, but a more complete analysis is necessary to assess these costs in relationship to the benefits. One approach to the assessment of benefits and costs is to view the projects as public investments. The benefits which result from the program are the return on the investment.

Within the public sector in the United States this approach to benefit-cost analysis has been most highly developed in the area of water resources. As far back as 1902, the *Rivers and Harbors Act* required that engineering reports for projects proposed by the Army Corps of Engineers include a discussion of benefits and costs. The *Flood Control Act of 1936* stated "that the Federal government should improve or participate in the improvement of navigable waters or their tributaries, including watersheds thereof, if the benefits to whomsoever they may accrue are in excess of estimated costs." Burkhead and Miner surveyed the elaborate procedure which included committee hearings for proposed projects and concluded that: "Benefit cost is used for project justification, not for the appraisal of outcomes."

During the 1960s benefit-cost analysis was applied to a whole range of governmental programs. The applications of benefit-cost techniques in the Defense Department received particular attention and led to their incorporation in the Planning-Programming and Budgeting System. Later these techniques were applied to a whole range of social programs.

Applying benefit-cost to human service programs presents some special difficulties, for example, evaluating the long-term impact of programs. Becker's theory about human capital has directed attention to lifetime earnings change as an indicator of program success, but other values may also be affected. Lifetime earnings may be difficult to estimate. Empirical data is a long time in coming and placing a value on these other outcomes may be difficult. One of the particularly difficult problems, especially related to health programs, is that of valuing human life.

One of the central questions in understanding benefit-cost analysis is the extent to which it is used within the decisionmaking context. The move from analysis to decision is critical in understanding the benefit-cost analysis.

The techniques for undertaking benefit-cost analysis within the water resources area are well-developed. The process requires extensive use of quantification in attaching values to the benefits and costs. Often the cost calculations are rather straightforward. The calculation of benefits may be more speculative. The success of applying benefit-cost analysis is in large part the result of the systematization of the process of calculating benefits. Benefits are classified as direct, indirect and intangible, and are relatively well-defined according to the specific project.

Thus the primary benefit of a hydroelectric plant is estimated in terms of opportunity cost—the difference in the cost of electric energy produced as compared with the cost of the most economic alternative source of supply, usually thermal power, that might have been produced on the same site. Associated costs for the hydroelectric plant would include the generators and penstocks. Secondary benefits are multiplier effects stemming from industries that supply the project area with goods and services and economic activities resulting from the processing, distributing and consuming of output of the project. Considerable disagreement exists as to whether these secondary benefits should actually be included in the calculation of benefits and costs. Intangibles include such items as impact on the esthetic quality of the landscape, enhancement of recreational opportunities, and human life itself.

While the problems of assessing indirect benefits and intangibles plague the evaluation of human service programs, it is interesting to see that they even affect the more highly developed area of water resources. The primary benefits in water resources are, however, readily quantifiable. The choice between a hydroelectric plant and other types of plants readily lends itself to quantification.

According to human capital theory, education and training programs can be evaluated in terms of the income streams of individuals who pass through these programs, since they should result in direct increases in individual income. But the estimation of these income streams may be subject to conjecture. Actual measurement requires a lifetime. In the health area, a greater obstacle is the valuation of human life. How can the benefit of a human life be quantified? In fact, an interesting decision of the United States Supreme Court has recently held that benefit-cost analysis in the area of health and safety cannot be required, because of the difficulty of computing the value of human life.

This problem of valuation of benefits is a great one. Another problem connected with evaluation is equating costs which are often incurred in the present with benefits that characteristically occur over time. This, of course, is characteristic of human service programs which have an impact on individuals and affect the individual over a lifetime.

This problem of comparing future values with present values is a real one. The most common way to handle the problem is to convert all values into present values by use of a discount rate. The discount rate represents the return that could have been realized if those same resources would have been put to some other use. The most important reason for using the discount rate is a productivity consideration: if the current resources allocated to this project were allocated to an alternative use, they might result in a higher rate of return. In addition, the future is uncertain and clearly current use is more valuable than future use. On the other hand, some individuals might prefer to receive benefits in future years. Similarly, from the point of view of future generations, value might be greater in the future than in the past. While strictly speaking, the use of the discount rate is not necessary to benefit-cost analysis, it usually becomes a central feature of calculations to compare alternative programs and investments.

A simple way of visualizing this approach is to consider any project as an investment at a particular time, $t(0)$. The benefit would be the return on the investment. In standard private sector investment decisions, the present value would be obtained by discounting future returns at a particular point in time by the current commerical interest rate. If, for example, the commercial interest rate were 10%, the present value of receiving $10,000 five years from today could be calculated by reducing its value by 10% for each of five years.

In general, the present value of future benefits at a given discount rate is given by the simple formula: $PV = A/(1+d)^n$, where A represents the future benefit, d represents the annual discount rate, and n the number of years from the present. In this example, $PV = 10,000 \div (1+.1)^5$

Selected Bibliography

Anthony, Robert N. and Welsch, Glenn A. *Fundamentals of Management Accounting.* Homewood, Illinois: Richard D. Irwin, Inc., 1974.

Becker, Gary. *Human Capital.* New York: Columbia University Press, 1964.

Burkhead, Jesse and Miner, Jerry. *Public Expenditure.* Chicago: Aldine and Atherton, 1971.

Copeland, Ronald and Dascher, Paul. *Managerial Accounting.* Santa Barbara: Hamilton Publishing Co., 1974.

Gruber, Murray, ed. *Management Systems in the Human Services.* Philadelphia: Temple University Press, 1981.

Henke, Emerson. *Introduction to Nonprofit Organization Accounting.* Boston: Kent Publishing Co., 1980.

Lohmann, Roger. *Breaking Even, Financial Management in Human Service Organizations.* Philadelphia: Temple University Press, 1980.

Lynch, Thomas. *Public Budgeting in America.* Englewood Cliffs, N.J.: Prentice-Hall, 1979.

Chapter 11.

Information Systems

1. Management and Information

The budgeting and accounting systems are important sources of information for management purposes. In fact, the arraying of program and cost information as they occur in benefit-cost analysis can be one of the most powerful uses of information available to management. The importance of information and its effective communication is a central theme of management experts. Mintzberg has even referred to the manager as an information processing system.

The informational role of the manager is closely related to the control function of management. In order to carry out fiscal and budgetary control as well as control program activities, the manager must obtain a variety of information. Management control is closely related to the ability of the manager to provide direction. In human service organizations a large amount of effort is expended in determining the eligibility of individuals for services, in obtaining payment for services, often from third parties, and in delivering services to individuals. Human service managers need to have information about these activities so they can determine the extent to which their organizations are functioning effectively. They also need the information to perform their functions of representation and advocacy.

These needs of management and the operational needs of the organization in fact coincide. The dependence of human service organizations on third party reimbursement reinforce the need to maintain records of individual contacts and treatment. The desire to document improvement in individual cases adds further burden to the information requirements of most human service organizations. Thus many organizations maintain individual client based records. These data may be used to evaluate the impact of services on the client population.

The amount of information that is retained is a function both of the detail and number of individual records. It should be evident, however, that record keeping can quickly mushroom and that the amount of information that is needed for even relatively small organizations can be significant. For this reason the use of automated data processing is becoming increasingly important in the human services. Most hospitals have an automated system for maintaining client records, for reimbursement and billing purposes. Even nursing homes, which are usually smaller, are beginning to install automated systems. Often, however, these systems will not include information about treatment. If human service organizations are part of larger organizations, such as local governments, they may participate in comprehensive automated systems for processing claims, accounting and budgeting. More often than not the human service manager depends upon one or more automated data processing systems.

The importance of information then flows both from the management role and the special orientation of human service organizations. The manager is respon sible not only for communicating with other individuals in the organization and serving as communications link, but also for structuring communication patterns in the organization. This role has been discussed above with respect to interpersonal communications. But written communications are equally important as they record, transmit and are processed in the information system of the organization.

An important task of management becomes the development and implementation of automated information systems to facilitate this process. These systems can have an important effect on overall management. Information and information systems are closely related to management planning and control. Information systems used in these processes are referred to as management information systems. They are specially designed subsystems that make use of organizationally derived data for management planning and control. They often summarize data from other subsystems that are relevant to management and correlate information about clients with information about finances.

Management information systems can provide a wealth of information to human service organizations, relating to: the pattern of service delivery, the acquisition and consumption of current resources, monitoring service characteristics, and reporting to funding agencies.

At the broadest level of planning, information systems can provide data on the attainment of organizational goals and policies and assist in long-range planning. At the operational level information systems can assist in determinations of eligibility and claims for reimbursement and help choose among alternative treatments.

Since human service organizations need so much data today for determinations of eligibility and claims, the introduction of automated systems may become an important priority in many organizations. These automated systems can be very effective in minimizing duplication of information-gathering through client interviewing and in generating required reports. Of course, their success depends upon the cooperation of agencies requiring reports and the careful design of the information-gathering process. Important issues of confidentiality are involved. Automated systems may eliminate some jobs and cause the redesign of others. Since a large portion of the work done by human service organizations involves data collection, effective use of information systems may free resources for other tasks, including direct service delivery.

2. What Is an Information System?

An information system is a mechanism for collecting, storing and processing information. The term can be used very broadly to describe the general way in which information is used in a particular organization. Or it can be used to specify a particular manual or automated system.

The advent of the computer has given greater priority to the formalization of information systems. While it is true that all organizations process information, often these processes are not well documented and occur independently. The capability of the computer for sorting and transforming data results in much greater attention given to relationships among information processes in organizations and an emphasis on integrating systems.

In fact, every organization must process information, or what is referred to more technically as data. Data are the facts and figures which allow organizations to move forward. To the extent that such information is quantifiable, it has much greater potential for analysis. This becomes particularly important when management seeks to use this information for decisionmaking purposes. It also facilitates automated processing. Using standard formulae, computers can calculate individual budgets for persons on welfare. They can determine eligibility based upon assets. They can add columns of figures for billing purposes and issue the appropriate claims.

Data processing may be defined as recording and transforming data into useful information for certain defined purposes. It can involve several different logical operations such as selecting, sorting, and mathematical calculation. The advantage of computers is their ability to perform many operations on data in a relatively short period of time at low cost. This allows for many applications in the human services. Once recorded, data can be retrieved as often as needed. This can greatly simplify many processes. In food stamps, computers can be used to establish an individual's eligibility, either by calculating on the basis of figures provided, or figures previously stored for another purpose. In public assistance, they may be used to ensure that the same individual has not been employed during the same period by certain organizations. In child welfare, the computer may track down missing parents. In medicaid, it may be used for establishing eligibility, determining benefit level and processing payments.

While information storage, retrieval and transformation are familiar concepts, it may be useful to set forth the distinct steps in data processing.

Steps in Data Processing

1. Data is recorded. In automated systems this requires that a file be created within the memory of the computer. Then the information is coded in the proper form and entered either by punched cards, typing into a terminal or sometimes using a tape that has been prepared by another computer.
2. Data is recalled. Once data is in the memory of a computer, it can be brought into the active part of the computer for processing.
3. Data is processed. Sometimes the data is merely recalled and printed out. More often, some operation is performed. Only certain categories of data may be selected or selected categories may be compared. Sometimes more complicated operations take place. Mathematical formulae may be used to transform the data.
4. A report is generated. Based upon the processing of data, a report is produced.

The results of automated data processing are everywhere. Utility bills, bank statements and payroll checks are typically produced this way. And the Internal Revenue Service monitors returns using data processing. More and more the clerical, computational and research activities carried on in the human services rely upon data processing. Many states are in the process of automating their social services, income maintenance and medicare systems and finding ways to combine their operations.

3. Client-Based Systems

A client-based system is a series of records providing information about individuals who are recipients of services provided by an organization. Typically human service organizations use these records to: 1) establish eligibility and benefits; 2) process payments and claims; and 3) evaluate individual progress in response to treatment. These records are an integral part of the operation of many human service organizations.

In some organizations, such as income maintenance centers, almost all the time and effort of employees is spent working with these records.

First, clients are interviewed. Then information is recorded. Next, eligibility and benefits are established by applying certain rules and formulae. Then benefit payments are processed. And finally eligibility and benefit levels are monitored over time.

In human service organizations which devote themselves to treatment, such as community mental health facilities, particular emphasis may be given to records about the outcome of treatment. But the functions of eligibility deter mination and payment must also be carried out and are part of the individual's record. Organizations which depend upon third party reimbursement, particularly health care facilities, must keep extensive records.

Not too long ago virtually all of these sytems were manual and were localized in a particular office. But because of the burdens on service delivery organizations in obtaining reimbursement and the efforts to institute greater control at the state level, the tendency to introduce automated systems has increased. Most hospitals and many other service delivery organizations have instituted automated systems for billing and reimbursement practices. Statewide systems of medicaid and medicare reimbursement have also developed. In addit ion, statewide systems have developed for the determination of eligibility for income supplements and food stamps and associated social services. A number of states are moving toward the development of systems which will handle several of these different programs simultaneously.

Automated systems can provide significant advantages. They can avoid duplication in record keeping and save costs in the storage and maintenance of files. If, by entering a client's name, a worker seeking to establish the client's eligibility can obtain information about the client which has already been verified, the task of establishing eligibility is greatly simplified. And time can be saved in recording and verifying information. Particularly when dealing with clients who are eligible for a number of benefits, the savings can be enormous. A problem which sometimes arises in such a system concerns the confidentiality of information and ensuring that access to client information is secure. However, such protections can be built into the system.

A second savings of automated systems can be in processing claims. An automated system can automatically generate bills and claims based upon the client's record, which provide treatment costs and identifying information. Similarly if information on treatment and outcomes is maintained, specialized reports can be generated which provide insight into the effectiveness of various treatments.

The savings which automated systems permit by avoiding duplication of information are a major stimulus behind current efforts by many states to establish links among information systems covering income maintenance, food stamps, and social services. Avoiding duplication in the generation and inputting of data can provide important economy. If a common data base could be established, individuals could establish their eligibility for several programs based upon the information supplied once and updated when needed. This cuts down on staff time and minimizes the opportunities for error. Secondly, the integration of the different systems will allow for greater coordination. Individuals who are eligible for more than one program can be notified. Those who are incorrectly receiving duplicate benefits can be identified also.

4. Designing and Implementing Automated Systems

The development and implementation of an automated client data processing system involves a complex process of interaction among line staff who will use the system and data processing professionals. Usually a project team is established, consisting of data processing professionals and those who will use the system. The process requires extensive documentation of existing information needs and the design of appropriate methods and procedures for transforming the information system to an automated one.

Again, in the implementation phase, the computer professionals and the line staff must work together to make the system work. Depending upon the capabilities of the in-house computer staff, both in time and expertise, outside consultants are often involved in such design and implementation efforts. Often the techniques of the systems analyst will point up aspects of the manual procedure which can be improved. The process of documentation and work flow analysis often illuminates areas of duplication and overlap.

But the role of the line staff cannot be overemphasized. They intimately understand the purposes of the data collection efforts and the uses to which they will put the data. The managers, of course, have a special responsibility to ensure that the design of the data processing system will yield the type of summary reports that they will find useful in performing the managerial function.

The process of design and implementation of a new automated information system is a long and complicated one, yet several distinct phases stand out. The first step is the selection of the study team and the announcement of the project. The next step is to delineate the specific information needs that are to be met by the system. What decisions could it affect? What information is currently gathered? What information is needed? The next step specifies performance criteria. In specifying these criteria, care should be taken to state them in quantitative terms so that the success of the system can be measured at a later time. Next the detailed design of subsystems takes place. This usually involves developing program descriptions, system flowcharts, input and output record layouts and a program flowchart. The next step involves the identifica tion of alternate equipment configurations. Then the alternative configurations are evaluated and one is chosen. An implementation proposal is developed and approved.

In a client-based system the data base consists of records of individuals who are served by the system. Since the system is only as good as the data base, care must be taken to produce an accurate data base. This involves, first, an interview process for obtaining information from the client. Next, a procedure is necessary for recording the information, followed by a procedure for verifying the accuracy of the information. Finally, the information must be placed in the data base. In automated systems it is possible for an individual obtaining information from a client to place it directly into a file, but ordinarily a two-step process is used, at least in the development phase, when the system is first being established. During the first step, the information is recorded and coded. During the second step, the information is placed in the data file.

A critical element in establishing the data base is deciding what informa tion will be placed in the file and designing the form that will be used to record the information. Of equal importance is deciding on the processes of verification that will be used and the steps by which the information will become part of the data base. Because of the tremendous capabilities of automated systems for processing information, the importance of obtaining an accurate data base cannot be overemphasized. Mistakes in creating the data base will result in mistakes in processing the data.

In designing the individual record, care should be taken to gather information that is needed and usable and to avoid gathering and storing unnecessary information. Of course, this rule is particularly important in large systems such as statewide systems which may have records for millions of individuals.

The content of the record reflects the purposes for which the record is being used. If the goal of the record is eligibility, the emphasis will be on identifying data and information about personal assets. Typically, a client will be asked to provide the name or names that are used, address, citizenship, date of birth, marital status, Social Security number, and ID number if one has already been assigned. In addition, any individuals who have legal responsibilities for the individual applying for assistance must be identified. Another major category of information involves current benefits from other government programs, including child care, medical care and education. The applicant must give detailed information about current and potential income and other assets.

The second stage of a client-based system is the establishment of eligi bility and benefit levels. This involves standard calculations, applying certain criteria established by regulation. An automated system can be constructed in such a way that these criteria will be automatically applied, once the basic data has been supplied. This is a great advantage in avoiding the mistakes that result when individuals make these calculations and apply regulations, often inaccurately. Additional cross-checking may be carried out automatically to ensure that determinations are consistent with the individual's other benefits.

The third aspect of the operation of a client-based system is the periodic reexamination of the benefit levels of individuals. Changes in benefit levels can result either from a change in the status of the individual or a change in the regulations for computing benefits. In the latter case the automated system can be programmed to carry out these calculations and directly change benefit checks. Where the status of an individual has changed as a result of other benefits, these changes can also be made automatically. Where an individual's assets or circumstance have changed, they must be placed into the data base and then adjustments in benefit level can be automatically made. The automated data system results in the elimination of much error and miscalculation built into a system which relies upon the calculating ability of individual employees.

A central problem in designing an automated system is determining the scope of that system. For human service organizations that operate independently in delivering services, this is not a major problem. An organization such as a hospital, nursing home or mental health facility would retain individual records for each individual who receives services. At a minimum, such records would retain basic treatment and cost data to allow for billing. The extent to which the automated system should contain treatment and outcome measures is sometimes a difficult question often involving cost considerations.

Another concern in the design of client-based systems is access and confidentiality. The information about clients, particularly if it involves treatment and response to treatment, may be highly confidential. The danger in placing this information in a computer file is that it may be difficult to limit access to those who need to know and who will not abuse the information. While security measures are possible to protect this information from unauthorized use, they must be carefully designed.

A special issue arises in the design of very large systems. Many state agencies are currently creating integrated systems to combine medicaid, income maintenance, and social services. In a recent court case a group of child care agencies in New York City bought legal action which limited the information they were required to provide about their clients for use in a statewide system. A careful calculation needs to be made regarding the benefits to be realized by combining these systems and the possible costs in making the system too large and unwieldy.

In conceiving of this overall design, attention must be given to the unique reeds of each operational unit and the prospects of overloading a system. Some delineation of subsystems is necessary with the eventual development of a common data base that can be drawn upon. A distributed data base can approach the advantages of a unified data base for certain purposes, while it retains the benefits of the independent nature of separate data base subsystems.

5. Management Information Systems

While client-based information systems are valuable for operations they also provide an ideal way for management to obtain feedback about organizational operations. This applies to first level supervisors who may want to keep track of the caseloads of those they supervise and to higher level executives in large organizations who may want to summarize data to predict future financing needs. In fact, the entire range of management planning and control efforts within an organization can be served by a management information system. These include strategic planning concerns such as setting organization goals and making projections for the future; managerial control functions, including budgeting and planning for new units and locations; and operational control functions, such as quality control and financial and personnel control.

In the design of a management information system (MIS), the first task is to define which managerial goals are to be furthered by the system. The next task is to investigate the extent to which currently available information should be supplemented to further those goals. While it may be desirable at times to revise information gathering practices as a result of management needs, available information should be used first.

In assessing the goals of such a system and the available data in the existing systems, the costs of generating reports should be carefully weighed. Ordinarily an MIS generates periodic reports prepared for managers summarizing data contained in the individual subsystems. Also a variety of reports are ordinarily available on a request basis. These reports often cross reference data from several subsystems. Thus, data from the accounting system about costs may be linked with program information to isolate the costs of specific programs and their outcomes.

While, in an ultimate sense, linking costs with services provided and their associated outcomes is the goal of most human service managers, often it is difficult to make these comparisons directly. Managers must often be satisfied with intermediate data. Cost comparisons may be possible between two different locations. Summary data on the amount of services may be provided. How well did preliminary decisions made about eligibility hold up over time? How long did it take to process the eligibility of such and such an individual? Another associated usage is the ability to prepare reports which may be required by superiors or funding agencies about the level of services provided.

Management information systems are dependent upon the information bases which support them. Thus the information system of an organization must be related to its own functions and environment. In the human services, the client-based information system described above, together with budgeting and accounting systems, form the data base upon which management information systems draw.

MIS reports can be viewed as reports required by higher levels in the organization, above the service delivery level. Ordinarily they are summary reports, combining information from individual records in a form that is useful to those operating at the higher levels of the organization. In order to understand the relationship between client- based records and possible MIS reports, consider the system described below, based upon a mental health facility.

Mental Health/Mental Retardation (MH/MR) Organization Reports List*

I. Reports to the State and County
   A. Intake and Proposed Service Plan (MH/MR): Registers entering patients with the county office MH/MR (monthly).
   B. Service Rendered Report and Invoice (MH/MR): Listing of treatment rendered to each patient by date, modality, and therapist discipline (monthly).
   C. Monthly Service Report: Information on admissions, discharges, and services rendered to catchment area and non-catchment area residents according to four target groups (children, adult, geriatric, mental retardation).
   D. Semiannual Summary Report: Frequency distribution of selected demographic variables on four target groups.

II. Reports to the Federal Government
   A. NIMH Monthly Patient Load: Census count on patients in drug programs.
   B. NIMH Inventory: Reports yearly statistics on admissions, treatments, movements, costs, etc. (annually).
   C. Continuation Grant: Statistics on caseload representativeness and treatment breakdowns (annually).
   D. Financial Inventory: An analysis of caseload for potential first and third party sources of revenue (annually).

---

*Reproduced with permission from James Sorenson and Michael J. Elpers, "Developing Information Systems for Human Service organizations," in Clifford Attkinson et al., eds., *Evaluation of Human Service Programs* (New York: Academic Press, 1978)

III. Reports to Management
   A. Population Report: Admissions, movements treatment and
       location of treatments by individual clinics and other treat-
       ment settings.
   B. Poverty Report: Percentage of admissions at or below cur-
       rent definition of poverty (family income by number of de-
       pendents), by census tract (periodically)
   C. Delayed Treatment Report: Average elapsed time between
       intake, proposed treatment plan and first treatment ren-
       dered for each treatment team and service (on request).
   D. Source of Referral Report: Frequency distribution of
       sources of referral by treatment teams and services, accord-
       ing to age, diagnosis, etc. (on request)
IV. Reports to Line Staff
   A. 90-day No-show: A listing of patients not seen in the past 90
       days.
   B. Open Case Listing: A listing of all currently open cases
       withinformation tailored for each of the following recipients
       (weekly).
       1. To Patient Coordinator: A listing showing the location
           of each patient, when, where, and by whom last seen
           and discharge status (sorted alphabetically within treat-
           ment team).
       2. To Team Administrator: A listing showing the current
           census of the team. Listing shows treatment-related in-
           formation (when, type of treatment, by whom ren-
           dered, sorted alphabetically by name, age, race, sex,
           address, etc.).
       3. To Emergency Room: Demographic and treatment re-
           lated variables on all patients currently being seen at
           center, used for referral and treatment decisions
           (sorted alphabetically).
       4. To Therapist: A listing showing all cases under care,
           used for information about effort and for correcting
           computer's files (sorted alphabetically by therapist).
       5. To Data Analyst: Computer Information Section—a
           listing showing admission and treatment information;
           used in the correction of data input.
V. Reports of Management Information Services Division
   A. To Computer Information Section
       1. Error Report: Lists all input documents rejected or
           flagged by computer for possible errors (weekly).
       2. Error Deck: A deck containing duplicates of cards re-
           jected by the computer (weekly).
       3. File Status Report: Technical data for the Management
           Analyst on the state of the data base.
       4. Admissions Report: A report on all previous admissions
           for each intake, the census tract, and all other patient

matching identification—to detect all non-apparent readmissions (daily).

5. History Listing: Identifying variables on every patient ever seen at the Center, showing present status, admission date, identifying variables, when, where, and by whom last seen, sorted alphabetically and by case number (weekly).

B. Operations Research Section
1. Treatment Activity Records: A set of cards comprising the previous week's encounter activities (weekly).
2. Cohort Data: Card output containing demographic variables on a cohort of admissions. Also cards for every treatment encounter of members of the cohort (quarterly).
3. Other Reports: (as requested).

C. To Patient Accounting Section
1. Weekly Transactions: A listing of treatment records submitted the previous week. Listing contains all information necessary for patient and third party billing. Records listed are those that have passed card edit (weekly).
2. Late Transactions: Same as above, except that it contains only those cards that have failed previous edits and have been corrected (weekly).
3. M.A. Eligibility: Listing of patients who are not currently eligible for medical assistance but appear eligible by virtue of income and number of dependents (periodically).
4. Daily Admissions: A list of previous day's admissions.
5. Open Case Listings: Demographic and treatment information used for billing and monitoring caseload (sorted alphabetically).

D. Reports to Research and Evaluation Section
1. Drop-outs: List of patient drop-outs, according to age, race, number of and types of treatments, for each treatment team and for each therapist (on request).
2. Missed Appointments: A listing of patients with missed appointments, containing selected patient characteristics (on request).
3. Other Summary Reports: (on request).

F. Reports to Medical Records Section
1. Missing Document Report: A listing of patients missing one or more intake documents (monthly).
2. Missing Item Report: A listing of which intake items are being omitted by which therapist.
3. Open Case Listing: Case listing showing demographic and historical information on each current patient:

used to respond to information requests from outside
agencies when legal and appropriate (sorted alphabetically by name).

First look at Category IV Reports to Line Staff. This is the basic information given to the line staff about the individuals under their care. This
includes a report to the team administrator, who may be viewed as the
first line supervisor. Now look at the reports generated by Category III:
Reports to Management. These reports summarize what is happening to
the total population in the facility, broken up by treatment unit. The
adminstrator is given critical information which allows for a comparison of
the services provided at different locations. The delayed-treatment report
provides an indication of delay in initiating treatment, which may be a
particularly troublesome problem in this facility and needs to be reviewed
periodically. Reports in Categories I. and II. are for state and Federal
agencies, and probably are built into the funding requirements. These are
similar to management reports, though not used for the management of
the organization itself. Category IV. comprises reports to the computer
information section, operations section, research and evaluation section,
and medical records section to ensure that records are updated and maintained on an accurate basis.

The variety and interrelationship of these reports should clarify the
close relationship between client records and management uses of these
records. The actual choice of management reports depends upon the
managerial control concepts in use. Management reports focus on service
levels, the outcomes of services and the costs associated with both. The
effective manager will be able to compare the services and costs among
different subunits. Thus a manager will be interested in the number of
consultations provided, the number of appointments kept and the number of individuals processed for intake. The manager will also be interested in the impacts of these services, as reflected in changes in the
individuals served, though sometimes this information may be difficult to
obtain. Examples are the number of welfare recipients who become partially or fully self-sufficient, the number of those admitted for mental
health reasons who are discharged and remain healthy over some given
period. Often special program evaluation techniques, which are discussed
in the next chapter, will be needed to assess impact data.

Another level of analysis involves evaluating service delivery and outcomes according to cost. Cost information by and large derives from the
budgeting and accounting subsystems. The calculation of benefits and
costs has been described in Chapter 10. Among the data sought are the
unit costs of providing services and achieving specified outcomes, the

types of fees generated by services and the comparative success of different organizational units in minimizing costs and maximizing revenues, as well as achieving cost effective outcomes.

MIS reports help management determine how well the organization is functioning and the extent to which goals are achieved. An important focus of MIS systems is cost information provided by the accounting subsystem. To the extent that cost information can be associated with specific program outcomes, which are themselves quantified, the usefulness of the MIS reports increases. In order for such a system to work, the accounting system must accumulate cost information based upon organizational units which are responsible for identifiable programs. Unless such information is available, the value of the MIS is limited.

While MIS provides an important tool for effective managerial control, the problems of tying costs to actual services and relating these services to client outcomes often requires the special techniques referred to as formal program evaluation. These formal techniques will be discussed in the next chapter along with how information systems are used by management in the process of program evaluation.

Selected Bibliography

Attkinsson, Clifford et al., eds. *Evaluation of Human Service Programs.* New York: Academic Press, 1978.

Barnard, Chester. *The Functions of the Executive.* Cambridge: Harvard University Press, 1938.

Cohen, S. et al. "New Ways of Looking at Management Information Systems in Human Services Delivery", *Evaluation and Program Planning*, 1979, Vol. 2, pp.49-58.

McLeod, Raymond, Jr. *Management Information Systems.* Chicago: Science Research Associates, 1979.

Mintzberg, Henry. *The Nature of Managerial Work.* New York: Harper and Row, 1973.

Chapter 12.

Program Monitoring and Evaluation

1. What Is Program Evaluation?

Recall the importance of information feedback in the *Program Evaluation and Review Technique (PERT)* described in Chapter 4. Program evaluation in that context referred to the feedback of information to the project manager about goal attainment. In fact, the term program evaluation is used more generally to refer to the process by which information is obtained by managers about the success of specific programs. In this sense, program evaluation is closely related to the monitoring function of management and the ability of the manager to obtain feedback about the progress of specific programmatic activity.

The sources of feedback that a manager obtains should be diverse. The manager should have a web of contacts that allow for the flow of information about program operations. These contacts should include both individuals at all levels of the hierarchy and those who are served by the organization or who are in a position to know about the organization. Particular attention should be given to the development of specific quantifiable indicators of goal attainment. The advantage of such indicators is that they provide regularly available, objective, baseline data for measuring tomorrow's performance against yesterday's performance. Sometimes the selection of these indicators is difficult. If the indicators are not carefully selected they can distort goal attainment. Yet a system of objective performance indicators is a valuable, indeed invaluable, aid in promoting goal attainment in human service organizations. Where a formal system is established to provide management with such information on a regular basis, the system can be referred to as a program evaluation system. A program evaluation system in this broadest sense, then, is a mechanism for charting the progress of an organization toward goal attainment by reference to a number of performance indicators. Its use in this broad sense should not be confused with more limited uses of the term program evaluation.

A second use of program evaluation which will be considered below involves experimental or modified experimental techniques for testing the impact of a particular program.

A third use of the term program evaluation is to refer to the process for evaluating specially funded government programs for improving social conditions. The rise of this usage is associated with the Great Society Programs, many of which funded local community organizations for obtaining certain specified goals, such as community development, improved educational attainment and job development and training. Often the Federal government provided funding to a number of projects, based upon written proposals which stated the objectives of the program. Gradually the term "funded program" came to be used more generally to refer to a project "funded" by a governmental or private grant.

As the Federal government and other agencies continued to provide funding for projects aimed at improving social conditions, the demand arose for demonstrating that these projects were successful and for differentiating among the more and less successful projects. Program evaluation was the term used for the process by which the success of projects was determined. In this sense program evaluation is a process for determining if a particular project, supported by grant funds, is adhering to the agreed upon project plan and attaining the results originally projected. Many funding processes require quite specific evaluation components, including in some cases the requirement of independent evaluation by an outside individual or group.

Since many human service organizations depend upon funded programs, the use of program evaluation in this sense is particularly important. The central task of program evaluation is to decide what the goals of programs are and then to go about determining the extent to which these goals are being met. This may seem like a simple task, but it is deceptively simple. For, in the real world, the goals of programs are often elusive, especially for human service programs. In fact, different groups often have in mind different goals for a program which they jointly sponsor.

2. Measuring Goal Attainment

As stated above, however, effective management in the human services depends upon goal specification. More and more managers are making special efforts to specify organizational goals. In funded programs, both the funding agency and the recipient are likely to direct considerable resources to ensuring that goals are specified.

Let us suppose that reasonably precise goals have been specified for a particular program. How does someone serving in a program evaluation capacity begin finding out whether some goal or set of goals has been reached? Sometimes the answer is obvious. If the goal of a school lunch program is to feed 1000 inner-city youths an adequate meal once a day during the school week, the confirmation of that goal would be the certified record of the contractor that those lunches have been delivered to the specified number of children at the specified quality level. But what if you were asked to determine if this particular program actually improved the school performance of these children, the original intent of the program? How would you determine program impact?

This simple example illustrates the difference between service goals, regarding the level of services to be provided, and outcome goals, regarding the impact of the program. This distinction is a critical one for personnel engaged in program evaluation. The issue of goal attainment is made more complicated by the fact that the measurement of service levels is often far easier than the measurement of outcomes and impacts of particular programs.

The measurement of goal attainment, whether in terms of services delivered or program outcomes, relies upon performance indicators. A performance indicator is an objective measure for determining whether a particular goal has been met. Performance indicators are not always obvious. Indeed, the development of appropriate performance indicators can be difficult for human services.

Distinctions can be made among performance indicators which provide measures of services provided (workload indicators), measures of program outcome (effectiveness indicators) and measures of services or outcomes related to costs (efficiency indicators). To clarify this distinction, refer to the figure below.

Performance Indicators in the Human Services

	Services Provided	Outcome	Output/ Input
EDUCATION	sessions completed	reading level	cost/change
RECREATION	benches repaired	satisfaction	cost/change in satisfaction
HALF-WAY HOUSE	residents served	% not returning within 12 months	cost/ rehabilitated person

The distinction between services provided and program outcomes and their associated performance indicators is central to an understanding of program evaluation. Ordinarily indicators of services provided are easier to define. Often indicators of outcome must be especially developed and may involve more elaborate program evaluation techniques using experimental or quasi-experimental designs.

Program evaluation may also be concerned with the process through which goals are attained. In process evaluations the central concern is how a particular program has been developed and implemented. However, process evaluation can be critical in understanding why a particular program does not succeed. Without an analysis of how the program was carried out, the program evaluation information may be useless in trying to redesign the program or suggesting alternative approaches. Another perhaps even more compelling reason for process evaluation and its associated examination of the input side of the program is that the quality of services is often determined in part by the character of the inputs. For example, the quality of therapy will in part be determined by the quality of personnel delivering the therapy.

While the tendency is to emphasize the outputs of programs, whether as services delivered or impacts, often evaluations do not detect differences in these areas. This is particularly true when evaluations are over short periods of time, when changes in outcomes may not be observable. Process evaluations which look at the implementation of programs and the organization of services as well as the quality of services may yield far more information that is relevant to management decisions about altering programs or adjusting them as they develop. These formative evaluation needs may in fact be much better served by process evaluations.

Since performance indicators have been identified as the heart of a system of program evaluation, much of the task of establishing a system of program evaluation must involve finding measures of performance. In measuring goal attainment, a variety of methods for collecting data are available. Carol Weiss, in *Evaluation Research,* suggests a number of different methods of collecting such data. They include interviews, questionnaires, observation, ratings, psychometric tests of attitudes, values, personality and norms, institutional records, government statistics, tests of information, skills and the application of knowledge, projective tests, situational tests, diary records, physical evidence, clinical examinations, financial records and documents. The use of these data sources is critical in developing and operationalizing performance indicators.

3. Data Collection Techniques

Interview data has a variety of applications in program evaluation. Interviews can be conducted with service recipients, service providers, and third parties. The advantages of this source of data are that it provides direct contact with the affected parties and the opportunity to gain much knowledge about a program in a short period of time. The major disadvantage is that the data may not be systematic and is subject to both the bias of the interviewee and the selective perception of the interviewer. Interview data is particularly important in process evaluation. If the data collection takes place after the fact, it may be the only available source. An example would be interviewing directors of community mental health centers to find out how the centers were set up and how their funding sources were coordinated.

When a study commences after events have occurred or when gaining direct access is too difficult or costly, interviews with those familiar with the process will be a good substitute for questionnaires or direct observation. Interviews can also be used to gather information from recipients or third parties about the quality or outcome of services. On the basis of such interview responses, an indicator of the quality or outcome of services could be used to compare services. For example, residents of a half-way house could be interviewed before they entered, when they left and one year later to arrive at attitudinal ratings relating to their personality, self-concept and attitude toward work.

Questionnaires are another source of data. They provide a mechanism for dealing more efficiently with a wider range of responses than interviews. They are particularly useful in measuring quality of service as judged by recipients, or in some cases by experts. Most training programs routinely request a rating of the quality of the training program. Where experts are familiar with a range of programs, for example, graduate programs in law or public administration, they may be asked to provide comparison ratings.

Questionnaires can also be used to measure program impact. For example, if a half-way house attempts to move its clients into full- time, self-sufficient jobs, a questionnaire distributed to individuals one year after leaving the half-way house might elicit information necessary to determine program impact in terms of level of employment and earnings. Questionnaires can be used to obtain systematic data about the process of establishing a program. A survey sent to a number of directors or other officials in a selected service delivery organization, such as a community mental health facility, might elicit basic data about the size, growth, and clientele of these centers. Another use of the questionnaire is in developing measures of perceived quality of service and in measuring attitudinal changes. Psychometric tests are often available for measuring attitudes, values, personality and norms. These tests make use of scales independently developed, which can be used to demonstrate change resulting from some program.

Direct Observation is another source of data for program evaluation.

Although it is costly to collect and requires a decision to collect data before the observed events occur, it can be a particularly valuable source of data. Because of the difficulties of gaining access to events and anticipating where to be at the right time, participant observation is a more frequently used technique. Participant observation avoids the necessity of introducing an outside observer into an ongoing real-life situation. Unfortunately, however, it increases the likelihood of observer bias.

Direct observation may also be used to gather data on program quality. Skilled observers can determine the extent to which a training program or a community mental health facility is well run. Sometimes observers may rely upon a standard rating procedure agreed upon prior to the actual observation. Direct observation is also useful as a way to gather data on program impact, although its use is more difficult here. Since program impacts often occur over a period of time, direct observation may be quite costly and sometimes impractical.

Institutional Records provide a good source of data, particularly when looking for indicators of change in the operation of programs and their impacts. Standard categories of data may be retained to document service levels. A community mental health facility might have information about the number of individuals receiving counseling and the nature of the counseling. Records would indicate the length of stay of individuals and the types of services administered, including frequency of counseling and other assistance. They would also indicate level of turnover in the client population. Where a training program is directed at bringing about institutional change, indicators should be selected for baseline tasks.

Government statistics provide a wealth of information about the ways in which jurisdictions and agencies actually operate. These data can provide a source of before-and-after comparisons of the effect of programs. By comparisons with government statistics, quality of services may be compared to comparable institutions.

Information Tests and other devices for establishing level of knowledge provide an important basis of judging the impact of training programs on individuals.

All of these various sources of data can contribute to a total system of program evaluation to provide information on quality of service, program outcomes, and the process of carrying out particular goals. An example of the establishment of such a system with respect to the program of Neighborhood Health Centers, established by the Federal government in the late 1960s, is described below. The Federal government sought to devise a system which would allow for comparisons among a number of different programs.

Evaluation of Neighborhood Health Centers

In the late 1960s, the Office of Economic Opportunity (OEO) sought to evaluate the Neighborhood Health Centers, created under the *Economic Opportunity Act of 1964*. Section 222(a)(4) of that act enumerated the factors to be included in a comprehensive health services program. By 1967, 33 OEO-assisted comprehensive health service projects were funded. A method for evaluating their success was considered critical. A program evaluation was conceived and put into operation.

The purposes of the Neighborhood Health Centers evaluation system was to address the following questions: 1. Are the program concepts being implemented? 2. Who is being reached, and just as important, who is not being reached? 3. What services are being provided and to whom? 4. What is the quality of the services? 5. How much do they cost? 6. How does the community accept and relate to these services? 7. What changes have occurred in the use of services?

With this series of questions as the basis, the next step in the development of the evaluation system was the delineation of a series of data-gathering activities in order to obtain information about these factors. A range of activities were developed involving a mix of independent staff oversight and data gathering by the facilities themselves.

Because of the small number of facilities involved, *site appraisal reviews* were selected to allow for direct observation by central office staff of funded projects. While such activities are a costly means of carrying out program evaluations, they have the advantage of allowing for independent review of the headquarters staff to see if the funded projects are really delivering what they are supposed to deliver. In this particular case, site appraisal reviews concentrated on the process of implementation, relationships to existing agencies and back-up health facilities, and degree of community involvement. These are the sorts of activities that would be difficult to capture using alternative methods such as surveys.

In order to assess the impact of these facilities on the quality of health in the area served by the new facility, *baseline health surveys* were conducted. These surveys measured patterns of health services utilization, including rates of hospitalization and disability. They also measured the extent and quality of preventive care. Attention was also given to establish baseline measures of quality of care among the new centers and comparable centers already in exis tence. This allowed for documentation of changes that occurred in the operation of the neighborhood health centers as they developed.

In addition, *ongoing data* about the utilization of services was gathered.

A standardized operational data system was developed which was useful to both local management and to federal monitors making comparisons among different localities. These operational data included cost data.

Finally, a series of *limited studies* were conducted of specific projects. These focused on whom the project was reaching, with what services, with what acceptance, and with what impact on family functioning.

As the program evaluation system became institutionalized a comprehensive systematic approach to data collection was developed, both to provide program evaluation information to the funding agency and to provide operational infor mation to the project leadership. This formalized information system fulfills five basic information needs: (1) patient utilization and registration, (2) management monitoring and control, (3) billing, (4) program evaluation and planning, and (5) research and reports. Basic input data are collected and retained so that the same data is not collected twice. All input data are processed and maintained in basic form so they can be combined as needed.

The key to a system of program evaluation is the actual collection of data. Ordinarily a series of forms are devised and responsibility for collecting and checking data is delegated. In this particular operational system, three different forms were used: a family registration form, an individual registration form, and a health services encounter form. The health services encounter form, reproduced below, is a sample of the type of information that is retained.

The health services encounter form illustrates how simplicity, clarity, and brevity combine to allow for accurate data collection. The simpler the form, the less likely are mistakes in recording data. During the introduction of data collection forms, an orientation or more formal training program is usually used. Especially during the initial period of implementation, a system for checking inaccuracies is a necessity.

In addition to the collection of raw data, a program evaluation system often includes the use of summary indicators of the quality of program aspects. A major rationale for the neighborhood health centers was to eliminate the fragmented care that poor people were forced to accept, because of the diverse locations at which individual members of the family received services. The indicator, comprehensiveness of care, was intended to measure the success of neighbor hood health centers in alleviating this problem. As the figure below indicates, the 33 neighborhood health centers were rated on the overall comprehensiveness of service based upon a number of factors including the range of medical, dental, and lab treatments available. Obviously, in collecting and pooling data, elements of subjectivity and error arise. The purpose of this particular example, is not exhaustive but it suggests how the elements of program evaluation work to provide systematic data on the operation and impact of programs. The difficulties in implementing such systems revolve around

DRAFT VERSION[*]

Name of NEIGHBORHOOD HEALTH CENTER
(City, State)

HEALTH SERVICES ENCOUNTER FORM

| 1 | 2 | 3 | 4 | | Y |
CENTER NO.   FORM NO.

(Space for Patient I.D. Card Imprint)
or

1. **Patient's Name** _____

2. **DATE**: _____

I.D. No. _____

3. **SITE OF ENCOUNTER:**
   1 = Center   2 = Home   3 = Hospital   4 = Other (specify) _____   5

4. **APPOINTMENT STATUS:**
   1 = Appointment   2 = Walk-In   3 = Direct Referral   4 = Other (specify) _____   6

5. **HEALTH CARE PROVIDER:**
   01 = Physician-Adult
   02 = Physician-Child
   03 = Obstetrician/Gynecologist
   04 = Psychiatrist
   05 = Other Physician Specialist
   06 = Psychologist
   07 = Nurse
   08 = Other Medical Provider
   09 = Dentist
   10 = Dental Hygienist
   11 = Other Dental Provider
   12 = Social Worker
   13 = Family Health Coordinator
   14 = Other Provider (specify) _____   7 8

6. **TYPE OF ENCOUNTER:**

   Medical Care
   01 = Episodic (including emergency)
   02 = Initial Health Assessment
   03-07 = Preventive Care:
   03 = Prenatal
   04 = Post partum
   05 = Well-Baby
   06 = Immunizations only
   07 = Other Preventive Care (specify) _____
   08 = Mental Health Care
   09 = Family Planning
   10 = Long-Term Care Management
   11 = Other Medical Care (specify) _____

   Dental Care
   21 = Initial Assessment
   22 = Preventive
   23 = Restorative
   24 = Other Dental Care (specify) _____

   30 = Social Service
   40 = All Other Care (specify) _____   9 10

7. **SELECTED ITEMS OF SERVICE AT THE CENTER:**
   Check circles for as many items as are applicable and enter numbers as appropriate for items 28 and 29.

A. X-rays (ordered)	B. Laboratory Tests (ordered)	C. Contraceptives	D. Dentistry	E. Prescriptions (issued)
11- ○ - Chest	17- ○ - Hematology	23- ○ - Oral Pill Rx Issued	26- ○ - Dental X-rays	30- ○ - Prescription Pharmaceutical (excluding oral contraceptive Rx)
12- ○ - Barium Swallow, Upper GI, Sm. Bowel Series	18- ○ - Urinalysis	24- ○ - I.U.D. Fitted	27- ○ - Prophylaxes	
13- ○ - Gall Bladder	19- ○ - Bac. & Para.	25- ○ - All Other	28- ☐ - Extr. (no. teeth)	31- ○ - Non-Rx Pharm.
14- ○ - Barium Enema	20- ○ - Serology		29- ☐ - Fillings (no.surf.)	
15- ○ - I.V. Pyelogram	21- ○ - PAP Smear			
16- ○ - Other X-rays	22- ○ - Other Lab Tests			

8. **EXTERNAL REFERRALS REQUESTED:**   Check as many as are applicable.

A. Direct Health Service	B. Indirect Health Service
32- ○ - Hospitalization	40- ○ - Food Stamps
33- ○ - Medical Consultation	41- ○ - Employment
34- ○ - Medical Management	42- ○ - Welfare
35- ○ - Dental Consultation	43- ○ - Medicaid/Medicare Registration
36- ○ - Dental Management	44- ○ - Vocational Rehabilitation
37- ○ - X-ray Procedures	45- ○ - Social Service
38- ○ - Laboratory Test	46- ○ - Other
39- ○ - Other	

Form 10-68

---

*Reproduced with permission from D.M. Nitzberg. "The Basic Neighborhood Health Center Data System. *American Journal of Public Health*, 1971, vol. 61, p. 1294-1306.

the problems of specifying easy and relatively error-free data and then evaluating the data and recycling that information into the management process. Thus the conceptually straightforward aspects of program evaluation become potentially confounding as managers attempt to design and make operational such systems.

Comprehensiveness of Care*

Center	Urban/ rural	Affiliation	Scoring MD range	Dental	Lab--x-ray	Quality
1	U	Med school	3	1	2/2	A
2	U	Med school	3	1	2/2	A
3	U	Med school	3	1	2/1	A
4	U	Med school	3	1	2/2	A
5	U	Med school	3	0	2/2	A
6	U	Med school	3	0	2/2	A
7	U	Hospital	3	1	2/2	A
8	U	Hospital	3	1	2/2	A
9	U	Hospital	3	1	2/2	A
10	U	Hospital	3	1	2/1	A
11	U	Hospital	3	0	2/2	A
12	R	Hospital	1	1	2/2	B
13	U	Hospital	2	1	2/1	A
14	U	Hospital	3	0	2/1	A
15	U	Health Dept.	3	1	2/2	A
16	R	Health Dept.	1	1	1/1	B
17	U	Health Dept.	3	1	2/2	A
18	U	Health Dept.	3	1	2/2	A
19	U	Health Dept.	3	1	2/1	B
20	U	Health Dept.	2	1	2/2	B
21	R	Health Dept.	1	1	-	B
22	R	Health Dept.	2	1	2/1	A
23	U	Community Corp.	3	1	2/1	B
24	R	Community Corp.	1	1	1/1	B
25	U	Community Corp.	3	1	1/1	B
26	U	Community Corp.	3	0	2/1	A
27	U	Community Corp.	2	1	2/2	B
28	R	Community Corp.	1	1	2/2	-
29	R	Community Corp.	1	1	2/2	B
30	R	Community Corp.	2	1	1/1	A
31	R	PPGP	2	0	2/2	A
32	R	PPGP	3	0	2/2	A
33	U	PPGP	3	0	2/2	A

*Reproduced from Gerald Sparer and Joyce A. Johnson, "Evaluation of OEO Neighborhood Health Centers," in Herbert C. Schulberg and Frank Bakers, eds., Program Evaluation in the Health Fields, Vol. II, P. 308, N.Y.: Human Sciences Press, 1979).

Often the line manager must rely upon others to design systems. Indeed the line manager may often find out to his or her consternation that a system of program evaluation has been designed which may be difficult to implement, provide little useful information, and not be used in the decision process. These types of systems give program evaluation a bad name. In fact, unless the system actually works and those who use the system see that it works and affects major management decisions, chances are that the system will fall into disuse quickly.

4. Quasi-Experimental Design

Having considered the uses of program evaluation, with particular reference to their applications to funded programs, managers should also be aware of the more formal use of experimental and modified experimental designs in program evaluation. Social science research has long used experiments as a way of increasing our knowledge about human affairs. Program evaluations using experimental and modified experimental modes are being increasingly used to extend our knowledge about the impacts of social programs.

The logic behind a true experimental design is classic and impeccable. If two groups of individuals are selected who are in all respects similar, except that one group is given the experimental treatment, after a period of time if there is a difference between these groups, the difference can be attributed to the experimental treatment. For example, if two groups of welfare recipients are alike in all respects, except that one group is allowed to keep a certain percentage of additional income earned, and at the end of several years that group has become partially self-sufficient while the other is totally dependent, the change can be attributed to being able to keep the additional income. Or if two groups of mentally ill patients are in all respects alike except that one group is receiving a new drug, and after five years the group receiving the drug has a much better recovery rate, the change can be attributed to that drug.

The trick, of course, is how to ensure that the two groups are alike in all respects. How can we be sure that the group which has become less dependent did not have more initiative to start with? How can we be sure that the group receiving the new drug was not a healthier group to start with? The key to the true experimental design is the selection of equivalent groups and this hinges upon a process of random selection of the groups from some larger group or population. Where random selection is not possible, equivalent groups are selected by some other method, approximating random selection. A frequent approach is the matching of two groups by ensuring that they are alike in their critical qualities.

As a specific example of a program evaluation using matched groups, consider the Upward Bound program. This is a Federally funded program designed to identify able high school students who would be unlikely to go to college because of low socioeconomic backgrounds or related problems of self-image. Often these difficulties are associated with a perceived inferior status of certain ethnic groups.

Typically, students are identified in their sophomore year of high school and are given special enrichment work at local colleges during the school year and during the summers. Special efforts are made in placing students. In addition, they are given small stipends. Enrollment in college terminates formal involvement with Upward Bound.

In order to evaluate the success of the program, the researcher chose to "match" Upward Bound students with their older brothers and sisters. He found that by and large these students did better than their siblings, but that their siblings often did well, too. Since the individuals selected by the program, although they did come from homes with below average deprivation, were not, by and large, the severely deprived individuals that were the original target of the program, their older siblings also had a high rate of college attendance.

In an effort to undertake a more detailed analysis of the benefits and costs of this program, Garms calculated the difference in expected lifetime earnings between the participants in Upward Bound and their own sisters and brothers. In the figure below, which lists the benefits and costs from the individual's point of view, the difference between discount rates of 5% and 10% differentiates net benefits from net losses. Note that the net benefits are the present value of lifetime benefits. From this example, you can see how important the discount rate is in determining the return on investment.

Would you view Upward Bound as a good investment? Walter Garms concludes that: "From the economic viewpoint, Upward Bound is at best a marginal program, and the justification for its continued existence must be sought in presumed benefits which are not accounted for here."

Some of the most telling criticisms of the application of benefit-cost analysis to public sector problems emphasize the inability of the analysis to deal with certain political dimensions of policy. Others have argued that these political aspects can be incorporated in a benefit-cost analysis if appropriate devices are used. While in theory it may be possible to accomplish this goal, in practice it presents formidable obstacles. It is difficult to quantify the political benefit of gaining or losing the support of some social group, or the aesthetic benefits of a park when compared to a parking facility. In fact, once benefit-cost analysis moves out of the economic marketplace, where all benefits and costs have a monetary value, it becomes less exact. Benefit-cost analyses are finding increasing use in the human services, especially where costs and benefits can be specified in monetary terms. Its limitations must, however, be clearly understood when it is used for decisionmaking purposes.

ANALYSIS OF THE UPWARD BOUND PROGRAM*

Benefits and Costs from Society's Viewpoint

	White		Nonwhite	
	Male	Female	Male	Female
Discount Rate 5%				
Benefits				
Lifetime income differentials (after taxes)	$7,020	$4,777	$5,491	$7,942
Cost Differentials				
Upward Bound Cost to Government	$1,811	$1,798	$1,922	$1,919
Upward Bound Cost to Colleges	260	257	275	275
Cost of Education	1,057	872	1,424	1,028
Extra Living Costs	260	225	379	267
Total Costs	$3,388	$3,152	$4,000	$3,489
Net Benefits	$3,632	$1.625	$1,491	$4,453
Discount Rate 10%				
Benefits				
Lifetime income differentials (before taxes)	$1,066	$1,560	$ 598	$2,609
Cost differentials				
Upward Bound Cost to the Government	$1,737	$1,724	$1,845	$1,842
Upward Bound Cost to Colleges	249	247	264	264
Cost of Education	852	724	1,183	856
Extra Living Costs	215	185	312	220
Total Costs	$3,053	$2,880	$3,604	$3,182
Net Benefits	-$1,987	-$1,320	-$3,006	-$ 573

*Reproduced with revisions from Walter Garms, "A Benefit-Cost Analysis of the Upward Bound Program," Journal of Human Resources, 1972, p.216.

Other types of quasi-experimental designs which are quite common include time series designs when an experimental group is compared to itself at different period of time and static state designs in which correlational analysis is used to discover potential links among different attributes in a cross section of individuals at a particular point in time.

The relaxation of conditions governing the use of comparison groups must be considered very carefully. At some point the groups are so different that the function of the comparison group is undermined. Thus, many program evaluators would not consider static state design within the purview of formal program evaluation. To others, before-and-after comparisons of one group without a comparison group fall outside of formal program evaluation. Wherever the line for formal program evaluation is drawn, these information sources can and should be used in what has been referred to more broadly as managerial program monitoring.

Program evaluation, ranging from basic monitoring involved in effective management, to the systematic approaches characteristic of the evaluation of funded programs, to the more sophisticated approaches of social science research is a potent managerial tool. The level and sophistication of the approach must be commensurate with the problems being solved. Increasingly, human services managers are being called upon to understand and use a variety of program evaluation techniques.

Selected Bibliography

Attkinsson, Clifford C. et al., eds.. *Evaluation of Human Service Programs*. New York: Academic Press, 1978.

Caro, Frank, ed. *Readings in Evaluation Research*. New York: Russell Sage Foundation, 1977.

Epstein, Irwin and Tripidi, Tony. *Research Techniques for Program Planning, Monitoring and Evaluation*. New York: Columbia University Press, 1977.

McGrundy, W. B. *Program Evaluation: A Conceptual Tool Kit for Human Service Delivery Managers*. New York: Family Service Association of America, 1979.

Rossi, Peter and Williams, Walter, eds. *Evaluation of Social Programs*. New York: Academic Press, 1972.

Schulberg, Herbert and Baker, Frank. *Program Evaluation in the Health Fields*. New York: Human Services Press, 1979.

Weiss, Carol. *Evaluation Research*. Englewood Cliffs, New Jersey: Prentice-Hall, 1972.

Wildavsky, Aaron. "The Self-Evaluating Organization," in *Speaking Truth to Power*. Boston: Little, Brown, 1979.

Chapter 13.

Survival in Hard Times

1. Toward a Developmental Approach

The knowledge and skills that have been considered in the preceding chapters are important to every human service manager. Managers who master communications, understand project planning, and can use the techniques of program evaluation will be able to function more effectively. Yet the key to managerial success is the adaptation of these skills and techniques to the circumstances in which a manager operates.

A manager needs to have clear goals and a means for reaching those goals. An important consideration is the relative emphasis on maintenance and change. Should a manager focus on doing the present job better or is there a different way of doing that job? Should the manager focus on improving the functioning of the existing staff, or should attention be focused on recruiting, developing and coordinating a new staff?

The need to acquire resources in a non-market situation shapes the pressures on the human service manager. The relative focus on maintenance and development goals is affected by the stability of funding sources. To the extent that the organization funding sources are stable, the tendency is to continue to support maintenance strategies, carrying out the current service goals and improving efficiency where possible. To the extent that funding is unstable, either rising or falling, developmental goals will predominate. Accordingly the manager will spend more time eliminating old programs and developing new programs and implementing these changes.

The 1960s and 1970s must have appeared to many human service managers a period of great testing and stress. New organizations were created under extreme pressures of time to respond to the new initiatives of the day. The rules that organizational entrepreneurs had to follow were changing daily. If it wasn't new federal legislation, it was new agency regulations.

As an example of these changes, consider the area of employment and training. Originally established under the *Manpower Development and Training (MDTA) Act of 1962*, employment and training programs were federally funded and administered by the Department of Labor to focus on retraining those displaced by automation. The *Economic Opportunity Act of 1964* introduced new employment and training programs for the unemployed and the hard-to-employ. This focus generally was adopted by the Department of Labor. But with the enactment of the *Comprehensive Employment and Training Act of 1973* to replace MDTA, the approval of programs was turned over to newly established local prime sponsors. In 1979 Private Industry Councils (PICs) were created and when the *Jobs Partnership Act of 1982* replaced CETA, the PICs assumed a new importance, seemingly replacing the prime sponsors in the policy area. In addition the state governments were given an expanded role.

The size of the organization the manager is heading and its autonomy from other organizations is critical in determining the appropriate mix of strategies. The autonomous manager operating at the head of a small community group will have much greater discretion than a manager heading a small unit in a county welfare department which is part of a state administered system subject to federal regulations. The manager's discretion is also affected by the client groups served, and the larger public demands and socioeconomic conditions. A successful manager knows when to exercise discretion and the risks in using that discretion.

The period of the 1960s and 1970s also presented great opportunities for growth. The entrepreneurial manager of community based organizations could reap tremendous success, first, directly through the community action programs under the Office of Economic Opportunity, and then through a variety of specific programs in education, employment and training and housing. By 1981, an era of natural contraction was heightened by the new Reagan administration budget cuts, presenting a particular trying time for the managers of human service organizations.

2. Environmental Uncertainty and How to Cope

The importance of developmental goals to human service organizations stems from their vulnerability in an uncertain environment. Just as the individual entrepreneur must be sensitive to changes in the market, the human service manager must be sensitive to changes in governmental programs. Perhaps the most distinctive aspect of human service organization operations is this vulnerability to the vagaries of public and private funding.

Strategies which strengthen the responsiveness of the organization will ultimately serve well. In the short run, the manager must have "antennae" tuned to anticipate change. This means staying active in professional circles and cultivating individuals with access to information within government. It also suggests a strategy of diversification so that the organization is not solely dependent upon any one funding source.

The specific strategy, of course, depends on the area of autonomy in which an individual manager operates. A community-based organization may have wide latitude, with a board of directors willing to pursue a variety of funding sources. A public agency such as an elementary school or a day care facility may have a narrow operating sphere. Yet even these organizations may search for additional functions and resources in times of adversity.

During the 1960s and 1970s, with the proliferation of social programs, the innovative or developmentally-minded human service manager could apply for a variety of funding from Federal, state, and local agencies. But many successful managers not only apply for new programs, but anticipate them and help develop them. Just like a business entrepreneur seeks to recognize new markets, the human service entrepreneur seeks to recognize and develop new programs.

A focus on new and developing government or privately funded programs is not sufficient, however. The developmentally-minded human service manager must be alert to new political positions that are developing among influential political leaders. These positions will have important effects on existing and new programs. Active political involvement is often helpful, both in terms of personal contacts and organizational affiliation. Despite the need for professionalism, many leaders of human service organizations find themselves deeply involved in politics and even political campaigning. The manager of a drug rehabilitation program or an employment and training project would be well advised to stay in contact with local political leaders. Their help can often be invaluable in encouraging support from governmental sources.

Political positions often reflect broad social movements and changing social problems. If these social problems and movements are understood, changes in political positions and government programs can often be anticipated. In fact, identification with a social movement may lead to new sources of support when those social movements gain power.

The administration of President Reagan with its emphasis on private sector initiatives may result in new opportunities for the growth of human services within the corporate setting or with the explicit support of corporate philanthropy. It is also likely that a new emphasis will be placed on services that are supported by user fees.

Finally, the human service manager will do well to watch overall economic conditions. In bad economic times, the resources available for human service programs will diminish. This is what happened during the Great Depression when state and local governments were no longer able to support welfare programs. In better economic times, government and private sources more readily fund human service programs. Of course, times of great need may also spawn great social movements. The New Deal rose on the ashes of the Great Depression.

The manager of human service programs should be a prophet and a gambler. To stay abreast of the environmental uncertainty that characterizes the human services is a task that requires great adaptability. Leadership requires developing organizational resilience and creating conditions that allow for adaptation to a changing environment.

3. Effective Implementation Through Self-Analysis

A manager selects goals and the means to attain them carefully. Consideration must be given to the goals which emanate from above and are suggested from below. The extent to which a manager's goals are realistic will affect organizational success. But selecting goals is only the beginning; the daily work of the manager focuses on goal implementation.

The manager should plan daily activities carefully to ensure that they will result in the attainment of the stated goals. To help you plan your own activities a guide to self-analysis is provided below. It is based upon a number of studies of managerial behavior which categorize the activities of managers. These patterns of interaction are defined by the daily occurrences within a manager's day. Activities may be classified in various ways. Following most studies of its kind, the form below emphasizes work by oneself at a desk, telephone contacts, informal meetings, including brief face-to-face encounters, and formal meetings. A record of these activities over time presents a picture of the manager's interaction pattern. While an accurate sampling of an individual's behavior should take place at intervals over an extended period, perhaps as long as a year, for purposes of self-diagnosis a week or two should suffice. Record your activities for a time period of at least 7-10 days, using the form provided below.

Having kept a diary of your patterns of interaction for a number of days, you are ready to analyze these patterns. In analyzing your patterns, no fixed rules exist. Scholars have noted considerable variation in the patterns of individual managers, depending upon the level held in the organization, type of organization, managerial function and personal characteristics. In assessing your patterns you should measure them against your own goals and abilities to achieve them. Pay particular attention to three aspects of these interaction patterns: (1) How much of your day is spent in each of the major categories of contacts? (2) How well do you spend your time within each of those categories? (3) Are the purposes to which you are devoting most of your time likely to result in the attain-

INSTRUCTIONS FOR COMPLETING INDIVIDUAL LOG OF MANAGERIAL CONTACTS

The individual log of managerial contacts is a self-analysis tool designed to allow you to better understand the use of your time and allocate it more effectively. For purposes of simplification, you are asked to deal with blocks of time during the day, at 2-hour intervals. For each of these 2-hour intervals, from 8 in the morning to 6 in the evening, you are asked to indicate the amount of time spent at desk work (DW), and the number of telephone contacts (TC), informal meetings (IM), and scheduled meetings (SM) that you take part in. Then you should indicate the approximate percentage of the 2-hour period that is devoted to each of these activities. The purpose of each activity should be indicated from among the following: policymaking (POL), informational (INF), bargaining and negotiation (BAG), authorization (AUT), implementation (IMP), counseling subordinates (COU). Try to select that category which represents the main focus of the activity. More than one category may be used.

Individual Log of Managerial Contacts   Name:

                                            Date:

Time	DW	% Purpose	TC	% Purpose	IM	% Purpose	SM	% Purpose
8-10								
10-12								
12-2								
2-4								
4-6								

ment of your goals? Let us consider each category in turn.

Relative Time Among Major Categories. Since you are analyzing your work patterns in two-hour blocks of time, you may average the percentages in each category (DW, TC, IM, SM) for each day to achieve a daily average of percentage of time spent in each category. Then the daily averages may themselves be averaged to obtain an overall percentage of time spent in each category. The total figures should add up to 100%.

While some romantic notions of managers may place them behind their desks, approving written requests or engrossed in deep thought and long-range planning, evidence indicates that the higher up in the organization, the less time is spent in written communication. The managerial task is an active task. Time in excess of 25% involved in desk work may indicate a failure to interact sufficiently with staff. Since a manager is the leader of a work group and often extends his activities beyond the work group, the central task of management is to achieve effective work group coordination. This means that the manager must spend a good deal of time in interactions with others which are fairly open-ended. He or she must be flexible enough to allow for the inevitable reactions and adaptations to everyday events. In general, managers spend over half of their time in informal interaction and discussion, encompassed in the categories of informal meetings (IM) and telephone contacts (TC). As managers move up the ladder there is a tendency to make greater use of the scheduled meeting. This results partly from the greater number of individuals with whom the manager may interact, including several levels in the organization and external contacts. A study of chief executives found that close to 60% of their time was spent in formal meetings. Our study of human service organizations has indicated a tendency to proliferate meetings, even at lower levels.

Your interaction patterns should reflect a balance between accessibility to other individuals and attention to the paper flow in the organization and formal meetings. One of the ways of paring your job to more manageable proportions, particularly if you find yourself working too many late nights is looking at the distribution of activities. Which category seems to be using too much time? Then take measures, for example, as suggested below to limit your time commitment in that area.

Increasing Efficiency Within Categories. Desk work can be reduced by streamlining the approval process or delegating approval, in both instances reducing the paper flow. The more effective use of secretarial support can also be helpful here. Telephone calls can be reduced by setting your own limits on the amount of time spent on individual calls. Polite responses are possible for cutting short "talky" associates. If calls interrupt other activities, a secretary formal meetings. Since being in the presence of the top leadership is a sought-after commodity within the organization, a dynamic is set into motion to increase the demand for meetings. While formal meetings are important in performing maintenance functions and also confer status, frequent, non-productive meetings can also undermine the effectiveness and the espirit within an organization. While managers at the higher levels spend large proportions of their time, close to 60% in formal meetings, this figure is probably an upper limit. Managers at the middle and lower levels of the organization should try to limit this portion of their day to substantially less.

The Purpose of Activities. While it is important to analyze your interaction pattern, it is probably even more important to evaluate whether the activities are directed at your managerial purposes. Before calculating the importance of the various purposes as listed in your diaries, how would you rank these respective purposes in assessing the needs of your particular managerial job. Rank the following purposes from 1 to 6: policymaking (POL), information exchange (INF), bargaining and negotiation (BAG), authorization (AUT), implementation (IMP), and counseling subordinates (COU). After you have stated your preferences, compare these with the actual preferences expressed in your diaries by adding the number of instances of each purpose over the course of the sample time period. How similar are your own projections to the actual findings of your diary? Are there changes you could make in your patterns of contacts to achieve a rating closer to your view of the importance of the respective purposes?

Before making any precipitous changes, be certain that they are truly justified. While many managers believe that they should spend much of their time making decisions, most studies indicate that somewhere between 5%-20% of their time is spent in decisionmaking and policymaking. A surprising amount of time is spend on information exchange. Most managers could probably benefit from more time spent counseling subordinates. In the human services, many managers find they spend an inordinate amount of time authorizing actions by others. This results from the excessive bureaucratization of the human services and is an area where many managers can effecuate real savings for themselves and their organizations.

4. Strategies for Creating a Responsive Organization

The uncertainties of the environment of human service organizations will be weathered best by an organization which has been built and reinforced with change in mind. This requires attention to both the individuals in the organization and the way they are organized. They should be individuals who are comfortable with change and who understand the environment around them. They should have the professional, social and political connections to the outside world that will alert them to developing changes. It is important that the organization have a feeling of dynamism and anticipation, rather than reaction and discouragement when changes arrive, as they always do.

To the extent that organizational subunits can be given discrete tasks for which they are responsible, their members will gain a sense of accomplishment and responsibility and seek new tasks. A sense of commitment to the organization and its goals is important, as is a sense that the organization stands for something and is worth preserving. Encouraging professional activities and leadership in professional organizations on the part of staff will help keep the organization in the shifting mainstream.

An acceptance of change within the organization should also be encouraged. Reorganizations should not be viewed as the end of the world. They should be accepted as part of organizational life. At certain times new individuals will be brought into the organization and others will leave, as the scope of programs changes. Efforts should be made to avoid bureaucratic rigidity by forming task forces and developing matrix forms of organizations in which individuals participate in more than one work group for different purposes. Individuals within the organization should be given a sense that they should be alert to new trends and that providing leadership in initiating new projects will be rewarded by advancement and support from above.

In the final analysis, of course, the responsiveness of an organization to change will depend in large part upon the quality of leadership, especially the vision of the top management. Managers who understand the present and can anticipate the future are best equipped to provide the leadership to ensure that their organizations will survive.

As the writing of this book concludes, the human services are facing a bleak future as government funding continues to decrease. The years ahead will be more trying than ever. But the ability to adapt to changing circumstances has always been the mark of the human service manager who survives and the organization which prospers. Good management and flexible management will be needed now more than ever.

Appendix A:

The Human Services

In order to understand the operations of the human services, it is useful to focus on specific program clusters. These clusters often have a common legislative foundation, coordinated government supervision and a group of common purposes. Each program cluster will be discussed from both historical and organizational perspectives. The focus will be on describing both their origin and their current administration. While in many of these areas there is a strong tradition of support for local control, the influence of Federal legislation and funding in determining their development and organization has been profound. The program clusters to be described are: 1) social security and public welfare; 2) child welfare; 3) education; 4) employment and training; 5) health; 6) mental health; 7) corrections and 8) care of special groups, including the aged, the handicapped and veterans.

1. Social Security and Public Welfare

Public assistance and social services constitute both the most visible and vulnerable foundation of the human service system in the United States. These programs aimed initially at the destitute have been broadened over the years. In the middle of the seventeenth century in both the colonies of Massachusetts and Virginia, local governments established relief based upon the *English Poor Law of 1601*. For those defined as needy and without family resources, the community assumed responsibility, providing either residence in an almshouse or income support for those with outside residences. The colonial administrations soon after began assuming responsibility for those without residence in a town. Where pauperism was associated with idleness, however, legislatures passed laws authorizing jailing, whipping, indenturing, and in a few instances, workhouses to earn relief.

During the nineteenth century the ranks of the needy expanded, as large immigrations and cyclical economic conditions left groups of unemployed. Following the *English Poor Law Amendments of 1834*, which channeled poor relief through almshouses, the states began authorizing local governments to establish similar institutions to be run on a contract basis by a private superintendent. These institutions served as residences for the indigent sick, the feebleminded, the mildly insane, the crippled and able-bodied poor. But soon the deplorable conditions in many of these institutions led to a movement toward the state administered asylum which became the basis for the state activities in mental health. These state asylums which were generally run independently by a Board of Trustees continued to develop throughout the nineteenth century, stimulated by the increasing demands of an industrialized society, increased immigration and the millions of individuals displaced and debilitated by the civil war and its aftermath. While many of these institutions began under reformist leadership they generally became more conservative giving up their claims of effective rehabilitation to assume a more custodial orientation. The Association of Medical Superintendents of American Institutions for the Insane was formed in 1844 to further the interests of directors of those asylums serving the mentally ill. In 1863, the Massachusetts legislature created the first statewide organization, the Board of State Charities to provide advice to state government and serve as a coordinative mechanism. During the remainder of the century most states established advisory and administrative boards in the area of social welfare.

But as a counterbalance to the activities at the state level, throughout the country and particularly in the larger cities, mutual aid societies and other private charities developed to deal with the problems of the needy. Beginning in 1877 Charity Organization Societies (COS) were formed in city after city by the wealthy upper-classes to provide coordination among the local charity institutions and to direct resources to the most needy and discourage pauperism. By the end of the nineteenth century, a two-tiered system of welfare had developed, where the first line of defense was the voluntary local society. The state asylum was considered a last resort for the most desperate cases.

During the early part of the twentieth century a movement developed to help poor children which was bolstered by the Children's Bureau authorized by Congressional action in 1912. The Children's Bureau was instrumental in developing a whole range of child health and welfare services. In 1911 Missouri adopted the first widow's pension law. By 1919 thirty-nine states had followed their lead. By the beginning of the New Deal, pensions for the needy aged had also been adopted by most states. Child welfare, mental health and care for the aged became differentiated from the general social welfare problem.

It was during the Great Depression and its aftermath that poverty was addressed directly by the Federal government. Faced with growing numbers of people without jobs, and an inability of state and local governments to provide the funds necessary to support them, the Federal government passed the *Social Security Act of 1935*. The basis of the act was the concept of social insurance, that workers should be protected through a contributory plan against social uncertainties such as unemployment and old age. But in its comprehensive form, the act formed the basis not only of a system of unemployment insurance and old age pensions, but of public welfare and social services. The major provisions included: 1. Continued Federal responsibility for providing work to employable persons; 2. Federal grants to the states to help them provide assistance to unemployable persons, mainly needy old people and dependent children; 3. A Federal-State system of unemployment insurance, supplemented by a work program for those who exhausted their benefits; 4. A Federal system of old age insurance; 5. Federal grants to the states to help finance public welfare and child welfare services; 6. A commitment to other forms of insurance in the future, including health insurance.

A three member Social Security Board administered the provisions of the act and eight bureaus were created, including most prominently the Bureaus of Public Assistance, Unemployment Compensation, and Federal Old Age Benefits.

The provisions assisting states in the development of a program to aid unemployable persons, such as the aged and dependent children were really an afterthought to the act itself. It was believed that these provisions were transitional until the contributory system was able to have its effects in the long run. The program to aid dependent children, however, became the basis of the most important public welfare program in the United States. By providing 50% Federal matching support to states, it provided the basis for a program that became increasingly attractive to the states. Although only 10 states established programs in the first year of operation, eventually all states participated. By 1938 all states had established programs for the aged. Federal funding provided an attractive incentive to the states, but also presaged a continuing controversy over Federal/state relationships. As the program developed over the years sometimes elaborate federal regulations were promulgated to govern the determination of eligibility and the operations of the program. Another provision of the same legislation authorized grants to help finance public welfare and child welfare services. These funds greatly facilitated the development of state welfare services.

The close link of these welfare programs with the social insurance concept of the contributory pension system has had a profound impact on the American system of cash support. From the beginning grants to the indigent were to be but one aspect of a larger program of social insurance.

And a major aspect of that program was to be a contributory pension system, and unemployment system. This link becomes quite important in later years when the Social Security Fund is tapped for programs of a social welfare nature and then in turn, is bolstered by direct Federal funds.

In 1939, under Reorganization Plan I, a major step toward coordinating social welfare programs was taken with the creation of the Federal Security Agency. The Social Security Board, the Office of Education, the United States Employment Service, the Public Health Service, the Civilian Conservation Corps, the National Youth Administration and the Works Progress Administration were all placed under one roof. In 1946 the Social Security Board was changed to the Social Security Administration and the Children's Bureau was placed within it. Then in 1953, the Department of Health, Education and Welfare (HEW) was created and the Federal Security Agency merged into it. As of 1957 the major operating agencies were: the Public Health Service, the Office of Education, the Social Security Administration, the Office of Vocational Rehabilitation, the Food and Drug Administration and St. Elizabeth's Hospital. The department also had nine regional field offices. After considerable pressure from the National Education Association, a major supporter of President of Jimmy Carter, the Carter Administration created a separate Department of Education and renamed HEW the Department of Health and Human Services.

In commenting upon the relationship between public welfare programs and the social security pension program, another program deserves mention, that of veterans' pensions. Following the first World War, Congress enacted a program of pensions for veterans. This program has survived to the present day and represents a formidable source of cash payments to individuals which some observers view as a special form of welfare.

These three cash assistance programs along with the Railroad Retirement Fund were in place before the Second World War and gained in scope and size throughout the next decade. By the 1980s they constituted a substantial portion of the total Federal budget and experienced some crises. During the 1960s the rolls of Aid to Families with Dependent Children (AFDC) increased dramatically as did the costs associated with them causing substantial burdens on state and local governments and giving rise to pressures for the federalization of the welfare system. During the 1970s, largely as a result of cost-of- living adjustments to the Social Security system, the fund supported by contributions became endangered and the expenditures began exceeding revenues. The growth of cash benefit programs during the 1970s is set forth below.

During the 1960s, the myth of the temporary nature of public welfare in American society, which had been implicit in the *Social Security Act of 1935* was layed to rest. With great fanfare, President Kennedy's Secretary for Health, Education and Welfare, Abraham Ribicoff, announced a new program to increase Federal support for social services which was to reduce the long-term costs of welfare. While the effect was to greatly bolster social services to the poor, the AFDC rolls nevertheless increased dramatically. In the period of 1962-67 the AFDC load rose almost 50% from 3.5 million to 5 million. In 1967 the result was Congressional pressure for increasing work incentive programs and child care programs to remove people from the welfare rolls.

No. 522. Federal Outlays for Income Security Benefits: 1970 to 1980

[For years ending June 30 except, beginning 1977, ending September 30]

CATEGORY AND PROGRAM	BENEFITS (mil. dol.)							PERCENT	
	1970	1975	1976	1977	1978	1979	1980	1970	1980
Total benefits	60,209	139,638	164,639	179,656	195,376	215,453	271,216	100.0	100.0
Cash benefits	48,567	109,585	128,763	138,299	147,909	161,732	200,307	80.7	73.9
In-kind benefits	11,641	30,053	35,875	41,357	47,467	53,721	70,909	19.3	26.1
Cash benefits	48,567	109,585	128,763	138,299	147,909	161,732	200,307	100.0	100.0
Social security	29,045	62,469	71,362	82,406	90,738	101,000	118,559	59.8	59.2
Old-age, survivors insurance	26,267	54,839	62,140	71,271	78,524	87,572	103,227	54.1	51.5
Disability insurance	2,778	7,630	9,222	11,135	12,214	13,428	15,332	5.7	7.7
Federal employee benefits [1]	5,768	13,986	16,703	18,426	20,677	24,768	27,846	11.9	13.9
Military retirement	2,849	6,242	7,296	8,216	9,171	10,279	11,920	5.9	6.0
Civil service retirement	2,518	6,825	8,055	9,257	10,570	12,011	14,719	5.2	7.4
Veterans benefits [1]	5,340	8,140	8,734	9,562	10,151	11,026	11,797	11.0	5.9
Disability dependency and indemnity	2,974	4,680	5,154	5,722	6,159	6,745	7,434	6.1	3.7
Veterans pensions [2]	2,255	2,739	2,859	3,113	3,239	3,521	3,585	4.6	1.8
Public assistance	3,868	8,672	9,803	10,059	10,921	10,601	13,720	8.0	6.9
Supplemental security income	(X)	4,081	4,440	4,618	5,234	4,782	6,411	(X)	3.2
Maintenance payments [3]	3,868	4,592	5,363	5,442	5,687	5,819	7,308	8.0	3.7
Unemployment insurance [1]	2,886	12,221	17,612	12,928	10,251	8,977	17,918	5.9	9.0
State programs	2,793	11,958	16,413	12,339	9,368	8,585	15,211	5.8	7.6
Railroad retirement	1,586	3,034	3,445	3,768	3,988	4,218	4,722	3.3	2.4
Other programs [1]	74	1,063	1,105	1,149	1,183	1,142	[4] 5,745	.2	2.9
Disabled coal miners	7	945	988	964	1,048	984	1,776	(Z)	1.0
Assistance to refugees	50	70	67	134	85	112	226	.1	.1
In-kind benefits	11,641	30,053	35,875	41,357	47,467	53,721	[5] 70,909	100.0	100.0
Food and nutrition [1]	1,590	6,468	7,714	8,278	8,500	10,205	13,978	13.7	19.7
Food stamps	551	4,357	5,266	5,028	5,133	6,443	9,117	4.7	12.9
Child nutrition [6]	481	1,956	2,396	3,176	3,267	3,385	4,043	4.1	4.8
Health care	9,576	[7] 21,518	25,896	30,674	36,067	[7] 40,763	[7] 49.989	82.3	70.5
Hospital insurance	4,804	10,355	12,267	14,906	17,513	19,898	24,288	41.3	34.3
Supplementary medical insurance	1,979	3,765	4,671	5,865	7,080	8,259	10,746	17.0	15.2
Medicaid	2,612	6,840	8,325	9,181	10,680	11,701	13,957	22.4	19.7
Military retirees care	181	548	633	721	794	869	966	1.6	1.4
Housing [8]	475	2,072	2,264	2,405	2,900	2,753	5,404	4.1	7.6
Public housing	(NA)	1,312	1,392	1,271	1,701	1,440	1,360	(NA)	1.9

NA Not available.   X Not applicable.   Z Less than .05 percent.   [1] Includes other benefits not shown separately. [2] Includes survivors pensions.   [3] Basically, aid to families with dependent children.   [4] Includes Basic and Supplemental Educational Opportunity grants.   [5] Includes low income energy assistance program.   [6] Includes special milk programs.   [7] Includes medical care for retired Public Health Service officers, not shown separately.   [8] Includes rent and mortgage interest supplements.

Ribicoff's change in the reimbursement rate for social service expenditures from 50 Federal/50 State, to 75 Federal/25 State had dramatic results. It meant that the ratio of Federal support for state support changed from 1-1 to 3-1. If a state maintained its existing effort it would draw triple the amount of aid it had previously drawn. Expenditures for services skyrocketed, though some states like Mississippi were forced to drop their services, because of the combined impact of the Federal requirement that social worker caseloads could not exceed sixty and spending limitations imposed by the state legislature.

Expenditures for social services continued to grow. For fiscal year 1969 they reached $354 million; by 1971, $1.7 billion and by 1972 when a ceiling was placed on further Federal expenditures, $2.5 billion. It is ironical that the Federal program which was sold as a way of reducing AFDC, by 1972 had almost reached 50% of the costs of AFDC itself. Meanwhile AFDC itself had doubled in the previous 3 years, far outstripping its 1962 costs.

The 1972 amendment to the *Social Security Act* which limited social services expenditures to $2.5 billion was refashioned as Title XX of the *Social Security Act* in 1974, establishing five goals for social services: 1) to encourage economic self-support and the elimination of dependency; 2) to achieve and maintain self-sufficiency to reduce dependency; 3) to prevent and remedy neglect, abuse, and exploitation of children and adults; 4) to limit institutional care by providing for community-based, home-based and other less intensive forms of care; and 5) to secure referral and admission to institutional care when other forms of care are not appropriate and to provide institutional services.

The period of the 1960s highlighted by the Great Society programs of the Johnson Era saw major increases in programs supporting dependent children and social services generally. Other legislation created the food stamp program and medical services for the indigent and elderly. Medicare and Medicaid are treated below under health programs. The Food Stamp Program like social service expenditures mushroomed quickly. Originally begun as a pilot program in 1961, it went national in 1964 at a cost of $31 million. Supported by a coalition of social welfare organizations and agricultural groups, it provided an opportunity for locally certified needy persons to buy a given amount of food stamps to expand their purchasing power. The program reached a plateau in 1976 but since 1978 has risen $1.5 billion per year. In 1977 a major change was enacted which provided the stamps free of charge resulting in a massive expansion of the program particularly among the very poor who had previously not participated. An increasing ceiling was set on expenditures at the same time, but the ceiling had to be lifted in fiscal 1980 to accommodate a rise to $8.8 billion fueled by increasing food costs. The Reagan administration has moved to cut back these expenditures. Along with food stamps a number of other food programs exist including the school lunch program, the milk subsidy program and food assistance for women, infants and children (WIC). These programs are handled by the Nutrition Subcommittees of the Senate and House Agriculture Committees.

During the 1970s, in response to the increasing welfare rolls and partly in response to the proliferation of programs, new pressures developed for a greater federal role in welfare. The concept of a negative income tax, consolidating the various grant programs became popular. The failure to establish a Congressional coalition capable of transforming the welfare system, stemmed both from conservative opposition to the increases in Federal responsibilities and the liberal fear of loss of specific programs. One of the results of these discussions, however, was the Federal take-over of several programs originally initiated in the *Social Security Act of 1935*. On January 1, 1974, the Supplemental Security Income (SSI) Program was implemented, under the *Social Security Amendments of 1972*, resulting in a complete Federal takeover of the programs of cash assistance for the aged, blind and disabled. The states continue to administer programs of aid to dependent children on a 50% matching basis with the Federal government and general assistance without Federal assistance to those who don't qualify for other programs. Within these programs there has been a movement for states to take over direct administration from the local governments and as of 1973 only 15 states had locally administered programs. Despite the modest claims for the *Social Security Act of 1935* it has proven a legacy which has remade our approach to cash support for the aged and needy.

2. Child Welfare

The welfare system which developed in the United States during the 18th and 19th centuries included children as well as adults. The Children's Bureau authorized in 1912 gave early recognition to the importance of child health and welfare and is the earliest example of a federal operating agency in the area of social welfare. As the American welfare system developed during the twentieth century, the progressives singled out widowed mothers, along with the aged, for special treatment. This special treatment formed the basis for inclusion within the *Social Security Act of 1935* of the special category of dependent children. The Federal subsidy providing for this category created the necessary incentive for a strong state effort. One result has been the strong association within the American welfare system of the welfare mother and the dependent child.

The concept of child welfare services apart from income support for dependent children is based upon a societal obligation for the health and welfare of children that extends beyond that due adults. Children were indentured out to master craftsmen even before they were placed in almshouses. And once in almshouses, children who were good workers were strong candidates for placement in homes where they would no longer be a burden on the state.

During the middle of the nineteenth century, immigration and industriali zation led to a large increase in the number of dependent children. A growing number of orphanages began to spring up and efforts increased to provide foster homes for displaced children. A pioneer in the foster placement field was Charles Loring Brace who founded the Children's Aid Society of New York. The debate has raged ever since as to the relative merits of home-based care, community- based care and institutional care. In 1975, Title XX of the *Social Security Act* was amended to provide services to individuals in institutions. But amendments in 1977 reflected recent trends to decentralization by limiting Federal support for institutionalized foster care cases. In addition, Federal support provisions were liberalized for those who adopt special children.

In the case of neglected and abused children, developments have been slower. The American reverence for the family and individual rights has been slow to give way to imposing the will of the state on children who are still in the custody of their parents. In this sense the United States was hampered by its inheritance of an English common law tradition giving fathers the legal right to their children, including the right to inflict arbitrary or severe discipline.

Nonetheless, driven in part by a desire to prevent abused and neglected children from becoming criminals, the formation of child protective societies began in New York in 1874. The New York State Society for the Prevention of Cruelty to Children (SPCC) was formed in the aftermath of a well-publicized child abuse case. These societies, working within the legal framework which they helped develop, removed children from deleterious environments whether they were almshouses, prisons or homes. Until the *Social Security Act of 1935* provided for state welfare agencies assuming responsibility for child protective services, they were provided by private voluntary agencies many of which became affiliated with the American Humane Association. In fact even after the passage of the *Social Security Act* many states limited these responsibilities to voluntary child welfare and protective services.

Private voluntary organizations perform a central function in this area and two national organizations, The Child Welfare League of America and the American Humane Association are particularly prominent. The Child Welfare League is a national voluntary accrediting and standard-setting organization established in 1920. The American Humane Association established in 1877 has been involved in the promotion of child labor laws, creation of special shelters, and the promotion of child protective services. In fact, many of its members are the local Societies for the Prevention of Cruelty to Children.

The laws governing child abuse and neglect vary from state to state. In most states children up to the age of 18 are covered though the limit is lower in some states and California has an age limit of 12. The definitions of child abuse also vary, though most focus on physical abuse. All states single out the medical profession as primarily responsible for reporting abuse, but in different states other professional groups such as social workers and school personnel may be given similar responsibilities. In all states the primary agency receiving the report of abuse is responsible to follow through on the case. And all states grant immunity against criminal or civil action for having filed such a report. The *Child Abuse Prevention and Treatment Act of 1974* established a National Center on Child Abuse and Neglect as part of the Office of Child Development, Children's Bureau. This has focused national attention on many of these problems and provided resources for research and technical assistance in this area.

A critical link in all involuntary cases of child care, including both cases in which an abused and neglected child is taken from parents and those in which the parents are superseded because of criminal activities of youth, is the Family Court. The original impetus for creating the family courts was the desire to remove children from the adult courts. The first such system was established in Illinois, in 1899, and within 18 years all but three states had passed legislation creating similar systems. Today serious questions are being asked about how well the system is working and consideration is being given both to limiting the cases diverted from criminal courts and increasing the use of non-incarceration alternatives for youth offenses.

In addition to services aimed at the care of neglected, abused children and youthful offenders, a broader concept of child welfare has found expression in programs such as public health and day care. This progressive tradition of child welfare was expounded by President Theodore Roosevelt who convened the first White House Conference on Children in 1909. By 1912 Congress had authorized the establishment of the United States Children's Bureau. The U.S. Children's Bureau was given broad responsibilities to investigate and report upon matters pertaining to the welfare of children, including such questions as infant mortality and children's diseases, orphanage, juvenile courts and dangerous occupations. The Bureau's activities have had a strong impact on child care practices throughout this nation.

The U.S. Children's Bureau was given responsibility to administer the *Owen-Keating Act of 1916* providing for the protection of child labor. In 1921 it began administering the *Sheppard-Towner (Maternity and Infancy) Act*. By 1927, 47 states had in turn set up child welfare bureaus. Opposition from private charities, the American Medical Association and states' rights advocates prevented the renewal of the *Sheppard-Towner Act*, which expired in 1929. But the concept of child welfare had been further legitimized and promoted.

Title V of the *Social Security Act of 1935* breathed new life into the U.S. Children's Bureau by establishing programs in Maternal and Child Health, Crippled Children's Services and Child Welfare Services all placed under the U.S. Children's Bureau. In 1946 the U.S. Children's Bureau became part of the Social Security Administration and was thereafter referred to simply as the Children's Bureau. Today its original emphasis on research, publication and dissemination of studies about children has expanded to include technical assistance and the administration of major grant programs.

The provision of day care for youth is largely associated in this country with the need to provide support for working women. The first day nurseries, as they were called were established during the first part of the nineteenth century. The idea spread, particularly after the Civil War, so that by 1898, the National Federation of Day Nurseries which was established that year claimed 175 member agencies. It was not until the 1920s that upper and middle class women participated in organized day care, which was recommended as a form of learning and play.

While the Federal government had established a limited number of day care facilities for working mothers after the Civil War, the first large scale government efforts occurred in 1933 under the Works Progress Administration (WPA) and was intended for teachers and related school personnel. During the Second World War, the Federal government once again moved to provide day care to women under the *Lanham Act of 1942*. Between 1942 and 1946, the Federal government spent over $50 million for 3,000 centers in 47 states which were closed at the end of the war. A small number of programs continued under the child welfare provisions of the *Social Security Act*. With the exceptions of the State of California and the City of New York, which created special legislation and funding, publicly supported day care largely disappeared until the mid 1960s.

Many states, had, however, expanded pre-school programs. By 1974 kindergarten programs had been mandated in 14 states and were eligible for state funding in all but two others. And 11 states provided some support for pre-kindergarten programs. Encouraged by liberalized funding and regulations, day care services were provided first for children of past, present or potential welfare recipients under Title IV A and XX of the *Social Security Act*. Project Head Start was a major new program originally administered by the Office of Economic Opportunity and later by the Office of Education to provide compensatory opportunities for children from poor homes. Additional programs specifically aimed at the poor were included in other poverty legislation, including *Title IV-C, Work Incentive Program, Concentrated Employment Act, Manpower Development and Training Act and the Elementary and Secondary Education Act of 1965*.

3. Education

Public education is unlike public welfare in that it is available to all children, rich or poor. Education has been an area that has strongly resisted Federal intervention. The public school system developed during the course of the 19th century within the United States with the formation of public school societies. Toward the latter part of the 19th century and early 20th century the states assumed a role both in chartering and financing the public schools. With the exception of the land grant colleges and the *Smith Hughes Act of 1917*, federal financing and involvement in education was non-existent. During the Second World War a major initiative was passed to help support educational institutions in areas of high concentrations of Federal installations. The *Lanham Act of 1940* and the *Veterans Readjustment Act of 1944* established precedents for federal assistance to education. In the late 50s and early 60s the *National Defense Education Act* became another important precedent. When President Kennedy took office a major priority became education. Despite plans for broad-based aid to education, a revision of the *Vocational Education Act of 1963* was all Kennedy could accomplish.

The *Vocational Education Act of 1963* continued and reinforced the system of vocational education which had been established by the *Smith Hughes Act of 1917*. That system had resulted in specially-designated vocational education schools which took on a separate character apart from the ordinary secondary school. This network at the local level was reinforced by state and Federal agencies which together formed a powerful force in the halls of Congress and which was supported by a number of lobbying groups, such as the American Vocational Assocation.

In the aftermath of Kennedy's assasination and the impetus for the Great Society, President Lyndon Johnson gave the country its first major new aid to primary and secondary education bill since the Smith Hughes Act of 1917 and followed it with aid to higher education. Title I of the In the aftermath of Kennedy's assasination and the impetus for the Great Society, President Lyndon Johnson gave the country its first major new aid to primary and secondary education bill since the *Smith Hughes Act of 1917* and followed it with aid to higher education. Title I of the *Elementary and Secondary Education Act of 1965* was not exactly the general aid to education bill that many had sought, but it did provide considerable funding to school districts around the country, tied to the number of low income students in a district. The passage of the *Elementary and Secondary Education Act of 1965* represented a victory for President Johnson in coordinating a diverse set of executive, legislative and interest group leaders. Before the legislation was submitted a major disagreement between two opposing interest groups, the National Catholic Welfare Conference and the National Education Association had to be reconciled. Other groups which were involved in the legislative process included the American Federation of Teachers, the Congress of Parents and Teachers, the National School Boards Association, the American Legion, the AFL-CIO, the Council of Chief State School Officers and the Council of Great City School Boards. This constellation of actors may be conceived of as a subsystem functioning in the area of national education policy which becomes activated with expanded or contracted membership depending upon the particular legislation being considered. Also these actors maintain contact on an ongoing basis to influence the implementation of Federal policy. Although the educational subsystem is particularly well articulated, similar subsytems can be identified in each of the other program areas under consideration.

Title I of the *Elementary and Secondary Education Act* has provided some interesting precedents in the development of Federal policy toward the states. The provision for independent evaluations of funded programs was a major departure that was to be followed in other subsequent Federal legislation. The controversy over the targeting of programs and the extent to which districts used Federal funds to replace previous programs rather than providing special additional programs of a compensatory nature were important instances of Federal efforts to define a role which still acknowledged the major role of the local educational systems.

Since the passage of the *Vocational Education Act of 1963* and the *Elementary and Secondary Education Act of 1965*, a number of other special programs have been passed at the elementary and secondary level. Among these are the *Emergency School Assistance Act*, the *Education for All Handicapped Children Act* and the *Bilingual Education Act*. These acts provide limited federal funding for programs and require states and local school districts to carry out certain mandates on their own. The Education for All Handicapped Children Act required all states and districts to provide free education for all handicapped children by September 1, 1978. Federal support meanwhile has accounted for approximately 12% of the costs of complying with this mandate. A similar approach in the bilingual education area, adopted by the Department of Education under President Carter, was suspended by President Reagan's Education Secretary Terrell Bell before taking effect. A similar approach of providing funding and adopting regulations that force local districts to incur costs was adopted in the *Emergency School Assistance Act (ESAA)* in the area of desegregation. The issues of desegregation and busing have remained controversial during this period and a series of measures have been passed by Congress to alleviate the burdens placed upon school districts by the courts. While the Federal courts, more so than the Federal bureaucracy have taken the lead in this area, the effect has been to impose considerable costs on school districts. States and local school districts are increasingly restive about this approach in which the Federal government mandates action by states and local districts, while only paying for a small part of the added costs.

For elementary and secondary education the locus of control remains largely at the state and local level. Most individual school units, the SDOs are run directly by the government. Private schools still flourish, however, and in fact have increased, particularly where integration has become a local issue; private schools have provided an option to parents who are not willing to send their children to desegregated schools. In some cities the press of integration in the face of a dwindling white student population had led to the flourishing of private and parochial schools as an alternative to predominantly black schools. An issue spurred by the Reagan administration; has been the support of non-public school through both direct grants and tax deductions.

As at the primary and secondary levels, Federal involvement in higher education has focused on funding, much of which flows to the students directly. The organization of higher education has been and remains different at the service delivery level. While in the Western part of the country the Federally supported public land grant institutions dominate, in the Eastern states, the private colleges remain exceedingly strong, particularly at the level of the most prestigious institutions. Public four-year colleges tend to be run directly by the states, while two-year colleges are often run by the local communities. The state college systems of California and New York are by far the largest and include several levels of institutions. By 1984 all but three states had statewide agencies for coordinating higher education. In some cases they are part of an education agency which ranges across all levels. State regulation of higher education, has been considerably less than that at the primary and secondary levels. In part this reflects differences in funding approaches, and the greater importance of private institutions of higher education.

Several revisions of the *Higher Education Act of 1965* occurred in 1972: (1) The scope of the act was expanded to address a range of postsecondary education including vocational and technical education; (2) A series of approaches to student aid were included, the most important being the Basic Education Opportunity Grant (BEOG), which provided direct funding to qualifed students on the basis of need; (3) The Act provided general aid to institutions of higher education based upon the number of BEOG students attending; (4) The Fund for the Improvement of Postsecondary Education was created to stimulate innovation; (5) Assistance was provided to the states in the planning and development of community colleges and occupational education; (6) The Act emphasized the importance of state governments in comprehensive planning and provided for the designation of postsecondary education commissions; and (7) A National Commission on the Financing of Postsecondary Education was created to study alternatives to the present system. Although several portions of the Higher Education Act were never funded, the effect has been to emphasize and solidify the progress of the states in upgrading higher education and its administration. States generally have a leading role in the area of higher education, both regulating private institutions and administering a system of public universities.

At the initiation of President Jimmy Carter a separate Department of Education was established starting with fiscal year 1979. The creation of the department represented a symbolic victory for the national recognition of education and fulfilled a campaign pledge to the National Education Assocation.

4. Employment and Training

Though today the first governmental efforts in the area of employment and training are believed to have taken place in the early 1960s, particularly the *Manpower Development and Training Act of 1962* and the *Economic Opportunity Act of 1964*, several major efforts in this field were contained in the *Social Security Act of 1935*. Legislation in the areas of vocational rehabilitation and job placement actually predated that Act, while vocational education legislation goes back to the early part of the century.

The *Vocational Rehabilitation Act of 1920* provided grants to the states to assist the disabled in training, guidance and placement. While these provisions were incorporated in the *Social Security Act of 1935*, the *Barden-LaFollette Act of 1943* separated vocational rehabilitation from the Social Security Administration Major changes were made in legislation passed in 1954 to strengthen vocational rehabilitation efforts.

The *Wagner-Peyser Act of 1933* established the Employment Service. With millions unemployed during the Depression, the *Wagner-Peyser Act* provided 50% matching funds to states to establish state offices for aiding in the search for employment. Almost from its inception, the Employment Service found itself underfunded, despite additional Federal funds tapped from the National Youth Administration and the Civilian Conservation Corps. But after two years of operation, with the passage of the *Social Security Act of 1935*, the Employment Service was given responsibility for providing services to the unemployed under the new unemployment insurance system. During the Second World War when the Employment Service was federalized, all funds came from appropriated Federal revenues. This precedent of full funding was incorporated in the amendment of 1949 to the *Wagner-Peyser Act* which made the Employment Service part of the social security system, with funding derived totally from a Federal unemployment tax on employers. At that time, the Bureau of Employment Security was transferred from the Social Security Administration to the Labor Department.

The tension between the separate functions of administering unemployment benefits and linking employers with job applicants has remained a part of the Employment Service. In the early 1960s the states were instructed to make a physical separation of the two functions. Separation at the Federal level was achieved when the Bureau of Employment Security was replaced by the Unemployment Insurance Service and the United States Training and Employment Service.

The Employment Service today is a large and well staffed nationwide mechanism containing some 2,200 local offices and a staff of over 35,000 persons. It has been complemented by a network of over 450 state/local prime sponsors responsible for the implementation of CETA and a large number of subcontractors providing training services. Its correct role with respect to employment and training policy has never been resolved. The unemployment insurance system has been extended in time of need to offer extra benefits. The extent to which the Employment Service should supplement private employment services has been unclear.

When the new Federal employment and training programs were created through the *Manpower Development and Training Act of 1962 (MDTA)*, the Employment Service was given a major role in providing services including placement to the unemployed. These programs had been foreshadowed in the *Morrill Act of 1862*, the *Smith Hughes Act of 1917*, the *Full Employment Act of 1946* and the GI Bill which provided some $14.5 billion of training funds for World War II veterans. MDTA and subsequently the *Comprehensive Employment and Training Act of 1973(CETA)* placed operational responsibility for employment and training programs under the Department of Labor. State and local prime sponsors were given an expanded role under the (CETA). Title II of CETA incorporated provisions of the *Emergency Employment Act of 1971* authorizing a $2.5 billion public sector jobs program and Title VI created a new public sector jobs program considerably larger. CETA also included several other titles and was subsequently amended to create Private Industry Councils (PICs) to coordinate job efforts in the private sector. The *Youth Employment Demonstration Projects Act of 1977 (YEDPA)* was a major initiative to address youth unemployment.

In 1982 in the face of rising unemployment the *Jobs Partnership Act* was passed. It eliminated the public sector jobs program and greatly reduced the use of stipends for trainees. It also strengthened the PICs and gave the states much greater authority. The prime sponsors were to be replaced by a more autonomous local unit.

5. Health

The establishment of the American Medical Association (AMA) in 1847 may be viewed as a landmark in the professionalization of doctors and a harbinger of their importance in influencing public policy toward health within the United States. Up to that time health was basically a private matter between the patient and the medical practitioner. With the exception of providing some medical services for those supported in state institutions, government remained apart from the health field. But during the second half of the nineteenth century, state governments became involved in the licensing of the medical profession and local governments began supporting hospitals directly. Already in 1939, a joint study by the United States Public Health Service and the United States Bureau of Census in the *Social Work Yearbook* for 1939 reported that nearly 47% of hospital income came from government sources. Also during this period as the American nation was transformed to an urban society, the problems of public health involving disease control gained attention.

Yet despite the growing involvement of government in health care, the United States lagged behind the advanced industrialized nations of Western Europe in comprehensive health services. Bismark's Germany adopted health care for industrial workers as early as 1883. England, as early as 1911, provided for health care for low income workers. But American governmental involvement in direct programs remained at the local level without any nationally coordi nated policy. Between 1915 and 1918, the American Association for Labor Legislation made concerted efforts to shephard its model medical care insurance bill through several state legislatures, but the AMA lobby opposed any plan of contributory insurance. Samuel Gompers, President of the American Federation of Labor, feared the government control of workers implied in such a plan. Again during the New Deal, President Roosevelt's Advisory Committee on Economic Security, created to draft the *Social Security Act*, announced that it was studying health insurance and included a provision in an early draft of the social security bill calling for a study and report to Congress. The reaction, led by the AMA, was so strong and critical that Roosevelt feared the Social Security bill would be jeopardized as well as his chances for reelection. Subsequently AMA reversed its former opposition to private health insurance plans. It endorsed Blue Cross and commercial hospital insurance and actively supported private insurance for surgical and medical expenses, such as Blue Shield. By 1949 over thirty million Americans were covered by such plans.

President Truman's strong advocacy of national health insurance in the late 40s was not able to overcome Congressional opposition spearheaded by the AMA. The idea propounded by Truman advisers of first obtaining a health care plan for those on Social Security was no more successful. It was not until the legislative genius of President Lyndon Johnson that Medicare was passed in 1965 as part of *Public Law 89-97*. Along with Medicare, an insurance program for those covered by Social Security, a separate measure was included to provide services for those receiving public welfare from Federal and state funds. This became known as the Medicaid Program.

Prior to 1965, the Federal government had already taken some initiatives in the health field. In 1946, the *Hill-Burton Act* was passed providing funds for hospital construction. Medical research was being supported through the National Institutes of Health. The *Hill-Burton Act* subsidized

25-30 percent of the post-war hospital construction. By 1964, Federal, state and local governments accounted for $7 billion of the $35.4 billion expended on health services.

The health care situation in the United States was drastically altered by the amendments to the *Social Security Act* which created Medicare and Medicaid. The result has been a major growth in public and private spending at all levels to meet the increasing costs of health services. By fiscal 1980 spending for health care by the Federal government had risen from its 1965 level of less than $2 billion to $52 billion. The Health Care Finance Administration which administers Medicare and Medicaid was budgeted for fiscal 1980 at $25 billion, close to half of the total budget of the Department of Health and Human Services. Its funding dwarfed that of the old, established Public Health Service and exceeded even the $19 billion going to the Social Security Administration by a substantial sum.

Predictably a major movement to cut the costs of health care has developed in the Congress and Executive. Cost cutting has focused on the direct monitor ing of hospital stays through Professional Standards and Review Organizations (PSROs) and the creation of Health Maintenance Organizations (HMOs) to avoid costly hospital stays through taking preventive action. Regional planning units have sought to reduce duplication. A series of other preventive measures, including the establishment of a Center for Disease Prevention and Control, have taken place.

Regional planning has been attempted by health service organizations created by the *National Health Planning and Resources Development Act of 1974*. That act established a number of priorities, including 1) Encouragement of group practice, health maintenance organizations and other organizational forms for the delivery of health services; 2) Provision of primary care for medically underserved populations; 3) Development of mechanisms for coordination and consolidation of institutional health services; 4) Training and increased use of physician assistants; 5) Promotion of improvements in the quality of health services; 7) Development of multi-level care institutions; 8) Promotion of disease prevention activities; 9) Adoption of uniform cost accounting and management; and 10) Development of methods of educating the public about preventive techniques and effective use of available health services. Despite the fact that over 200 health service agencies are functioning and that over 80% have been approved by the Department of Health and Human Services and nearly all states have completed health plans, the units are still quite weak and have been caught in a cross fire of complaints since their establishment.

The detailed administration of the Medicare and Medicaid systems has fallen to state departments of health and social services. Indeed they have moved in some cases to involve private contractors in the task of ensuring that providers are paid in a timely fashion. The result has been a tremendous boon to state and local involvement in health services with many community-based facilities appearing in various parts of the country. These facilities have been particularly prominent in the field of mental health as described below.

Meanwhile, the private and voluntary hospitals have been incorporated in the health care system through increasing reliance on federal funding. The future of health care remains uncertain in the face of competing demands for a national system of health care, increased local autonomy and demands by health providers for greater autonomy and less regulation.

An associated issue is that relating to the training of health care person nel. In 1963 the *Health Professions Education Assistance Act* was created pursuant to PL 88-129. Federal loans and scholarships were made available to students in medicine, dentistry, osteopathy, optometry, podiatry, pharmacy and veterinary medicine. Amendments during the 1960s expanded coverage and authorized aid for training nurses and allied health professionals. In 1970 the Carnegie Commission predicted a critical shortfall of skilled physicians running as high as 50,000. A direct result was the Comprehensive Health Manpower Act of 1971. In the period since then, serious questions have been raised about maldistribution and overspecialization. The Carter administration predicted a surplus of doctors during the 1980s and suggested that the program be phased out. Whether or not that will happen remains to be seen.

6. Mental Health

While during Colonial times, the insane stayed with family or friends or were housed in local jails or poorhouses; beginning in the 1830s, state after state constructed specialized asylums to house them. This early history is recounted by David Rothman in *The Discovery of the Asylum*. This outpouring of activity was a reflection of the prevailing medical wisdom that insanity was based upon organic malfunction and could be easily corrected. One early superintendent claimed that 82.25% of all patients recovered. Indeed spurred on by a system in which their own promotions and tenure as well as their institutional appropriations were contingent upon a state legislature's perceptions of good results, the superintendents of asylums almost universally reported high rates of success with patients. Despite the claims, however, by the middle of the century, the reforming spirit in which the asylums had begun had clearly been dampened. Institutions throughout the country, though strongly supported by the states, were burdened by an overloaded population and the pretensions to rehabilitation gave way to the realities of custodial care.

The progressive era resulted in some reform and the founding of the National Committee for Mental Hygiene in 1909 had ameliorating influences. But the conditions of state institutions have been subjected to extensive criticism ever since and encouraged the deinstitutionalization movement of the 1970s which saw many patients in state mental hospitals released. During the twentieth century, the far reaching advances in knowledge about mental illness and the influence of the two world wars have increased the level of attention to mental illness.

Title VI of the *Social Security Act* which provided grants to states for establishing local health districts had a beneficial impact on state and local efforts to deal with mental health. It also set a precedent for the enactment of the *National Mental Health Act of 1946*, which established the National Institute of Mental Health, provided grants to states for improving mental health services and provided grants to universities, hospitals and other public and private institutions for research and training. Mental health legislation ordinarily is the responsiblity of the Health Subcommittee of the Senate Labor and Human Resources Committee and the Health and Safety Subcommittee of the House Education and Labor Committee. Major interest groups include the National Council of Community Mental Health Centers, the National Association of State Mental Health Directors and the Mental Health Association.

During the post World War II period a two-tiered system developed. Public institutions tended to be long term and custodial. Once individuals entered, they rarely left. Private institutions performed the bulk of remedial services. Public health facilities for veterans were somewhere in between. Recognition of the desperation of the plight of the state facilities and skyrocketing costs raised questions about the advisability of a change in strategy. By 1951, 330 community mental health clinics had been established throughout the country. The *Community Mental Health Centers Act of 1963* and its revision, the *Community Mental Health Centers Act of 1975*, reoriented the entire mental health delivery system.

Largely as a result of this legislation, the emphasis began focusing on community mental health facilities and the states adopted massive programs of deinstitutionalization, moving individuals out of residential care facilities. Between 1969-1976, Federal grants to community mental health centers totaled $1.7 billion. The result was a dramatic reversal from the 1940s when 75% of those treated in the mental health area were hospitalized. By the late 1970s only 25% of those treated were hospitalized. Deinstitutionalization was fueled by both therapeutic doctrine, which emphasized community placement as a form of treatment, and cost considerations. One result has been the concentration of many former residents of mental health facilities in the cities, in certain neighborhoods, which has had social repercussions.

Mental health, though certainly an integral part of the health field, represented in the early 1970s approximately 15% of total health expenditures. Its development in conjunction with the state institutions has served to maintain its distinctive character and has reinforced it as a state responsibility. As the growth of community based facilities takes place, a reintegration with other health services may be seen. Problems of management are certainly similar in health facilities of all kinds. To the extent that long term mental health facilities tend to deal with a more stable clientele over longer periods of time they more closely resemble nursing home facilities and correctional facilities, than general purpose hospitals.

7. Corrections

Correctional services, like mental health services, run the gamut from long term care facilities to outpatient service centers associated with probation and parole. During the early days of the American experience, correctional services were virtually non-existent. Penalties for criminal offenses involved fines or public display for the most part and actual sentencing in a correctional institution was rare. Indeed it was not until the 1820s when the penitentiary movement developed within the United States that prison sentences became a regular part of correctional activities. The extent to which correctional institutions retain their rehabilitative focus is a question that is not easily answered. Many critics argue that so-called correctional institutions are not really concerned with effecting improvement, but are basically custodial. A similar controversy raged recently in the mental health field which in part led to deinstitutionalization. In any case, during the course of the 19th century the prison system spread rapidly from state to state and it soon became the dominant mode for the punishment of convicted criminals.

In 1878, the practice of probation was formally initiated in Boston and it gained wide acceptance. Probation replaces incarceration, usually subject to certain conditions placed upon the offender and has been applied in a variety of ways to youth as well as adults. Parole refers to conditional release from an institution prior to the expiration of the prison term. The parole officer helps to effectuate the transition from incarceration to the free environment.

In 1899, the first juvenile court was established which attempted to emphasize the treatment of youth in a rehabilitative way. The juvenile courts allowed for treating youth outside of the criminal law and established a separate set of youth facilities differing considerably from a prison, both in terms of its younger population and in its more relaxed atmosphere. Some critics continue to argue however, that incarceration in youth prisons is basically custodial and a way of denying youth the due process protection available in regular criminal proceedings.

The importance of correctional management and its place within the larger criminal justice system was forcefully recognized by the President's Commission on Law Enforcement and the Administration of Justice in the late 1960s. Direction and monies began flowing with the *Omnibus Crime Bill*. Yet the 1970s have witnessed major examples of the failure of correctional institutions and increasingly militant responses on the part of inmates who have on several ocasions seized control of the institutions. The earlier emphasis on the rehabilitative function of correctional institutions seems to be giving way lately to a more sober and limited view of the role of prisons. Effective custody seems to be emphasized to a greater extent today.

It may be that a growing distinction is developing between the use of probation, parole, short term incarceration and community-based rehabilitation programs and longer term institutionalization which is used for basically custodial purposes. This trend emphasizes a range of measures and institutional settings in which to deal with convicted criminals. It seems likely, in any event, that state leadership in this area will continue, with perhaps greater coordination with local authorities. Federal efforts at direct service delivery are more circumscribed and deal with certain limited federal offenses.

8. Care of Special Groups

While most of the major human service programs have been covered, three additional groups deserve special mention. Most of the programs which affect them can be included in one of the categories above, but some cannot and these groups have a special prominence in human service programs. These are the aged, the handicapped and veterans.

The aged have a special place in the American scheme of human services. They are the individuals who benefit from the pension aspects of the social security system, from veterans' benefits and more recently from Supplement Security Income (SSI). A measure of the extent to which this group has been accepted as a legitimate recipient of government largesse is the pledge of President Reagan, representing conservative Republican ideology, in the 1980 presidential campaign not to tamper with the Social Security system. The aged also have been central in the Federal government's effort to subsidize health care. Despite the American hesitancy to engage in social welfare programs, assistance to the elderly finds ready political support. This is attested to, also, by the *Older Americans Act of 1965* which provides assistance in a variety of areas such as income, health, housing, social services and transportation. Under the allotment procedures adopted in 1973, in order to qualify for funding, the state must be divided into planning and service districts. In each area, public or not-for-profit agencies are designated to coordinate the delivery of services. Specific programs include nutrition, housing, counseling, recreation and consumer education.

A group which has found even greater acceptance than the aged is veterans. Over the years, but particularly during and after World War II they have been awarded an array of benefits which is both extensive and offered gratefully without stigma. The 58 regional centers of the independent Veterans Administration are evidence of the special treatment of this group. Each includes office space for the veterans groups such as the American Legion, Veterans of Foreign Wars and Disabled American Veterans, organizations which constitute powerful lobbying forces. Recently the Veterans of Foreign Wars became the first to form a political action committee, apparently fearing a diminution of its traditional strength. Veterans' benefits include disability payments for those injured in war, readjustment benefits, including extensive educational benefits, pension benefits and health care. The bulk of these benefits assist veterans without service connected disability. Veterans' benefits currently total over $21 billion annually and an estimated 40% of the population is eligible for benefits. The Senate and House Veterans' Affairs Committees are invariably cordial in their treatment of proposed legislation.

The handicapped have also achieved increasing recognition. Special programs exist for cash payments, vocational rehabilitation and education. The *Social Security Act of 1935* provided for cash assistance to the blind. Starting in 1954 a system of Social Security Disability Insurance has expanded until by 1960 it provided assistance to all disabled, regardless of age, who could not qualify for aid as dependent children or for old age assistance. Its increasing costs have led to the suggestion that it be supported from general tax revenues. Federal assistance to the states for vocational rehabilitation of the disabled dates back to the *Vocational Rehabilitation Act of 1920*. Recent federal legislation increases state obligations to provide for the education of the handicapped as described above.

9. Operating in the Human Services System

The main program clusters constituting the human services system have already been described. Clearly, cash assistance to the needy, including the elderly, is an important basis of this system both from an historical point of view and functionally today. But clearly, too, education and health care have distinctive and important roles. In all these areas the SDOs are the heart of the system and for the most part, with the exception of the Social Security system, are operated at the state and local levels. In every area, however, the federal government does have SDOs of its own and in the very significant areas of social security and veterans' benefits a wholly Federal delivery system exists. More importantly the Federal government provides major subsidies in every area and influences policy to a considerable extent. An understanding of the mechanisms for the determination of Federal policies and the ways in which they influence the performance of SDOs is critical for successfully operating in the human services system. Equally important in many areas is the operation of the states, both in the exercise of their regulatory functions and in providing financial resources and direction. In some cases such as mental health, the state itself carries out a large proportion of the service delivery activity. And in those areas like health care and employment and training where most of the SDOs are non-governmental organizations, an understanding of state and local regulation and coordination is critical.

While the human service manager may be particularly concerned with the operation of human services within a specific program cluster, knowledge of other clusters and indeed the entire range of human services is helpful in maintaining a broader perspective.

Selected Bibliography

Coll, Blanche. *Perspectives on Welfare: A History.* Washington, D.C.: U.S. Government Printing Office, 1969.

Cyert, Richard M. *The Management of Non-Profit Organizations.* Lexington, Mass.: Lexington Books, 1975.

Davis, Michael and Hirsch, Joseph. "Medical Care," *Social Work Yearbook,* 1939, p. 240.

Derthick, Martha. *Policymaking for Social Security.* Washington, D.C.: The Brookings Institution, 1979.

Duffee, David. *Correctional Management.* Englewood Cliffs, New Jersey: Prentice-Hall, 1980.

Greenblatt, Milton, et al. *The Patient and the Mental Hospital.* Glencoe, Illinois: The Free Press, 1957.

Kahn, Alfred J. and Kamerman, Sheila B. *Social Services in the United States.* Philadelphia: Temple University Press, 1976.

Kovner, Anthony R. and Newhauser, Duncan. *Health Services Management.* Ann Arbor: Health Administration Press, 1978.

Lieberman, E. James. *Mental Health: The Public Health Challenge.* Washington, D.C.: American Public Health Association, 1975.

Litwack, Eugene and Meyer, Henry. *School, Family and Neighborhood.* New York: Columbia, 1974.

Mencher, Saul. *Poor Law to Poverty Program.* Pittsburgh: University of Pittsburgh Press, 1967.

Nathan, Richard P. *The Plot That Failed.* New York: John Wiley & Sons, 1975.

Roby, Pamela. *Child Care–Who Cares.* New York: Basic Books, 1973.

Romanyshyn, John. *Social Welfare: Charity to Justice.* New York: Random House, 1971.

Rothman, David. *The Discovery of the Asylum.* Boston: Little, Brown & Co., 1971.

Slavin, Simon, ed. *Social Administration: The Management of the Social Services.*

New York: Haworth Press and the Council on Social Work Education, 1978.
Steiner, G. *The State of Welfare.* Washingon, D.C.: The Brookings Institution, 1971.
Walter, William and Ellmore, Richard, eds. *Social Program Implementation.* New York: Academic Press, 1976.
White, R. Clyde. *Administration of Public Welfare.* 2nd Edition. New York: American Books Co., 1950.
Zald, Meyer, ed. *Social Welfare Institutions.* New York: John Wiley, 1966.

MANAGING THE HUMAN SERVICES IN HARD TIMES

David A. Bresnick

MANAGING THE HUMAN SERVICES IN HARD TIMES is the outgrowth of a major university-agency collaborative effort, involving the largest human service agency in the country and a School of Business and Public Administration. Over 1,000 administrators participated in the effort which resulted in the development of agency specific curricula to teach the basic skills that managers need.

Adapting this approach for use with a wider audience, Professor Bresnick authored a monograph for Project Share under contract with the United States Department of Health and Human Services, entitled, "A Practical Approach to Human Services Management."

This full-length book is a greatly expanded version now accessible to human service managers throughout the country. While maintaining the hands-on approach of the training program, it provides a comprehensive framework applicable to human service managers operating in a variety of organizations: social service, hospitals, residential care, education, training, childcare and mental health.

In addition to providing you with an overview of the basic areas of managerial knowledge it provides specific models and guidelines for such activities as: conducting meetings, project management, staff development planning, problem solving, budgeting, fiscal controls, information systems and program evaluation.